Teacher Educators and Professional Developm

This book focuses on the professional development of teacher educators, forming a definitive and expert resource for all those interested in this area of professional learning. It offers an in-depth overview of existing international research and professional development initiatives in the area of teacher educators' learning.

The book highlights relevant research on the topic, identifies the lessons learnt from recent initiatives and indicates ways forward for teacher educators' professional learning internationally. It provides a unique combination of seven years of pan-European collaborative work, resulting in a book with clear relevance and appeal to both academics and practitioners internationally. The book conceptualises teacher educators' professional development in order to deepen understanding of how and why learning occurs and conducts empirical research into the professional development needs of teacher educators internationally using quantitative and qualitative methods to redress gaps in existing research.

This book will be of great interest to academics, researchers and post-graduate students in the fields of teacher education and professional development and learning.

Ruben Vanderlinde is a Professor at the Department of Educational Studies at Ghent University in Belgium where he coordinates the research group Teacher Education and Professional Development.

Kari Smith is Professor of Education and Head of the National Research School in Teacher Education at the Norwegian University of Science and Technology (NTNU).

Jean Murray is a Professor of Education in the School of Education and Communities at the University of East London in England.

Mieke Lunenberg has expertise in the professional development of teacher educators. She has had a leading role in multiple projects for supporting the professional development of teacher educators and has written a considerable number of publications on this theme.

Routledge Research in Teacher Education

The Routledge Research in Teacher Education series presents the latest research on Teacher Education and also provides a forum to discuss the latest practices and challenges in the field.

Europeanisation in Teacher Education
A Comparative Case Study of Teacher Education Policies and Practices
Vasileios Symeonidis

Study Abroad for Pre- and In-Service Teachers
Transformative Learning on a Global Scale
Laura Baecher

Becoming Somebody in Teacher Education
Person, Profession and Organization in a Global Southern Context
Kari Kragh Blume Dahl

Professional Learning and Identities in Teaching
International Narratives of Successful Teachers
Edited by A. Cendel Karaman and Silvia Edling

Teacher Quality and Education Policy in India
Understanding the Relationship Between Teacher Education, Teacher Effectiveness, and Student Outcomes
Preeti Kumar and Alexander W. Wiseman

Teacher Educators and their Professional Development
Learning from the Past, Looking to the Future
Edited by Ruben Vanderlinde, Kari Smith, Mieke Lunenberg and Jean Murray

For more information about this series, please visit: https://www.routledge.com/Routledge-Research-in-Teacher-Education/book-series/RRTE

Teacher Educators and their Professional Development

Learning from the Past, Looking to the Future

Edited by
Ruben Vanderlinde, Kari Smith,
Jean Murray and Mieke Lunenberg

Routledge
Taylor & Francis Group

LONDON AND NEW YORK

First published 2021
by Routledge
2 Park Square, Milton Park, Abingdon, Oxon OX14 4RN

and by Routledge
52 Vanderbilt Avenue, New York, NY 10017

Routledge is an imprint of the Taylor & Francis Group, an informa business

British Library Cataloguing-in-Publication Data
A catalogue record for this book is available from the British Library

Library of Congress Cataloging-in-Publication Data
Names: Vanderlinde, Ruben, editor. | Smith, Kari, 1949- editor. | Murray, Jean, 1955- editor. | Lunenberg, Mieke, editor.
Title: Teacher educators and their professional development : learning from the past, looking to the future / edited by Ruben Vanderlinde, Kari Smith, Jean Murray, Mieke Lunenberg.
Description: Abingdon, Oxon ; New York, NY : Routledge, 2021. | Series: Routledge research in teacher education | Includes bibliographical references and index.
Identifiers: LCCN 2020052428 (print) | LCCN 2020052429 (ebook) | ISBN 9780367480349 (hardback) | ISBN 9780367769086 (paperback) | ISBN 9781003037699 (ebook)
Subjects: LCSH: Teacher educators--Training of. | Teacher educators--Professional relationships. | Education--Study and teaching.
Classification: LCC LB1707 .T4229 2021 (print) | LCC LB1707 (ebook) | DDC 370.71/1--dc23
LC record available at https://lccn.loc.gov/2020052428
LC ebook record available at https://lccn.loc.gov/2020052429

ISBN: 978-0-367-48034-9 (hbk)
ISBN: 978-0-367-76908-6 (pbk)
ISBN: 978-1-003-03769-9 (ebk)

Typeset in Bembo
by Taylor & Francis Books

Contents

Illustrations

Figures

Tables

Contributors

Yvonne Bain is a Professor in the School of Education at the University of Aberdeen, Scotland. Her professional responsibilities include the strategic development of new initiatives in teacher education and overseeing the post-graduate taught programmes and professional learning developments for educators. Her initial teaching career started in secondary schools. She has been in higher education for many years supporting initial teacher education of student teachers and the on-going professional learning of teachers and lecturers in schools and in further education colleges. Her scholarly and research interests are in the professional development of educators and online learning. She is a member of the InFo-TED Council.

Amanda Berry's work focuses on the development of teachers' knowledge and the ways in which that knowledge is shaped and articulated through teacher preparation, beginning teaching and in-service learning. Amanda's research concerns the ways in which teachers' and teacher educators' learning can be studied from an insider perspective, as a means of enabling and empowering teachers and developing collectively understood knowledge of practice. Amanda has published extensively in the above areas, including books, handbook chapters, international journals and academic texts. She is current Editor of *Studying Teacher Education*, an international journal of self-study; former Chair of the American Education Special Interest group in Self-study of Teacher Education practices; and Associate Editor of *Research in Science Education*.

Gerry Czerniawski taught humanities, business studies and sociology in schools and colleges in London before gradually moving into teaching in higher education within the political sciences and education at the Open University, the University of Northampton, London Metropolitan University and London University's (now UCL) Institute of Education. In 2006 he joined the University of East London where he is currently Professor of Education. He has been Programme Leader for secondary PGCE/GTP/Schools Direct humanities courses and runs the doctoral programmes in education. Gerry holds a National Teaching Fellowship from the Higher

Education Academy and is a Trustee, Director and Council Member of the British Educational Research Association (BERA). He is the Lead Editor of The BERA Blog, Chair of The British Curriculum Forum and a Principal Fellow of the Higher Education Academy.

Bregje de Vries currently works as a teacher educator and researcher in the Teacher Education Institute of the Vrije Universiteit Amsterdam (VU). Her main research interests are related to the professional development of teachers as designers of innovative learning arrangements, and teachers as practitioner researchers. She is also the Coordinator of a professional development program for teacher educators at the VU and concerned with the support of teacher educators to register as professionals.

Jurriën Dengerink had been a Staff-Member of Educational Development in the Department of Teacher Education at the Vrije Universiteit Amsterdam (VU), until his retirement in 2018. He was co-leader of several projects in which they developed a professional standard, certification procedure and a web-based knowledge base to support the professional development of teacher educators in the Netherlands. He coordinated a Dutch professional development program for teacher educators, was involved in policy as Secretary of the National Board of Teacher Education Departments of Research Universities in the Netherlands and is (co-)author of several articles and a review study about the profession of teacher educators and editor of a book on teacher development.

Ainat Guberman is Head of the Research Authority at the MOFET Institute in Tel Aviv, Israel. She is a Lecturer at David Yellin Academic College of Education, as well as in the Department of Education at the Hebrew University, both located in Jerusalem, Israel. Dr Guberman is a council member of the International Forum of Teacher Educators Professional Development. Her main fields of interest are teacher educators' professional development as well as cognitive development in early childhood. Her book *Graphic texts: Literacy enhancing tools in early childhood* authored with Eva Teubal was published in four languages: English (Sense), Chinese (Psychological Publishing), Spanish (Paidos) and Hebrew (MOFET).

Shotaro Iwata is an Associate Professor in the Department of Education Design for Teacher Educators Program in the Graduate School of Humanities and Social Science at Hiroshima University, Japan. He teaches physical education methods courses and runs international teacher education and lesson studies research projects. He also has a Doctor/Master of Education degree from the Graduate School of Education at Hiroshima University, Japan. His research work is grounded in supporting teachers as professional learners and teacher educators of professional learning communities as lesson study, and in investigating teacher educators' professional development that enhances the teaching and learning of physical education.

Geert Kelchtermans studied educational sciences and philosophy and obtained a PhD from the KU Leuven in 1993, with a narrative-biographical study of teachers' professional development. He is working as a Full Professor at that same university, where he chairs the Centre for Innovation and the Development of Teacher and School. His research interest focuses on the complex interplay between individual educational professionals (and their development throughout the career) on the one hand and their institutional/organisational working conditions on the other. Recent research topics include: teacher educator professionalism; teacher induction and network analysis; micro-politics in school developments; the role of artefacts in the implementation processes of educational innovations; and organisational routines.

Warren Kidd is a Senior Teacher Educator at the University of East London. He is Subject Leader for Secondary Social Sciences and Humanities ITE and also a Principal Fellow of the HEA (PFHEA) and an Academic Associate. His research interests explore the identities and craft practices of novice teachers, teacher educator learning and identities, digital ethnographies and action research. He was a Council Member until 2019 of The International Forum for Teacher Educator Development (InFo-TED).

Kazuhiro Kusahara is a Professor of Social Studies Education at Hiroshima University, Japan, currently serving as Director of Educational Vision Research Institute. He received his BA, MA and PhD in curriculum and instruction at Hiroshima University. Most of his scholarly writing concerns the teacher education and rationale of citizenship education among social studies teachers. His research has been published in several peer-reviewed journals, including *Journal of Social Studies Education in Asia* and *Journal of Japanese Educational Research Association for the Social Studies*. He has edited books on the research methodology. Professor Kusahara has taken office as Secretary General of the Japanese Educational Association for the Social Studies. He is also active in the social studies profession. He has been a consultant of the public schools for professional development using the method of lesson study, and acting member of the advisory board on national curriculum revision in junior high school.

Mieke Lunenberg's expertise is the professional development of teacher educators. She has had a leading role in multiple projects for supporting the professional development of teacher educators. She has taught in a program for teacher educators and has given workshops and lectures for colleagues in Australia, Belgium, Germany, Japan, Netherlands, Norway, South Africa, Switzerland and United States. One of her foci is self-study research, and she has supported several colleagues who studied their own practices. Mieke has written a considerable number of publications on the professional development of teacher educators and was an Editor of *Teaching and Teacher Education*, among others. She is a Founding Member of InFo-TED.

Ann MacPhail is Assistant Dean of Research in the Faculty of Education and Health Sciences at the University of Limerick, Ireland. Her research interests include the professional learning needs of teacher educators, teacher educator research practices, (physical education) teacher education, the enactment of the teacher education continuum and instructional alignment.

Andrea McMahon is the Head of Education, Training and Development in the School of Education and Communities at the University of East London. Before moving into the university sector, she was a teacher and manager in further education for a number of years. Her research interests are in the higher education-further education interface, professional development and teacher education.

Paulien C. Meijer is Full Professor Teacher Learning and Development at Radboud University Nijmegen, the Netherlands. She is the Scientific Director at the Radboud Teachers Academy and supervises the research programme Cultivating Creativity in Education: Interactions between Teaching and Learning. Together with her research team, she publishes in high-indexed scientific journals in the field of teacher education and teacher learning, with specific attention for the cultivation of creativity in education. She supervises PhD students in this area and teaches a variety of courses in the teacher education programmes of her university. She is Member of the International Forum on Teacher Educator Development and a former Chair of the International Study Association of Teachers and Teaching (ISATT).

Jean Murray is a Professor of Education in the School of Education and Communities at the University of East London in England. Her research focuses on the sociological analysis of teacher education policies, research and practices internationally. Jean has written well over 200 books, chapters, journal articles and official reports on these issues and has also run many educational research projects. She has taught at all levels of higher education and in schools, as well as being an educational consultant on teacher education and professional learning for governments, non-governmental organisations and universities across the world. She has been an active member of the academic community in the United Kingdom and internationally for more than twenty years.

Helma Oolbekkink-Marchand is a Professor at the School of Education within HAN University of Applied Sciences. Her research focuses on the professional development of teachers and teacher educators, and she has a special interest in teachers' professional identity and agency. She is a Board Member of the Dutch Teacher Educators Association (VELON) in which she is involved in initiatives related to the professional development of teacher educators. Within InFo-TED, she has been involved in the development of the program of the Summer Academy.

Mary O'Sullivan recently retired from the University of Limerick, Ireland, where she served as Dean of the Faculty of Education and Health Sciences and Professor of Physical Education and Youth Sport. Previous to that she was Associate Dean of Education and Professor of Physical Education at Ohio State University in the United States. Mary is currently Chair of the National Council for Curriculum and Assessment (NCCA) in Ireland. Mary's research interests have been on teaching, teachers and teacher education policy and practice with a particular interest in physical education curriculum and pedagogy.

Frances Rust currently serves as Adjunct Professor at the University of Pennsylvania-GSE. She is Professor Emerita at New York University-Steinhardt and Scholar in Residence at the New York University (NYU) Metro Center. She obtained her doctorate at Teachers College at Columbia University and, since 1985, she has directed teacher education programs at Teachers College, Manhattanville College, Hofstra University, NYU and the University of Pennsylvania. She has published widely on topics related to teacher preparation, teacher professional development, teacher-driven action research and school improvement. She has given invited addresses in Europe, Israel, China, Canada, and throughout the United States, and regularly consults with universities and non-governmental organisations on the design and implementation of teacher education programs.

Kari Smith is Professor of Education and Head of the National Research School in Teacher Education at the Norwegian University of Science and Technology (NTNU). She has had a long career as a teacher, teacher educator and researcher. Currently her main teaching activities are within doctoral education, students and supervisors. Her research interests are assessment, more specifically assessment for learning, teacher education, novice teachers, and professional learning of teachers and teacher educators. Smith has published widely within these areas. She was the Coordinator of InFo-TED from the start (2013) until 2019.

Hanne Tack is Doctor-Assistant at the Department of Educational Studies at Ghent University in Belgium. Her research interests focus on teacher education in general, with a particular interest in teacher educators' professional development, promising instructional and professional development strategies in teacher education, and the research competences of (student) teachers (educators). These research interests are also visible in Dr Tack's engagements as JURE coordinator of EARLI SIG 11 'Teaching and Teacher Education', as Council Member of InFo-TED, as Editorial Member of *Tijdschrift voor Lerarenopleiders*, and in active contributions on international conferences, publications in SCCI-journals and practice-oriented publications. In August 2017, she defended her PhD dissertation 'Towards a better understanding of teacher educators' professional development: Theoretical and empirical insight into their researcherly disposition'. Dr Tack is experienced with large-scale quantitative survey studies, mixed-methods designs and intervention studies.

Marit Ulvik is Professor at the Department of Education at the University of Bergen, Norway. She is a Teacher Educator in a postgraduate programme for secondary school teachers and is responsible for educating school-based mentors. Furthermore, she is a leader of the research group Teacher Professionalism and Education. Her main research interest is professional development, including research on teacher educators, teacher education, newly qualified teachers, mentoring, action research and teaching. She has published in national as well as international books and journals.

Eline Vanassche is a Tenure Track Professor at the Faculty of Psychology and Educational Sciences at KU Leuven in Flanders, Belgium. She is a former Marie Skłodowska-Curie fellow at the University of East London and Assistant Professor at Maastricht University. Her research interest includes teacher educators' professionalism and its development throughout their careers. She has a particular interest in the interaction between teacher educators and the socio-structural contexts of their work. Her more recent work turns to positioning theory and frame analysis to understand what a teacher educator 'may do and not do' in the complex relationships with trainees and school-based mentors.

Ruben Vanderlinde is a Professor at the Department of Educational Studies at Ghent University in Belgium where he coordinates the research group 'Teacher Education and Professional Development'. His research interests are in the field of educational innovation, teacher training and professionalisation, and the integration of information and communication technologies (ICT) in education. He publishes widely on these topics, both in ISI listed journals and more practitioner-oriented journals. Dr Vanderlinde is methodologically experienced in mixed method research, and currently uses social network analysis in his research projects. He teaches Educational Innovation and Pedagogy of Teaching in the Bachelor's and Master's degree of Educational Sciences, and Teaching Methodology in the Teacher Training degree. He is one of the founding members of InFo-TED (International Forum for Teacher Educator Development), and since 2019 has been the Chair of this group of international scholars.

Sheeba Viswarajan is a Senior Lecturer in Teacher Education (Secondary) at the University of East London. She teaches on postgraduate teacher education programmes and works with a range of school partners to train both chemistry and physics teachers. She runs the Subject Knowledge Enhancement course for chemistry, the first of its kind in England to be approved by the Royal Society of Chemistry. She is pursuing her doctorate in the 'Effectiveness of practical work under the new GCSE curriculum'. Her interests are in reducing cognitive load in lessons and in improving learning, especially from practical work.

Amber Walraven is Assistant Professor at the Radboud Teachers Academy at Radboud University in Nijmegen. She is the coordinator of the one-year Master of Education program that educates academic prospective and in-service teachers for the senior grades of Dutch secondary education. Her research focuses in particular on ICT in education, professionalisation of teachers in the field of practice-oriented research, and recently on adaptive expertise of teachers and teacher educators.

Foreword

This is a thoughtful, important, and, to my knowledge, unique book about the education and professional development of teacher educators in a European context. Of course, there are now many books, reports and special issues of journals that provide an international look at particular aspects of initial teacher education or compare the goals, approaches and outcomes of teacher preparation models in two or more countries. While this book joins the ranks of these extant cross-national volumes in certain ways, it is unique in its focus on teacher educators, its pan-European perspective and in terms of the wide scope of the contribution the book makes to how we think about who teacher educators are, what they are expected to do, and what their professional learning needs are within today's exceedingly challenging political and policy climate.

In the context of a discussion about major trends in teacher education and growing international recognition of the importance of teacher educators, the book begins with a very useful discussion about multiple types of teacher educators, based primarily on the location of their work, the roles they take up and the routes through which they enter teacher education. In this spirit, I begin my remarks about this valuable new book with two vignettes about teacher educators. Despite the fact that these vignettes come from the United States and both of them occurred many years ago, I believe that they touch on some of the complex – but under-studied – issues related to the learning needs and entry pathways of teacher educators that this book so ably illuminates and considers in depth.

Vignette I: teacher/teacher educator

On almost the same day she began her course of study as a brand new doctoral student in language and literacy at a school of education at a major research university in an urban area, a young woman also began her career as a teacher educator at a small liberal arts college nearby. She was hired to teach courses in reading/language arts and children's literature to undergraduate elementary education majors and also supervise seniors in the program who were completing their one-semester period as student teachers in local schools.

As an adjunct faculty member in the tiny elementary education department at the college, she was given a pile of prior syllabi for the courses she would teach, including information about the already-purchased text books that were to be used in the courses, but she was also assured she could make the course her own by adding new ideas and changing the details of assignments. To assist her in supervising student teachers, she was given a checklist for classroom observations, which reflected criteria that were to be the basis of each student teacher's final evaluation.

This young woman had been hired after an interview with the head of the program and on the basis of her experience. As her resume indicated, she had taught reading/language arts and social studies to elementary school children for seven years just prior to leaving teaching in order to begin doctoral study, and although the interviewer did not know this, she was a teacher who was well-regarded by parents and teachers at her school. Once the semester began, she had the opportunity to ask any questions she had of the head of the program. The following year, she was hired to teach the same courses in the undergraduate and graduate level initial teacher education programs at the university where she was doing her doctoral work.

Vignette 2: professor/teacher educator

On the first day of his new job as an assistant professor in the department of educational research and measurement at a school of education at a medium-size research university in a different urban area, a young man also became a teacher educator. With a PhD in Measurement, Evaluation and Statistical Analysis, the young man had been hired to teach courses in psychometrics to graduate students and to bring his expertise in quantitative educational research and statistical analyses to improve doctoral research across the school.

During his first semester on the job, the young man did indeed teach graduate-level psychometrics. However, based on the fact that he had both undergraduate and master's degrees in psychology, he was also assigned to teach a course in child development to students in their first year of the elementary teacher education program. Although he had no teaching experience at any level, he was given no information about the larger teacher education program and no supervision as a teacher. The only guidance he received was a textbook on child development written by a fellow faculty member and the former class syllabus.

To teach the course, the young man managed to stay one chapter ahead of the students, drawing on the information in the book, his background in psychology and his day-to-day experience as an attentive father with a three-year old and a five-year old at home. The following year, a measurement course the young man was scheduled to teach failed to meet enrolment requirements and was cancelled, meaning that the young man again needed another assignment to fulfil his teaching load. He was assigned to supervise several high school student teachers in mathematics. He was given no training. With the goal of being polite to the classroom teachers, he observed the student teachers several times over the course of the semester, making notes about things like clarity of presentations, eye contact and decorum.

Like many other teacher educators in her generation, the young woman in the first story – myself, as some readers will have realised – went on to become a teacher education scholar and practitioner, now with more than 40 years of national and international experience in multiple aspects of teacher education research, policy and practice. In contrast, the young man in the second story, who years later became my husband, has worked for nearly 40 years as a researcher and practitioner in the field of measurement, evaluation, statistics and assessment. It is worth noting, however, that he continued to teach child development courses to teacher education students for the first five years of his career, but he never thought of himself during this time as a teacher educator and was not aware of the larger issues or the considerable scholarly work about teacher education that existed in this field. He learned to be a teacher (and, by default, for a while, a teacher educator) through experience and through what he picked up on the job. Interestingly, however, years later, he began to study and work to enhance his own teaching through longitudinal statistical analyses of his course evaluations and his students' drawings of the experience.

Clearly both of these stories of new teacher educators took place a long time ago, and a great deal has changed, including the fact that now many institutions and organisations in countries around the world attend more systematically to the education of new teacher educators, and a body of rich international scholarship about teacher educators has developed.

Despite the age of these two vignettes, however, they still serve to introduce some of the issues that this new book deals with in great depth and with great complexity: Who counts as a teacher educator? What are the various roles and responsibilities that teacher educators take on? What does it mean to be a teacher educator without understanding or acknowledging that role? Does it make sense to assume that because one is a (good) teacher, then he or she will be a (good) teacher educator? Does it make sense to assume that because one knows content material, then he or she can teach that content to teacher candidates? What are the complex learning needs of teacher educators in various circumstances and at different career points? What kinds of organisations, forums and projects support the learning needs of teacher educators in various countries?

Of course, some of these questions have been around for many years, while some of them represent new ways of thinking about teacher educators and their critical role in the learning of new teachers and their students. The value of this unusual and important new book is that it brings so much light to bear on these and other important questions about teacher educators Very importantly, the book considers these questions in the context of the rapidly changing geopolitical climate wherein there has been unprecedented attention from leaders at the highest levels of policy to the importance of teacher educators in the learning of teachers and ultimately in the learning of their students.

This book is the product of an unusual and very forward-thinking colla-borative group, referred to as InFo-TED (The International Forum for Teacher Educator Development). InFo-TED is a working group of international tea-cher education scholars and stakeholders who have come together over the last seven years to study, support and disseminate information about teacher edu-cators' professional learning and development. With the support of funding from the EU, the group was founded by the four editors of this book with the intention of figuring out ways to enact the ambitious agenda regarding the education and development of teacher educators put forth in the European Commission's 2013 report, *Supporting Teacher Educators to Improve Learning.* Now with more than 20 active researchers from six European countries (Bel-gium, England, Ireland, the Netherlands, Norway, Scotland) as well as working colleagues in Australia, Israel and the United States, the group has achieved a remarkable set of accomplishments, one of which is this book.

Teacher educators and their professional development: Learning from the past, looking to the future is a distinctive volume with a clever organisation that alternates between groups of chapters that focus on developments and initiatives related to teacher educators' learning in Europe, and three 'Interlude' chapters about the professional development of teacher educators in Australia, Japan and the United States. One of the major strengths of this book is that it does not attempt to reduce the complexity of the issues related to the education and development of teacher educators. Rather the various chapters in the book collectively make the point that in order to enhance the education of teacher educators, many different kinds of scholarly, practice-related and policy tasks are necessary, establishing definitions and designing conceptual frameworks, analysing existing literature, conducting new research, drawing from case stu-dies, evaluating initiatives, and disseminating knowledge frameworks.

Impressively, across the chapters, the book manages to carry out these mul-tiple tasks with insight and clarity. Of particular note along these lines is the book's generative conceptual framework for understanding the development of teacher educators, which is provocatively contrasted with a standards-based approach; the rich, asset-based framework links the developmental, perspectival and dynamic aspects of professional development as they play out at different levels from personal to global.

In addition, the book presents new analyses from a mixed-methods study about the professional learning opportunities valued by teacher educators based on a large-scale survey and follow-up interviews conducted in six countries, revealing the critical importance of understanding professional development as a duality of formal and informal learning. In addition, the book self-critically and thoughtfully assesses the impact of the collaborative work of the InFo-TED project through four different country-based case studies and through thoughtful analysis of its Summer Academy. As the authors point out, these show that an international project can support development across countries, but even more importantly, these cases reveal that advancing the professional learning of teacher educators is to a great extent context-specific, given the widely varying historical, geopolitical, economic and institutional trends that both unite and divide the various nations and the widely-varying experiences of different teacher educators.

Marilyn Cochran-Smith
Cawthorne Professor of Teacher Education, Lynch School of
Education and Human Development, Boston College

Chapter 1

Teacher educators and their professional development

Jean Murray, Kari Smith, Ruben Vanderlinde and Mieke Lunenberg

Introduction

For over two decades, the work of teacher educators and the subsequent importance of their professional development have been the focus of increased attention from practitioners and researchers (see Izadinia, 2014; Loughran, 2014; Cochran-Smith et al., 2019). Significantly, international policy makers have also realised how central this occupational group is in both teacher education and in improving schooling systems; because of this, their professional development has become of particular importance.

In 2005, the Organisation for Economic Co-operation and Development (OECD) published the report *Teachers Matter* stating the importance of teachers for improving student learning. It took another eight years, however, before the European Commission acknowledged officially that those who teach the teachers – the teacher educators – also matter in pan-European policy making. Their report reads:

> Teacher educators are crucial players for maintaining – and improving – the high quality of the teaching workforce. They can have a significant impact upon the quality of teaching and learning in our schools. Yet they are often neglected in policy-making, meaning that some Member States do not always benefit fully from the knowledge and experience of this key profession. It also means that teacher educators do not always get the support and challenge they need, for example in terms of their education and professional development.
>
> (European Commission, 2013, p. 4)[1]

A major emphasis in official reports (e.g., OECD, 2018) is that, because of socio-economic, cultural and technological changes in all societies globally, schooling and teacher education both need to respond rapidly to ensure that education remains relevant and meaningful to social needs.

This chapter opens with a brief analysis of teacher education policies, but any such attempt needs to take account of the broad changes taking place globally.

professional development should take on relevant/changing topics

These are clearly many and complex, and it is beyond the remit of this chapter to discuss them at length. We note, however, that in the last two decades, wide-ranging and frequent socio-economical, geo-political and technological changes have brought unexpected, global challenges for educational policy makers and practitioners. These factors form powerful background influences on how education 'reforms' for teacher education are devised, implemented and evaluated; those reforms in turn have significant implications for teacher educators and for their professional development.

Pre-service teacher education is now a policy driver to change schooling through often fast-changing policy requirements and the systematic politicisation of teacher education. Kosnik et al. (2016) identify eight types of international teacher education 'reforms'. Seven of these are about pre-service teacher provision; they can be grouped into two inter-linked categories: 1) increased, external regulation and surveillance; and 2) reforms re-focusing curriculum content, format and/or the location of pre-service programmes. All these reforms have had implications for the demographics and work of teacher educators and, consequently, for their professional development needs.

Examples of Kosnik et al.'s (2016) second category of reforms include moves towards more 'research-based' modes of teacher education. Trends include: more emphasis on the importance of research in curricula, the growth of master's level programmes and teaching moving from colleges to universities. These trends have changed teacher education, the location of teacher educators' work and their professional development in many countries. For example, in Ireland, teacher educators' work has moved from colleges of higher education to universities. In Norway a move to master's level courses is one of the drivers behind NAFOL (Nasjonal forskerskole for lærerutdanning), a professional development programme that enables teacher educators to gain doctorates in order to be able to supervise master's students (Smith, 2020).

But at the same time, other reforms have aimed to make teacher education more 'practical', with 'two main ways of achieving this … proposed: (a) enhancing the theory-practice connection in campus courses; and, (b) linking the campus program more closely with the schools' (Kosnik et al., 2016, p. 273). This 'practicum turn' (Mattsson et al., 2011) has certainly been a noted feature of teacher education policy internationally (OECD, 2012, as cited in Kosnik et al., 2016; European Commission, 2015). This turn has been implemented differently in various countries. For example, in parts of the United States and in England, it has resulted in 'a hyper-emphasis on clinical practice – extensive immersion in the field, *(and)* limited (or no) emphasis on research or "theoretical" course work' (Goodwin & Kosnik, 2013, p. 335). Here, traditional, higher-education based pre-service routes are often under threat, school-led training proliferates and teacher educators may see themselves as living in an educational landscape that is subject to criticisms (Cochran-Smith et al., 2019). But in parts of continental Europe, the 'practicum turn' has involved following a model in which 'research-informed practice' and 'specialist training schools' are part of pre-service provision in both universities and schools. One example here is in the Netherlands, where teacher educators from higher education institutions and mentors collaborate to provide 'research-rich' teacher education (Van Velzen et al., 2019).

Internationally, teacher educators have acknowledged to be a heterogeneous occupational group (Izadinia, 2014), working in many roles to support pre- and in-service teachers, usually from within a higher education institution. There has been a well acknowledged 'problem of definition' (Ducharme, 1993, p. 2) in discussing this group, partly because of the diverse roles and work patterns within the field and issues around self- and communal-ownership of the term 'teacher educator'. Certainly, determining who is a teacher educator can be challenging because the term is so blurred, multidimensional and often context dependent (Murray, 2017; Smith & Flores, 2019). For the purposes of clarity, here we have adopted the inclusive definition that 'a teacher educator is someone who contributes in a formal way to the learning and development of teachers' (Snoek et al., 2011, p. 652).

To explore this issue further, we present definitions of three different types of teacher educators, generating our analysis from the location for work and the roles undertaken. These are inevitably somewhat simplistic, given the complexity of the field. In our three types, we have not, for example, included community-based teacher educators (White, 2019) or university academics in disciplines outside education, cited by the European Commission (2013) as teacher educators because they teach the teachers of the future in under-graduate subject degrees.

The first type is what we term the 'traditional group' of teacher educators – that is, people employed within higher education institutes of some kind. Defined by Ducharme (1993) as 'an ill-defined and poorly understood segment of the higher education faculty populations' (p. 3), this occupational group were once seen as 'hidden' and under-researched (Maguire, 1994). Since the 1990s, however, research on teacher educators, their identities and their practices as teachers and researchers has grown steadily (Izadinia, 2014). Large-scale research studies on the career pathways and qualifications of this type of teacher educator are rare[2], but smaller-scale work shows that individuals usually enter higher education work through one of two main routes: either what Davey (2013) terms the 'practitioner pathway' (moving into academia after working as a school teacher, frequently without a doctorate); or the 'academic pathway' (entry into teacher education comes after PhD study, sometimes without experience of school teaching). In some countries, for example, the United States and Israel, most teacher educators enter on the 'academic pathway'; in others, for example, the United Kingdom and the Netherlands, entry is usually on the 'practitioner pathway'; in other countries, for example, Norway and Australia, entry patterns are either mixed or rapidly changing.

In terms of work, Lunenberg et al.'s (2014) systematic review concluded that this 'traditional group' of teacher educators has at least six different roles: teacher of teachers, researcher, coach, curriculum developer, gate-keeper and broker. There are, of course, other roles within work patterns: for example, Maguire (1994) notes the often gendered and intensive work of caring for students or academic 'house-keeping' in bureaucratically inclined universities; Ellis et al. (2013) identify the work of 'relationship maintenance' between schools, students and the university. But teacher educators are usually not required to undertake all these roles during their working lives. Depending on the exact work pattern then, teacher educators' roles and identities – and therefore their professional development needs – will vary.

One example here is the variable requirement for active engagement in research. Contractual arrangements and associated career structures in some universities value research activities over pedagogical practices. Some teacher educators, with heavy teaching loads and/or engagement in supporting the student practicum, may then face challenges in becoming and remaining research active (Smith & Flores, 2019). This is often particularly so for those entering from school teaching. Beyond institutional demands, teacher educators' dispositions and senses of agency are also important. Tack and Vanderlinde's (2014) typology identified teacher educators' 'researcherly disposition', defined as 'the habit of mind to engage in research and thus to produce both local knowledge and public knowledge on teacher education' (p. 301). These authors argue that teacher educators need to invest in their own professional development to develop such a 'researcherly disposition'.

Our second type of teacher educator is that of mentors or supervising teachers, that is those who work within a school to oversee students' practicums or guide newly qualified teachers. Mentors have long been central to high quality teacher education, but their importance in providing high quality learning has become more widely recognised since the generation of more inclusive definitions of teacher educators as an occupational group. As we identify below, the professional development needs of this type of teacher educator have been extensively researched since the early 1990s. More recent initiatives to develop mentors' pedagogical skills have included Van Velzen et al.'s (2019) research in the Netherlands on enhancing modelling skills, and a Norwegian programme for enhancing mentoring skills and practice-orientated research (Smith & Ulvik, 2015).

The third type is that of school-based teacher educators. The emergence of this type can be clearly traced to the development of school-led models of teacher education in the last decade. Working sometimes in partnership with higher education institutes and sometimes autonomously, this group takes on nearly all of the roles identified above for the traditional group of teacher educators (White, 2019), with the possible exception of research. Identified as 'hybrid teacher educators' by Zeichner (2010, p. 90), Czerniawski et al. (2019) further describe these educators as having 'hybrid, poly-contextualised identities' (p. 171). White (2019) shows some of the benefits and challenges that this type face in their dual roles as teacher and teacher educator. Little is known about the professional development needs of this emerging group, although

White (2019) states that these include pedagogical approaches such as explicit modelling.

Tendencies and directions in existing research

Research on professional development or learning for teacher educators is a relatively young and under-researched area (Lunenberg et al., 2014; Ping et al., 2018). This is in many ways surprising because, as stated above, teacher educators are now considered to be central to the improvement of both teacher education and schooling systems. Of the small number of available research studies, the majority focus on teacher educators based in higher education (what we refer to above as the 'traditional group' of teacher educators), exploring their learning needs when working within universities or colleges.

Professional development for school teachers is, however, a far more extensive area, within which there is much research on professional development for mentors. This mentor development literature dates back to the development of school-university partnerships, including the establishment of Professional Development Schools by the Holmes Group in the United States in 1990 and the formal requirements for universities to work in partnership with schools in England from 1992, but it is also an on-going and rich area of work internationally (Van Velzen et al., 2019; Hobson & Maxwell, 2020). As we have noted above, however, a noticeable deficit is studies on the professional development needs of school-based teacher educators.

We make no claims to a comprehensive literature review here, but based on reading 100 research studies on teacher educators' professional development from 2000 onward, we know that this research usually sits within interpretivist or practitioner research/self-study paradigms, using some type of qualitative methodology. There are a number of common substantive themes. For example, Lunenberg et al. (2014) found that most of the 137 studies they analysed were focused on teacher educators in roles as teachers of teachers; there were far fewer studies on other roles, for example, researcher or coach. They concluded that more coherence between studies was needed to create solid knowledge about professional development for *all* teacher educator roles. They also noted that quantitative research studies were scare. And, whilst this situation is slowly changing (Tack & Vanderlinde, 2014; Czerniawski et al., 2017), this recommendation is still valid.

A systematic review by Ping et al. (2018) of what, how and why teacher educators learn analysed 75 research articles and concluded that, whilst research on teacher educators' professional learning is growing fast, the field is fragmented in focus. In line with Lunenberg et al. (2014), Ping et al. conclude that this is largely because first, there is no clear knowledge base deemed essential for teacher educators' work, and second, the forms of professional learning undertaken are diverse. Using the categories of content, activities and reasons for learning, they record content emphases on the 'pedagogy of teacher education' and 'doing research', particularly practice-orientated scholarship. Like Lunenberg et al. (2014), this review found that one research/practice priority is to focus on learning to support the diversity of professional roles undertaken. Ping et al.'s (2018) analysis of 'activities' shows that elements of reflection and collaboration inform the types of learning undertaken. They also record the reasons for undertaking professional development to be primarily 'internal', that is, intrinsically rather than extrinsically motivated.

Czerniawski et al.'s (2017) international empirical study of teacher educators' professional development (see chapter 3) concludes that 'much more needs to be done to foster (*teacher educators'*) professional learning needs'. These authors also identify that professional development as a passive and instrumental act of 'being done unto' (e.g., receiving content knowledge from others) is unlikely to be productive.

Other studies of teacher educators' professional learning indicate how important informal and formal learning in the workplace is (McNamara et al., 2014), since this clearly takes place in professionally and personally relevant contexts and is close-to-practice. It also involves experiential workplace learning (defined here as that learning which takes place alongside work but is not its primary goal). Such learning for teacher educators, however, is not well theorised compared to the strength and depth of conceptualisation found in other professional fields (McNamara et al., 2014). Acknowledging this conceptual gap in knowledge of teacher educators' professional learning is important when considering teacher educators as a group dually positioned as both workers/employees *and* learners/scholars. Addressing this gap may provide better understanding of how workplaces can offer rich and contextualised opportunities for learning about being a teacher educator.

One example of professional learning from practice in the workplace is self-study research, which has a long tradition amongst teacher educators. Cochran-Smith et al. (2019), for example, state that the prominence of self-study has meant that 'a significant number of university teacher educators in the US has been involved in a kind of self-education through ongoing inquiry and research' (p. 13). Self-study research, together with other types of qualitative research, has, of course, contributed significantly to the existing knowledge about teacher educators' practices and professional learning. As Cochran-Smith et al. (2019), state about teacher educators' self-education through self-study research, however,

> unless… this happens in the context of an edgy critical community wherein members find ways to get beneath the surface and interrogate their own and others' assumptions, the value of this self-education can be limited, sometimes simply confirming current practice, and often not getting very far toward teacher educators' deep learning and unlearning, which is critically needed.
>
> (p. 13)

Self study = not helpful (handwritten annotation)

Self-study may then be either a rich and productive source of self-education for teacher educators or a 'false friend' that neither develops learning from/in practice nor contributes to the shared knowledge about the professional development of teacher educators (Zeichner, 2007).

To date, many studies of teacher educators' professional development have focused on induction into teacher education or on early career stages (Murray, 2016). Of particular interest here has been development during the transition from school teaching to higher education work in countries where this pattern of entry into teacher education is common (Murray & Male, 2005; Van Velzen et al., 2010). For a significant period of time, induction into teacher education was assumed to be unimportant. Zeichner (2005) states that the assumption was that 'if one is a good teacher of primary or secondary school students, this expertise will automatically carry over to one's work with novice teachers' (p. 43). In fact, the transition into teacher education is routinely portrayed as challenging and multifaceted, with professional development often necessary to support the generation of new senses of identity as teacher educators and the generation of new knowledge bases and pedagogical skills.

Studies of induction are often highly contextualised and share the general methodological characteristics of most other research on teacher educators' professional development, as identified above. In addition, most of this research is undertaken either by those who are – or have recently been – beginning teacher educators, or by more experienced teacher educators with strong interests in professional development. This is not to imply that any of these characteristics are *necessarily* problematic; much of the research on beginning teacher educators, for example, has contributed greatly to understanding the field from insider perspectives. But the limitations do mean that the findings of the studies should be read with consideration of the contexts within which they were generated, the researcher positionality and the research methods used. A further issue is that there are very few longitudinal studies, even though some of the research indicates that transition may be a long process (Murray & Male, 2005). Similarly, there is an overall lack of longitudinal studies across the career course.

As we have identified, there are few quantitative, large-scale studies in this field; most of the available research on teacher educators' professional development tends to be small-scale, unfunded, and practice-based; conducted and reported by teacher educators who are practitioners and/or researchers and policy makers in the field; focused on specific and often highly contextualised activities, identities and practices; and frequently based on self-study or self-report methods, such as interviews and focus groups. As indicated above, this is not to imply that these characteristics of teacher education research are *necessarily* problematic in themselves, but, as Zeichner (2007) identifies, it does make it difficult to achieve the coherent accumulation of research findings and therefore the capacity for impact and improvement in teacher educators' professional development nationally and internationally.

In summary, research in this area tends to focus overwhelmingly on the needs of teacher educators based in higher education, but often only considering a limited range of their roles (predominantly the pedagogy of teaching teachers) and career stages (with studies of induction and early career the most common). In a fragmented field of study, the many and various forms of professional development are not well understood, in part because of weak conceptualisation. This is a particular omission in relation to workplace learning. There is a shortage of longitudinal studies across the career course and of teacher educators' professional development needs in mid- and late career. These omissions indicate directions for future research.

As later chapters of this book elaborate, it is not possible to design a blueprint for *all* teacher educators' professional development as the needs are complex, multidimensional, multifactorial and context dependent. We would, however, note one imperative for all: in today's globalised, world teacher educators have the responsibility to prepare teachers for working in multi-ethnic, multilingual and multicultural classrooms. Much of the literature about this comes from Anglophone contexts (see, e.g., Yuan, 2017; Lampert & Burnett, 2016; Ellis & Maguire, 2017) where diversity has been on the political and research agendas for decades. But in these and other national contexts, this is an issue that is still under-researched, not least because the ethnic homogeneity of teacher educators does not resemble the multi-ethnicity of the classrooms in which pre-service students may work during the practicum and later as teachers. We suggest then that all stakeholders in education need to address two questions: what professional development provision is required to enable teacher educators to become confident in preparing teachers for diverse contexts?; and how can teacher educators themselves engage in this area of professional learning, which for some may be a new, challenging responsibility?

Our overview illustrates a fundamental, over-arching problem about teacher educators' professional development: currently provision is still too dependent on small-scale, ad hoc, intermittently funded and local initiatives. This situation is clearly unsatisfactory and indicates an imperative to create differentiated and systematic professional learning provision for this key occupational group. In their review of teacher educators' professional development in four countries, Cochran-Smith et al. (2019) assert that, despite some innovations,

> it also clear that in none of these countries is there a comprehensive and deliberate approach to the education of teacher educators that simultaneously acknowledges the full range of teacher educators – from university course instructors to university-based supervisors of practicum experiences to school-based mentors and cooperating teachers – and that also provides the social, intellectual, and organizational contexts that support teacher educators' continuous learning.
>
> (p. 14)

We agree, once again underlining the importance of organised action to redress this situation. But in addition to calling for that 'comprehensive and deliberate approach' to professional development at the level of national systems, we would also stress how vital it is to consider the institutional contexts that often play significant roles in the focus and organisation of provision, and the individual work, agency and dispositions of participating teacher educators (Tack & Vanderlinde, 2014). These are all themes taken up in later chapters of this book.

InFo-TED's contribution to knowledge of teacher educators' professional development

In 2013, the four editors of this book founded the International Forum for Teacher Educator Development (InFo-TED). They then invited a group of experienced teacher educators from across Europe to join the InFo-TED Council. The organisation aims to develop knowledge and understanding of teacher educators' professional development internationally and to share these findings broadly. While its focus has mainly been on Europe, colleagues from other countries including Israel, the United States and Australia were also involved in InFo-TED as critical friends. Additionally, colleagues from many other nations have participated in regional meetings and in international learning events. Research results have been shared in publications and conference presentations.

This book details the achievements of InFo-TED. In summary, these were: the development of a conceptual model of teacher educators' professional development to deepen understanding of how and why learning occurs and to develop a shared language; a set of learning and design principles for professional development activities; a large scale study into the professional development needs of higher education-based teacher educators internationally, using quantitative and qualitative methods; and a series of international dissemination events.

The conceptual model and the learning and design principles were the basis for developing and sustaining a web-based portal as a knowledge repository for teacher educators' professional development. This consisted of building blocks and blogs to sustain online and blended leaning. These also formed the foundation for developing, implementing and evaluating face-to-face learning events that took place in regional meetings and, notably, at an international Summer Academy in 2018 for experienced teacher educators, with the second iteration originally planned for 2020 but now postponed to 2021.

This book details seven years of learning by the InFo-TED group, offering an evidence-base for guiding policy makers, academics, practitioners, researchers and other stakeholders involved in considering professional development for teacher educators. It draws together research and professional initiatives in the field and uses these strands to contribute new knowledge and understanding. It is academically rigorous, but with relevance for practitioners and policy makers involved in the design, implementation and evaluation of professional learning.

Eight chapters of this book report on different aspects of InFo-TED's work in Europe and Israel. Three interlude chapters are written by critical friends of the project, reporting on teacher educators' professional development in Australia, Japan and the United States, and reflecting on the implications of InFo-TED's work for these national contexts. The final chapter reflects on what has been learnt and outlines paths for the future.

Chapter 2 presents a model conceptualising teacher educators' professional practices, taking those practices as its starting points. The authors contrast this approach with previous work on the development of professional standards, arguing that the latter approach risks over-looking the complexity of teacher educators' daily work. This is a discussion that requires further debate with all stakeholders.

Chapter 3 systematically integrates both the qualitative and quantitative findings from an international and comparative professional development survey among higher education-based teacher educators from seven countries. It shows the many similarities and nuanced differences in teacher educators' professional learning needs. The study also adds to the rapidly developing research base about the professional learning of higher education-based teacher educators.

Chapter 4 presents an overview of the relative absence of organised professional learning of teacher educators in Australia that on the one hand is cause for concern, but on the other hand promotes the ownership of professional learning among others by self-study research and networking. In that context InFo-TED can be marked as an initiative that brings together teacher educators who want to build their own professional learning pathways and support each other. Extending the network of teacher educators involved in InFo-TED beyond Europe would be worth exploring.

Chapters 5 describes the increasing number of professional development initiatives for teacher educators by teacher education institutions, national organisations and international networks that evoke the question of what design principles guide these initiatives. As professional development for teacher educators is only recently described in the literature, no clear sets of design principles yet exist. This chapter offers a set of 12 principles and makes a plea for more design-based research on teacher educators' professional development.

Chapter 6 tackles the idea that teacher educators need specific knowledge for teaching teachers, acknowledging that research about the construction of such knowledge bases is scarce and sometimes contested. The chapter then analyses examples of two different knowledge bases, comparing contexts, the building of structure and contents, the creation of ownership, and the implementation and usage.

Chapter 7 offers an overview of different types of research on teacher educators in Japan since 2010. It discusses the influence of the Japanese political context and of European concepts on this trajectory. According to the authors, the principles of learning and design for teacher educators, the development of knowledge bases, and research by teacher educators are ways in which InFo–TED has inspired professional learning in Japan.

Chapter 8 reports on the design and implementation of the Summer Academy for teacher educators. Given the different pathways, expertise and contexts of the participants, a pedagogical technique called storylines was used in which teacher educators shared and reinterpreted their professional identities. This technique encouraged experienced teacher educators' development by building links between teaching and research, and supporting international learning and co-operation.

Chapter 9 examines the professional trajectories of four higher education-based teacher educators from Ireland, Israel, the Netherlands and Norway. Here personal characteristics and institutional and national contexts all interact to shape teacher educators' professional development. The findings show that there is formal as well as informal support in the local and national contexts, but also that pressures for research publication are rising.

In chapter 10 the author states that an enhanced focus on professional learning would support teacher educators in the United States to become 'architects of the teaching profession' and 'catalysts for educational change'. InFo-TED activities are a possible inspiration here, but as this chapter shows, to develop a nationally appropriate approach requires attention to the historical and cultural factors shaping the educational landscape of the US today.

Chapter 11 discusses how workplace learning is a major source of development for teacher educators. It is then important to know how learning away from the workplace can become integrated with workplace learning. The chapter summarises what patterns of learning occurred at the Summer Academy, and discusses how and why such patterns can lead to longer-term learning, with high relevant for practice.

Chapter 12 analyses the influence of the InFo-TED project on national initiatives for teacher educators' learning in four European countries. The analysis shows that it is possible for an international project such as InFo-TED to strengthen national initiatives, by emphasizing the importance of good connections with key stakeholders. The chapter closes with the identification of specific factors for achieving influence.

Chapter 13 summarises the main themes and issues across the book and discusses these in relation to future research, professional development practices and educational policies. Four important foci emerge: school-based mentors, innovative research methods, diversity and inclusion, and, particularly urgent since the Covid-19 pandemic, learning through and with technology.

Notes

1 The optimism created among teacher educators did, however, not last long. In our opinion, the good intentions of the 2013 report have not been sufficiently followed up by policy makers (InFo-TED, 2019). In Europe, the main focus at the EU level,

as well as at national levels, has continued to be on the structure and content of teacher education.
2 Large-scale studies of the demographics of teacher educators were conducted in the United States (the Research About Teacher Education [RATE] surveys, as cited in Ducharme & Ducharme, 1996) and Australia (as cited in Grundy & Hatton, 1995).

References

Cochran-Smith, M., Grudnoff, L., Orland-Barak, L., & Smith, K. (2019). Educating teacher educators: International perspectives. *The New Educator*, 16(1), 5–24.

Czerniawski, G., Guberman, A., & MacPhail, A. (2017). The professional developmental needs of higher education-based teacher educators: An international comparative needs analysis. *European Journal of Teacher Education*, 40(1), 127–140.

Czerniawski, G., Kidd, W., & Murray, J. (2019). We are all teacher educators now: Understanding school-based teacher educators in times of change in England. In A. Swennen, C., Kosnik, & J. Murray (Eds.), *International research, policy and practice in teacher education* (pp. 171–185). Springer.

Davey, R. (2013). *The professional identity of teacher educators: Career on the cusp?* Routledge.

Ducharme, E. R. (1993). *The Lives of Teacher Educators*. Teachers College Press.

Ducharme, E., & Ducharme, M. (1996). Development of the teacher education professoriate. In F. Murray (Ed.), *The teacher educator's handbook: Building a knowledge base for the preparation of teachers* (pp. 691–714). Jossey-Bass.

Ellis, V., Glackin, G., Heighes, D., Norman, M., Nicol, S., & Norris, K. (2013). A difficult realization: The proletarianisation of higher education-based teacher educators. *Journal of Education for Teaching: International Research and Pedagogy*, 39(3), 266–280.

Ellis, V., & Maguire, M. (2017). Teacher education pedagogies based on critical approaches: Learning to challenge and change prevailing educational practices. In D. J. Clandinin, & J. Husu (Eds.), *The SAGE handbook of research on teacher education* (Vol. 2, pp. 594–608). SAGE.

European Commission. (2013). Supporting teacher educators for better learning outcomes. https://ec.europa.eu/assets/eac/education/policy/school/doc/support-teacher-educators_en.pdf.

European Commission. (2015). Strengthening teaching in Europe: New evidence from teachers compiled by Eurydice and CRELL, June 2015. Education and Training. https://ec.europa.eu/assets/eac/education/library/policy/teaching-profession-practices_en.pdf.

Goodwin, A. L., & Kosnik, C. (2013). Quality teacher educators = quality teachers? Conceptualizing essential domains of knowledge for those who teach teachers. *Teacher Development*, 17(3), 334–346.

Grundy, S., & Hatton, E. J. (1995). Teacher educators' ideological discourses. *Journal of Education for Teaching*, 42(1), 7–23.

Hobson, A. J., & Maxwell, B. (2020). Mentoring substructures and superstructures: An extension and reconceptualisation of the architecture for teacher mentoring. *Journal of Education for Teaching*. 46(2), 184–206.

Izadinia, M. (2014). Teacher educators' identity: A review of the literature. *European Journal of Teacher Education*, 37(4), 426–441.

Kosnik, C., Beck, C., & Goodwin, L. (2016). Reform efforts in teacher education. In J. Loughran, & M. L. Hamilton (Eds.), *Handbook on Teacher Education* (pp. 267–308). Springer.

Lampert, J., & Burnett, B. (Eds.). (2016). *Teacher education for high poverty schools.* Springer.

Loughran, J. (2014). Professionally developing as a teacher educator. *Journal of Teacher Education,* 65, 1–13.

Lunenberg, M., Dengerink, J., & Korthagen, F. (2014). *The professional teacher educator: Roles, behaviour, and professional development of teacher educators.* Sense Publishers.

Maguire, M. (1994). *The job of educating teachers* [Unpublished doctoral dissertation]. University of London.

McNamara, O., Murray, J., & Jones, M. (Eds.). (2014). *Workplace learning in teacher education.* Springer.

Murray, J. (2016). Beginning teacher educators: Working in higher education and schools. In J. Loughran, & M. L. Hamilton (Eds.). *International handbook on teacher education* (pp. 35–70). Springer.

Murray, J. (2017). Defining teacher educators: International perspectives and contexts. In D. J. Clandinin, & J. Husu (Eds.), *International handbook of research on teacher education* (pp. 1017–1033). SAGE.

Murray, J., & Male, T. (2005). Becoming a teacher educator: Evidence from the field. *Teaching and Teacher Education,* 21(2), 125–142.

Mattsson, M., Eilertsen, T. V., & Rorrison, D. (Eds.). (2011). *A practicum turn in teacher education.* Sense Publishers.

Organisation for Economic Co-operation and Development. (2005). Teachers matter: Attracting, developing and retraining effective teachers. https://www.oecd.org/education/school/34990905.pdf.

Organisation for Economic Co-operation and Development. (2018). Education at a glance 2018: OECD indicators. https://www.oecd-ilibrary.org/education/education-at-a-glance-2018_eag-2018-en.

Ping, C., Schellings, G., & Beijaard, D. (2018). Teacher educators' professional learning: A literature review. *Teaching and Teacher Education,* 75, 93–104.

Smith, K. (2020). Expansive learning for teacher educators: The story of the Norwegian national research school in teacher education (NAFOL). *Frontiers in Education,* 5(43), 1–12.

Smith, K., & Flores, M. A. (2019). Teacher educators as teachers and as researchers. *European Journal of Teacher Education,* 42(4), 429–432.

Smith, K., & Ulvik, M. (2015). An emerging understanding of mentors' knowledge base. In H. Tillema, G. J. Westhuizen, & K. Smith (Eds.), *Mentoring for learning* (pp. 299–312). Sense Publishers.

Snoek, M., Swennen, A., & van der Klink, M. (2011). The quality of teacher educators in the European policy debate: Actions and measures to improve the professionalism of teacher educators. *Professional Development in Education,* 37(5), 651–664.

Tack, H., & Vanderlinde, R. (2014). Teacher educators' professional development: Towards a typology of teacher educators' researcherly disposition. *British Journal of Educational Studies,* 62(3), 297–315.

Van Velzen, C., Volman, M., & Breckelmans, M. (2019). There is no need to sit on my hands anymore! Modelling and scaffolding as mentoring tools during co-teaching. In J. Murray, A. Swennen, & C. Kosnik (Eds.), *International research, policy and practice in teacher education: insider perspectives* (pp. 155–170). Springer.

Van Velzen, C., van der Klink, M., Swennen, A., & Yaffe, E. (2010). The induction and needs of beginning teacher educators. *Professional Development in Education,* 36(1–2), 61–75.

White, S. (2019). Teacher educators for new times? Redefining an important occupational group. *Journal of Education for Teaching*, 45(2), 200–213.

Yuan, H. (2017). Developing culturally responsive teachers: Current issues and a proposal for change in teacher education programs. *World Journal of Education*, 7(5), 66–78.

Zeichner, K. (2005). Becoming a teacher educator: A personal perspective. *Teaching and Teacher Education*, 21(2), 117–124.

Zeichner, K. (2007). Accumulating knowledge across self-studies in teacher education. *Journal of Teacher Education*, 58(1), 36–46.

Zeichner, K. (2010). Rethinking the connections between campus courses and field experiences in college and university-based teacher education. *Journal of Teacher Education*, 61(1–2), 89–99.

Chapter 2

This week : 2

A conceptual model of te educator development

An agenda for future research and practice

Eline Vanassche, Geert Kelchtermans, Ruben Vanderlinde and Kari Smith

Ways of seeing and *not* seeing teacher educator professionalism

Teacher educators are no longer the under-researched and poorly understood occupational group Loughran and Russell (1997) they once were claimed to be. The amount of research on their professional identities, work and development has grown steadily, as evidenced, for example, in a recent special issue on *Teacher educators as teachers and as researchers* (Smith & Flores, 2019) and in Ping et al.'s (2018) systematic review of 'what, how, and why teacher educators learn' (p. 93). The growing research attention is grounded in the 'recognition of their centrality in the pedagogies and practices of pre-service or initial teacher education' (Vanassche et al., 2019, p. 478) and acceptance of the premise that the work of educating teachers requires particular professionalism (i.e., knowledge, skills and beliefs), which is qualitatively different from that developed as an experienced classroom teacher. Murray and Male's (2005) distinction between second-order and first-order practice helps to appreciate the difference between the work of teaching and the work of teacher education (see also Murray, 2002). 'As second-order practitioners teacher educators induct their students into the practices and discourses of both school teaching and teacher education' (Murray & Male, 2005, p. 126). The work of educating teachers to teach thus demands the capability to simultaneously maintain two perspectives: the perspective of the teacher educator and the classroom teacher. That is, 'teacher educators design instructional environments conducive to students' learning, they support learning processes, and select curriculum materials, pedagogies, and assessment strategies, but this teaching is always intended to support student teachers' learning about teaching (see also Kelchtermans, 2013)' (Vanassche et al., 2015, p. 345; see also Vanassche, 2014).

With this growing research attention for the specific nature of second-order professionalism also come initiatives designed to secure, upscale or control such professionalism. The realisation that teacher educators are 'the single most

factor' (European Commission, 2013, p. 54) influencing the quality
ent teachers' learning alerts policy makers to the need for teacher edu-
rs' knowledge and skills to be 'of the highest order' (p. 54). A particular
utgrowth of this situation is the increasing investment in approaches to
strengthen the credentials of teacher educators and the recent development of
teacher educator standards in many jurisdictions (e.g., Australia, Flanders, Germany, Ireland, the Netherlands, Turkey and the United States). Standards serve
to benchmark the minimum levels of achievement for teacher educators. 'It
makes clear what they should know and be able to do... and it guarantees a
level of quality in teacher education, especially when standards are combined
with certification or registration processes' (Vanassche & Berry, 2019, p. 9) as is,
for example, the case in the Netherlands (see also Koster & Dengerink, 2001).

Our contention is that whilst these standards are a noteworthy and
encouraging sign of public recognition of the importance of teacher educators'
work, they also deflect our attention from core characteristics of the professionalism invested in the work. As Vanassche and Berry (2019) have argued,
standards represent a specific, and arguably predominant, way of seeing (Burke,
1935) teacher educator professionalism that attends to particular aspects of such
professionalism, but also elides other aspects. This is exactly what a way of
seeing *does*: it focusses attention in one area, but also presents blind spots in
other areas. In particular, standards tend to frame and treat teacher educator
professionalism as a technical attribute that is acquired, possessed and performed
by the individual teacher educator (Vanassche & Berry, 2019).[1] Standards
evoke the notion of general, context-free knowledge and skills that travel with
the competent individual from one situation to the next. Teacher education is
then *seen* as a function of the individually competent teacher educator who has
the necessary knowledge, skills and attitudes to perform a task at the required
standard. Such a way of seeing, however, cannot explain persisting paradoxical
truths (Lingard, 2016) about teacher education, such as a teacher educator
being competent one day with one student, but not the next; or highly competent teacher educators regularly combing to form an incompetent team. Such
observations show that individual competence is necessary but not sufficient to
explain effective (broadly defined) teacher education. Put differently, what is
learned in teacher education is not in complete control of the teacher educator
and their competences; it emerges as a consequence of the relationships with
student teachers and colleagues (including mentors in schools), which are in
turn shaped by the resources and constraints in broader socio-cultural and
institutional contexts (Vanassche et al., 2019). Professional standards are struggling to keep the relational and contextual aspects of the work in view.

In addition to the standards' incapacity to speak to the complexity of the
practices it seeks to support, a second and perhaps more fundamental concern
with this way of seeing teacher educator professionalism is, as Kelchtermans
(2013) has argued, its prescriptive orientation. Standards serve as a normative
blueprint to describe the content and further development of teacher educator

professionalism and measure to assess whether an individual meets the registered criteria for 'professional' practice. With a set of professional standards also comes the possibility for distinguishing between 'professional' and 'unprofessional' teacher educators (or 'expert' teacher educators and those who are 'still developing' the required professionalism), and the associated need for an institution that monitors and assesses performance, and in so doing effectively 'puts itself "above" the blueprint' (Kelchtermans, 2013, p. 90). This effect remains true also when, as is the case in some countries, members of the teacher educator community are involved or manage this institution. It is simply inherent to the logic of the standards. In fact, such a prescriptive stance, as will become clear below, contradicts the very idea of teacher educators as professionals, as we have come to understand it. *Book takes issue w/ standard requirements*

The starting point for the conceptual model presented in this chapter is a different one. That is, we aim to present a model to conceptualise, study and actively support teacher educator development, which takes as its central unit of analysis not the 'mental sediment' of individual teacher educators' professionalism (i.e., knowledge, cognition, competence, etc.), but the actual enactment of their professionalism in teacher education practices and all the complexities these entail. In doing so, we intend to provide a descriptive and communicative account of teacher educator development, rather than a prescriptive one. As such, the conceptual model presented here serves, on the one hand, as a simple map to delineate the object of interest (i.e., teacher educator development). On the other hand, the model delivers a shared language that demonstrates and makes public (i.e., opens up for critical debate) the richness of the professionalism that it seeks to support, and that is able to frame the issue of teacher educator development across the diversity in educational systems and institutional arrangements in which teachers are being educated. Although we are fully aware of the normative, political and professional stance communicated in this mapping and choosing of a language, the model does not serve to prescribe particular types of or directions for development, nor should it be used to assess teacher educators' professionalism or serve as the basis for the accreditation of targeted induction and continued professional development programmes.

Having first elaborated the rationale for developing a conceptual model of teacher educator development, we now move on to present the model and its theoretical underpinnings. We conclude the chapter by summarising the agenda for future research and action embedded in the model.

Conceptual model of teacher educator development[2]

Figure 2.1 presents the conceptual model. It serves to visualise our way of seeing teacher educator professional development. The model draws on a systematic study of the developing body of research and a series of structured discussions and exchange of practice-based experiences with teacher educator

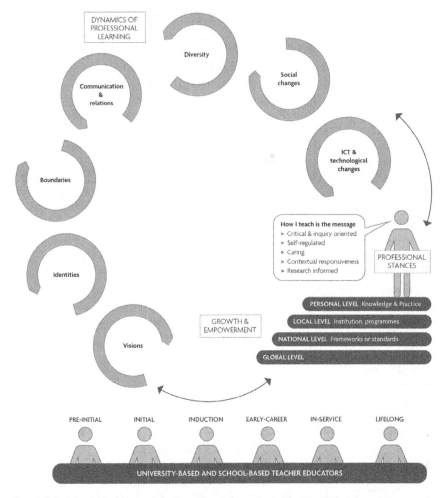

Figure 2.1 A conceptual model of teacher educator professional development

development among the community of the International Forum for Teacher Educator Development (InFo-TED). As hinted at above, the starting point for the professional development of teacher educators, in our opinion, needs to be their practice. We start from the assumption that acting teacher educators have good reasons for doing their job the way they are doing it. Such a starting point then gives a positive appreciation of the practice in which teacher educators *enact* their expertise. This is radically different from a deficit approach in which teacher educators' practices would be evaluated against the normative outline of the necessary competencies (e.g., professional standards) or evidence-based 'best practices'.

Our 'practice-based' approach (Kelchtermans 2013), in contrast to the 'blueprint' approach, starts from the idea that the actual practice reveals *who* a teacher educator is and what she or he really stands for. In terms of the Argyris and Schön's (1978) distinction, our stance implies that we do not start from the 'espoused theory' (the reasons people provide for their action) but rather from the 'theory in use' (the ideas, principles and beliefs that lie underneath what one is actually doing and, as such, can only be revealed by that practice). Teacher educators' sense of professional self or identity needs to be seen as reflected in their actions. In other words, the teacher educator as such only *emerges* in his or her practice (Kelchtermans, 2013).

In taking actual practice as the unit of analysis, we acknowledge that teacher educators' professional actions and decisions communicate particular professional messages. That is, 'how I teach is the message' (Russell, 1997). Based on our review of the literature and understanding of the field, such professional messages likely include being inquiry-oriented (reflective, looking for evidence, critically making explicit one's stance), self-regulated, contextually responsive and research-informed. In their teaching practices, teacher educators inevitably model teaching: they cannot *not model*, because student teachers will automatically observe them and judge the relationship between their words and actions (Loughran, 2006). From that starting point, the concentric circles (see Figure 2.1) reflect the movement and dynamics of professional learning, as well as professional learning's inevitable situatedness in a particular context. The point of departure for professional development needs to be the enacted practices by the individual teacher educator (personal level), as a reflection of his or her professional normative choices and judgment about what is or has to be the appropriate action in that particular situation. The professional knowledge of teacher educators combines solid theoretical knowledge with practical skills, inter-personal communication competence and experience. The enacting of such a complex set of knowledge takes place within the teacher educator's professional space, which is created by the situation and rarely repeats itself. Personal judgment, personal knowledge and beliefs, as well as the repertoire of skills and attitudes of the individual professional, are central for teacher educators in reflecting on and understanding their practices. *personal learning*

Individual practices, however, are always situated in particular local contexts (e.g., teacher education institutes, universities, training schools) and within specific programmes and curricula as part of the educational system in a particular country. This system also includes different partnerships with other organisations (e.g., training institute/training schools, but also professional organisations). Next, the practices by the teacher educators in their diverse organisational or local contexts are framed and influenced by national policy measures (including national frameworks or guidelines, standards and evaluation procedures). We do not think, however, of the relationship between the standards and the teacher education practices as linear and deterministic. Policy prescriptions are always interpreted, negotiated and translated into particular practices in the local organisational

always comes back to policies/policymakers

context in which a teacher educator is working. For that reason, the central goal of teacher educator development is personal empowerment to successfully design and enact their practices. Empowerment implies on the one hand acknowledging teacher educators' work and the expertise it reflects, and on the other hand creating opportunities to further develop and improve the expertise.

Since teacher educators' expertise often remains hidden (Livingston, 2014) or implicit, often reflected only in their practices, their professional development needs to include efforts to make that implicit expertise explicit and to create opportunities to share it with others. This, at the same time, will inevitably imply collegial discussion, forcing the teacher educator to critically reflect on and possibly modify his or her expertise. So becoming aware of and making one's expertise public is an essential constituent of professional development, similar to what Sachs (2015) calls the learning approach (in relation to teachers). Practitioners actively express their opinions and knowledge, and become involved with creating a knowledge base for their occupation as a process of establishing the profession. Finally, we situate teacher educators' practices in a global level in order to stress the relation with supra-national (e.g., Organisation for Economic Co-operation and Development [OECD]) and societal evolutions.

The increasing diversity of modern society is reflected in schools and constitutes multiple challenges for teachers and therefore also for teacher educators who are supposed to prepare teachers for this diverse reality in schools (e.g., Mills & Ballantyne, 2010). Pupils are not only diverse in the traditional categories of individual capacities or socio-economic backgrounds, but also increasingly in culture, language, ethnic identity, nationality and home situation. Teacher educators inevitably operate in complex networks of different groups and individuals (including students, parents, partner school staff, colleagues, policy makers). Their positioning in these networks, their willingness and capacity to cross traditional boundaries and to engage with a diversity of people (communication and relations), without losing sight of the bigger picture and purpose of their work, are all important domains for professional learning. Achieving this capacity to respond to and engage with diverse perspectives, influences and relationships requires confidence and at the same time a self-critical stance on the part of the teacher educator. Tack and Vanderlinde (2014) speak about a 'researcherly disposition' as the habit of mind to engage in research and thus to produce both local knowledge and public knowledge on teacher education. In addition, it requires conscious development of different identities, or put differently, a coherent system of different ways to conceive of (and understand) oneself in the profession (Kelchtermans, 2009).

Finally, professional development for and among teacher educators should include exposure to big ideas or world views, including not only different theoretical frameworks on education, teaching and becoming a teacher, but also more fundamental ethical, political and theoretical concepts and positions. This exposure to and study of different conceptual frameworks and theories will also operate as a strong impetus to self-critically become aware of and analyse one's normative ideas (and the ways in which they are enacted in or reflected by one's practices). It is clear that this self-critical reflection or engagement with different normative views is not a neutral intellectual endeavour, but it is our sense that taking such a perspective must and will help teacher educators to be able to develop a normative stance in their practice as well as the capacity and willingness to take responsibility for it. It is further obvious that the stance taken eventually results in the need for teacher educators to develop a researcher's attitude towards their own practice (individual or collaborative with peers from the same or other institutes). In other words, the professional development of teacher educators as we see it demands an attitude and self-positioning in the tradition of the 'reflective practitioner' (Schön, 1983; McHatton et al., 2013).

In order to develop one's professionalism, and also to improve one's practice (individual or collective), this reflective stance needs to be pushed regularly into real research activities in that practice. Such research activities are key elements of teacher educators' professional learning. Loughran (2014) speaks about a teacher educators' career as a 'research journey'. Teacher educators have to engage in research to improve their knowledge about teaching, their knowledge about students' learning, their own teaching and teacher education in general. Research thus needs to constitute an inherent part of the core practices of a teacher educator: teaching about teaching. Cochran-Smith (2005) has referred to this as 'working the dialectic'. Examples and methodologies to draw on are the long-standing international traditions of action research, teacher as researcher or self-study in teacher education practices (e.g., Altrichter et al., 2008; Cochran-Smith & Lytle, 2009; Loughran et al., 2004; Noffke & Somekh, 2008).

The continuum at the bottom of Figure 2.1 prompts a broad, inclusive definition of teacher educators in line with key policy documentation (European Commission, 2013). That is, we think about teacher educators as working in both schools and universities,

> encompassing a wide spectrum of positions in the educational system and field, and implies that we are aware that teacher educators enter the profession with different backgrounds. Some, for example, enter having worked as teachers, some as researchers with or without a PhD, and others may come from a variety of education-related roles.
>
> (Vanassche et al., 2015, p. 348)

The description of the phases on top of the continuum stresses the importance of thinking of teacher educators' practice as not only situated in a spatial context (e.g., an organisation or institute), but also in a temporal context. Understood from the position of the individual, this implies that professional development always needs to take into account one's career or biography, a position that is influenced by experiences from the past as well as expectations for the future (Kelchtermans, 2009). Teacher educators often enter the job from very different pathways, and their needs for development will be different depending on the career stage. Again, and similar to the influence from the organisational or institutional context, we do not think of career stages or phases as strict determinants of teacher educator's development, but rather as temporal elements of the context against which teacher educators give meaning to their experiences, feel particular needs for professional learning and/or make sense of what is offered to them in professional development opportunities.

Towards an agenda for future research: two key priorities

The proposed model not only provides a shared language for communication and collaboration across institutional and national boarders, it also serves as an overview of what we believe are core characteristics of teacher educator development to be explored in future research.

There is first and foremost a need to systematically account for the contextualised nature of teacher educators' work and development. The organisational and institutional contexts in which teacher educators enact their professionalism and develop professionally are significant (e.g., Tack & Vanderlinde, 2018; Vanassche & Kelchtermans, 2014, 2016). For example, the ability to 'stand by one's views and argue them convincingly' (Koster & Dengerink, 2001, p. 348; professional standard for Dutch teacher educators) is deeply compromised if one's personal views of teaching imply a covert or public critique of the operating curriculum policy in the programme. A point in case is Vanassche and Kelchtermans' (2016) case-study of a teacher educator who participated in a two-year professional development project and whose beliefs about teaching deeply conflicted with the operating curriculum policy at his institution. The researchers' narrative reconstruction of his experiences over the course of the project showed this was not just a technical difference of opinion about the goals and means of teacher education; it inevitably also involved issues of power and loyalty that had a strong impact on this teacher educator's professional identity, work and development.

As highlighted in the conceptual model, teacher educator development is never just a matter of 'upscaling' the technical knowledge and skills invested in the work but always represents a complex dynamic of the individual teacher educator and his or her working context. At the same time, we acknowledge that the field as a whole is currently lacking the appropriate conceptual and methodological tools to unpack the mediating role of context in teacher educators' work and development. In particular, there is a need for a thoughtful combination of theories of professional learning (e.g., adult learning, reflective learning, career-long learning) that place the individual learner at the centre of activity, with more 'systemic' or institutional frameworks that conceptualise the learning and actions of individuals as shaped by the broader socio-cultural and institutional structures involved in teacher educators' work and development. In our plea to give centre stage to actual teacher education practices for conceiving of teacher educator development, 'we have tried to operationalise this contextualised character of teacher education in a manner in which teacher educators globally can identify and instantiate' (Vanassche et al., 2015, p. 360).

Staying true to the proposed practice-based approach to professional development, there is also a need for thorough and detailed empirical descriptions of actual teacher education practices and all the complexities these entail. An interesting account of practice to start from is, for example, the supervisory conferences conducted with mentors and student teachers after lesson observations on school placements. These have been recognised as a distinctive aspect of teacher educators' work (see, e.g., Valencia et al., 2009; Williams, 2014), but at the same time also remain one of the most difficult agendas for teacher educators to understand and enact (see, e.g., Bullough & Pinnegar, 2004; Ben Harush & Orland-Barak, 2019).

One of the reasons why these supervisory conferences are so complicated is because they present a coming together of different understandings of teaching and learning about teaching, as well as different contexts of teacher education (i.e., the school and the teacher education context). Supervisory conferences thus inevitably bring to bear teacher educators' (and student teachers' and mentors') view of good teaching, as well as teacher educators' ability to work towards the improvement of teaching practice, making this an excellent site for studying teacher educators' professionalism and opportunities for further development.

Towards an agenda for action

The proposed model for teacher educator development not only offers implications for future research, but also immediately suggests a framework to actively work on (i.e., further develop and support) teacher educator professionalism.

A practice-based approach to the professional development of teacher educators demands, as highlighted above, first and foremost a researcher's attitude (Kelchtermans et al., 2014) and what Grossman et al. (2009) labelled as 'pedagogies of investigation', that is, finding ways to share and critically investigate accounts of practice in honest dialogue in a community of practitioners. *The Self-Study of Teaching and Teacher Education Practices* community (e.g., Loughran et al., 2004) offers a starting point for how we might understand and conceptualise these pedagogies of investigation. Self-study research is a way of purposefully examining personal teacher education practice and its shaping forces (i.e., including elements of one's professional biography and the context of the teacher education institute as an organisation), as well as the relationship between one's teaching as a teacher educator and student teachers' learning.

The reflective and investigative attitude in self-study research is a more thorough and explicit variant of what Cochran-Smith (2003) labelled 'inquiry as stance'. The latter refers to 'the positions teachers and others who work together in inquiry communities take toward knowledge and its relationships to practice ... the metaphor is intended to capture the ways we stand, the ways we see, and the lenses we see through' (Cochran-Smith, 2003, p. 8; see also Cochran-Smith & Lytle, 1999, p. 289). Inquiry as stance refers to a particular way of looking at and relating to professional practice. Taking the perspective of inquiry as stance means teacher educators generating local knowledge of practice, acknowledging and taking into account its relational and contextualised qualities, and interpreting and interrogating the research of others. It involves making problematic teacher education practice both on a personal and a public level (Cochran-Smith & Lytle, 1999). Its research agenda – building on the model put forward in this chapter – might focus on making problematic teacher educators' personal knowledge and beliefs about good teaching underpinning their practices (as an important element of teacher educators' sense of self), their student teachers' learning, as well as the broader institutional context in which these teacher education practices operate.

Central to a researcher's attitude is the recognition and positive appreciation of the complexity, messiness and unpredictability that characterises teaching and teacher education that also formed the basis of the proposed conceptual model. In reflecting upon one's practice, not a 'quick fix', but a deepened understanding and knowledge of the complexity of the situation and becoming better informed about the different possibilities to act and respond pedagogically in that situation is central. That is,

> for the problematic to be seen as problematic, teacher educators must accept the responsibility of teaching in ways that continually focus attention on not only what is being taught, but also on the complexity of how and why it is taught; regardless of the perceived success or otherwise of the practice at that time.
>
> (Loughran, 2006, p. 42)

A more refined understanding of the complexity of teaching about teaching adds to the possibility that teacher educators will be able to deliberate more effectively between different opportunities to act.

A researcher's attitude operates best in concert with others (e.g., colleagues) as it is essentially dialogical: it manifests itself in forms of professional dialogue, conversation, critique and inquiry with others (Kelchtermans et al., 2014). Investigating practice works best in a community of colleagues that in turn try to enact a researcher's attitude, from a collective moral commitment to the education of the next generation of teachers. Having an audience not only helps to open up new opportunities for action and understanding of one's practice but also holds the basic conditions for generating a pedagogy of teacher education that is clearly grounded in practice, yet extends well beyond that local practice in relevance.

On a more systemic level, we encourage policy makers to establish an awareness of and act toward the need for and creation of more coherent national infrastructures for the professional development of teacher educators, in whichever education setting they work, and the diversity of their roles in supporting the initial education, induction, and career-long learning of teachers.

(International Forum for Teacher Educator Development, 2019, p. 6)

There is a need for professional development support through trusted communities of practice (Clemans et al., 2010) on a regional, national and trans-national level. 'The time of the isolated teacher educator belongs to the past, and "communities of practice" reaching far beyond the local context are today both technically possible and expected' (Kelchtermans et al., 2018, p. 130).

Notes

1 This chapter aims to critically question the emerging discourse of professional standards for teacher educators, recognizing that standards are constructed, and therefore select and deflect. This is an exercise in making standards unfamiliar and uncovering the theoretical constructs and motivations that underpin them, in order to guard against naive and uncritical acceptance of standards in policy and practice. This is not withstanding the explicit attempts in some contexts to firmly keep the ownership of the standards with the professional community (e.g., the Netherlands) or purposeful avoidance of the term 'standards' and its static connotations (e.g., the 'developmental profile for teacher educators' in Flanders). Beyond this, inherent in the use of the 'way of seeing' metaphor is acknowledgment of the fact that this is not a simple binary opposition. Each alternative way of seeing presents new blind spots and selects and deflects. We invite the community to critically engage with this alternative way of seeing and draw attention to what it invokes and what it elides.

2 This paragraph is a slightly extended reprint from Kelchtermans et al. (2018). Towards an 'international forum for teacher educator development': An agenda for research and action. *European Journal of Teacher Education, 41*(1), pp. 125–129 (published online on 4 September 2017, copyright Association for Teacher Education in Europe, published by Routledge, Taylor & Francis Group, Informa Group Plc, available online: https://doi.org/10.1080/02619768.2017.1372743).

References

Altrichter, H., Feldman, A., Posch, P., & Somekh, B. (2008). *Teachers investigate their work: An introduction to action research across the professions* (2nd ed.). Routledge.

Argyris, C., & Schön, D. (1978). *Organizational learning: A theory of action perspective.* Addison-Wesley.

Ben Harush, A., & Orland-Barak, L. (2019). Triadic mentoring in early childhood teacher education: The role of relational agency. *International Journal of Mentoring and Coaching in Education,* 8(3), 182–196.

Bullough, Jr., R. V., & Pinnegar, S. (2004). Thinking about the thinking about self-study: An analysis of eight chapters. In J. Loughran, M. L. Hamilton, V. K. Laboskey, & T. L. Russell (Eds.), *International handbook of self-study of teaching and teacher education practices* (pp. 314–342). Kluwer.

Burke, K. (1935). *Permanence and change: An anatomy of purpose.* New Republic.

Clemans, A., Berry, A., & Loughran, J. (2010). Lost and found in transition: The professional journey of teacher educators. *Professional Development in Education*, 36(1–2), 211–228.

Cochran-Smith, M. (2003). Learning and unlearning: The education of teacher educators. *Teaching and Teacher Education*, 19(1), 5–28.

Cochran-Smith, M. (2005). Teacher educators as researchers: Multiple perspectives. *Teaching Teachers*, 21(2), 219–225.

Cochran-Smith, M., & Lytle, S. (1999). Relationships of knowledge and practice: Teacher learning in communities. In A. Iran-Nejad, & C. Pearson (Eds.), *Review of research in education* (pp. 249–305). American Educational Research Association.

Cochran-Smith, M., & Lytle, S. (2009). *Inquiry as stance: Practitioner research for the next generation*. Teacher College Press.

European Commission. (2013). *Supporting teacher educators for better learning outcomes*. https://ec.europa.eu/assets/eac/education/policy/school/doc/support-teacher-educators_en.pdf.

Grossman, P., Hammerness, K., & McDonald, M. (2009). Redefining teacher: Re-imagining teacher education. *Teachers and teaching: Theory and practice*, 15(2), 273–290.

International Forum for Teacher Educator Development. (2019). *The Importance of teacher educators: Professional development imperatives* [White paper]. https://info-ted.eu/wp-content/uploads/2019/10/InFo-TED-White-Paper.pdf.

Kelchtermans, G. (2009). Who I am in how I teach is the message: Self-understanding, vulnerability and reflection. *Teachers and Teaching*, 15(2), 257–272.

Kelchtermans, G. (2013). Praktijk in de plaats van blauwdruk. Over het opleiden van lerarenopleiders [Practice instead of blueprint: Educating teacher educators]. *Tijdschrift Voor Lerarenopleiders*, 34(3), 89–99.

Kelchtermans, G., Vanassche, E., & Deketelaere, A. (Eds.). (2014). *Lessen uit LOEP: Lerarenopleiders Onderzoeken hun Eigen Praktijk* [Lessons from LOEP: Teacher educators research their own practice]. Garant.

Kelchtermans, G., Vanderlinde, R., & Smith, K. (2018). Towards an 'international forum for teacher educator development': An agenda for research and action. *European Journal of Teacher Education*, 41(1), 120–134.

Koster, B., & Dengerink, J. (2001). Towards a professional standard for Dutch teacher educators. *European Journal of Teacher Education*, 24(3), 343–354.

Lingard, L. (2016). Paradoxical truths and persistent myths: Reframing the team competence conversation. *Journal of Continuing Education in the Health Professions*, 36(1), 19–21.

Livingston, K. (2014). Teacher educators: Hidden professionals. *European Journal of Education* 49(2), 218–232.

Loughran, J. (2006). *Developing a pedagogy of teacher education: Understanding teaching and learning about teaching*. Routledge.

Loughran, J. (2014). Professionally developing as a teacher educator. *Journal of Teacher Education*, 65(4), 1–13.

Loughran, J., & Russell, T. L. (Eds.). (1997). *Teaching about teaching: Purpose, passion and pedagogy in teacher education*. Falmer.

Loughran, J., Hamilton, M. L., LaBoskey, V. K., & Russell, T. L. (Eds.). (2004). *International handbook of self-study of teaching and teacher education practices*. Kluwer.

McHatton, P. A., Parker, A. K., & Vallice, R. K. (2013). Critically reflective practitioners: Exploring our intentions as teacher educators. *Reflective Practice*, 14(3), 392–405.

Mills, C., & Ballantyne, J. (2010). Pre-service teachers' dispositions towards diversity: Arguing for a developmental hierarchy of change. *Teaching and Teacher Education*, 26(3), 447–454.

Murray, J. (2002). Between the chalkface and the ivory towers? A study of the professionalism of teacher educators working on primary initial teacher education courses in the English education system. Collected Original Resources in Education (CORE), 1–550.

Murray, J., & Male, T. (2005). Becoming a teacher educator: Evidence from the field. *Teaching and Teacher Education*, 21(2), 125–142.

Noffke, S. E., & Somekh, B. (Eds.). (2008). *The SAGE handbook of educational action research*. Sage.

Ping, C., Schellings, G., & Beijaard, D. (2018). Teacher educators' professional learning: A literature review. *Teaching and Teacher Education*, 75, 93–104.

Russell, T. L. (1997). Teaching teachers: How I teach is the message. In J. Loughran, & T. L. Russell (Eds.), *Teaching about teaching: Purpose, passion and pedagogy in teacher education* (pp. 32–47). Falmer.

Sachs, J. (2015). Teacher professionalism: Why are we still talking about it? *Teachers and Teaching*, 22(4), 413–425.

Schön, D. A. (1983). *The reflective practitioner. How professionals think in action*. Temple Smith.

Smith, K., & Flores, M. A. (2019). Teacher educators as teachers and as researchers. *European Journal of Teacher Education*, 42(4), 429–432.

Tack, H., & Vanderlinde, R. (2014). Teacher educators' professional development: Towards a typology of teacher educators' researcherly disposition. *British Journal of Educational Studies*, 62(3), 297–315.

Tack, H. & Vanderlinde, R. (2018). Capturing the relations between teacher educators' opportunities for professional growth, work pressure, work related basic needs satisfaction, and teacher educators' researcherly disposition. *European Journal of Teacher Education*, 42(4), 459–477.

Valencia, W. S., Martin, S. D., Place, N. A., & Grossman, P. (2009). Complex interactions in student teaching. Lost opportunities for learning. *Journal of Teacher Education*, 60(3), 304–322.

Vanassche, E. (2014). (Re)Constructing teacher educators' professionalism: Biography, work- place and pedagogy [Thesis dissertation, University of Leuven].

Vanassche, E., & Berry, A. (2019). Teacher educator knowledge, practice, and S-STTEP research. In J. Kitchen, A. Berry, H. Guðjónsdóttir, S. M. Bullock, M. Taylor, & A. R. Crowe (Eds.), *Second international handbook of self-study of teaching and teacher education practices*. Springer.

Vanassche, E., & Kelchtermans, G. (2014). Teacher educators' professionalism in practice: Positioning theory and personal interpretative framework. *Teaching and Teacher Education*, 44, 117–127.

Vanassche, E., & Kelchtermans, G. (2016). A narrative analysis of a teacher educator's professional learning journey. *European Journal of Teacher Education*, 39(3), 355–367.

Vanassche, E., Kidd, W. E., & Murray, J. (2019). Articulating, reclaiming and celebrating the professionalism of teacher educators in England. *European Journal of Teacher Education*, 42(4), 478–491.

Vanassche, E., Rust, F., Conway, P., Smith, K., Tack, H., & Vanderlinde, R. (2015). InFo-TED: Bringing policy, research, and practice together around teacher educator development. In C. Craig, & L. Orland-Barak (Eds.), *International teacher education: Promising pedagogies (part C)* (Vol. 22, pp. 341–364). Emerald.

Williams, J. (2014). Teacher educator professional learning in the third space: Implications for identity and practice. *Journal of Teacher Education*, 65(4), 315–326.

Chapter 3

Researching the professional learning needs of teacher educators

Results from international research

Gerry Czerniawski, Ann MacPhail, Eline Vanassche, Marit Ulvik, Ainat Guberman, Helma Oolbekkink-Marchand and Yvonne Bain

Introduction

The two-part sequential mixed study described in this chapter provides an international and comparative needs analysis through a survey of 1,158 higher education-based teacher educators in the countries participating in the International Forum for Teacher Educator Development (InFo-TED): Belgium, Ireland, Israel, the Netherlands, Norway, and the United Kingdom. Follow-up interviews were also carried out with 61 participants who took part in the survey to enable a deeper understanding of the survey data findings. The teacher educators who participated in this study belong to the 'traditional group' described in chapter 1: those who work in higher education institutes, whether universities or teaching colleges. As that chapter explains, the professional learning[1] of higher education-based teacher educators is deemed more valuable when facilitated not just through formal provision and organised programmes, but also through informal workplace learning (Boyd et al., 2011; Murray et al., 2017). Highlighting the many similarities, across different jurisdictions, in teacher educators' professional learning needs, the chapter draws attention to the realities of this work, its many nuanced differences and what an understanding of both can tell us about the professional learning needs of this group of teacher educators. The chapter, for the first time, combines a systematic integration of both the qualitative and quantitative findings from both parts of the study to provide contrast and depth to our findings.

The chapter starts by introducing the reader to literature on the complexities associated with higher education-based teacher educators' roles and professional development. An understanding of these complexities is essential when examining the professional learning needs of the participants in this study. After describing the methodology, the chapter then presents findings from the overall study. The discussion, deriving from the study as a whole, begins to address issues pointed at in chapter 1: the relative lack of large-scale research into the professional learning of higher education-based teacher educators, particularly beyond the induction phase.

The careers of higher education-based teacher educators

Becoming a teacher educator is a complex and challenging endeavour and one hereto situated within a paucity of reported professional development opportunities. As chapter 1 explains, previous attempts to describe teacher educators' work (Lunenberg et al., 2014; Swennen et al., 2010) have cited a variety of roles, each of which require professional development: teaching, coaching, facilitation of collaboration between diverse organisations and stakeholders, assessment, 'gatekeeping', curriculum development, research and critical inquiry. The lack of induction into these roles experienced by so many teacher educators is well documented (Murray et al., 2011; Van Velzen et al., 2010). Teacher educators' professional learning needs may differ from each other depending not only on the roles they have but also on their personal background, institution and country. Whether recruited mainly from schools or universities (Griffiths et al., 2014), both groups may encounter different transitional experiences influencing their own unique professional learning needs vis-à-vis their roles.

Furthermore, as chapter 1 explains, institutions of higher education have experienced 'the university turn' and the 'practice turn' differently, depending on their country's policies as well as their own agenda and mission, and may have different expectations of their academic staff. A distinction can, for example, be drawn between colleges of higher education and universities whereby the latter may[2], in some locations, be associated with greater levels of research activity.

As many of the authors in this book have highlighted, the transition from teacher-to-teacher educator is not something that happens immediately. Acknowledging the problematic (yet desirable) use of the term 'teacher educator' in schools, many former school teachers have gained significant experience as teacher educators when mentoring student and newly qualified teachers. Many experienced teachers in schools will also have provided training and development opportunities to their colleagues (e.g., through carrying out observations, mentoring, workshops). But moving into higher education employment for the first time can still leave many experienced teachers feeling deskilled, isolated and insecure about the expectations of their performance as novice university employees (Labaree, 2003; Van Velzen et al., 2010). As school teachers, their job would be focused on the development of learning and teaching and associated activities, but in higher education there are additional and competing demands. Writing about early career researchers in general, Laudel and Glaser (2008) argue that the job of an academic, working in large organisations like universities, consists of three (not one) interrelated but largely independent careers:

1   A cognitive career – the development of a research trail and knowledge base (made up of published articles, grants, bids);
2   A community career – developed through the participation in the knowledge production and academic communities associated with their discipline (e.g., reviewing journal articles for publishers, membership of subject associations, editorial teams, etc.).
3   An organisational career – the specific performance expectations of the employer institution (e.g., the career path as identified by the university job specification).

Laudel and Glaser (2008) argue that the nature of these three careers accounts for why many academics feel 'decoupled' from their employer organisation. For teacher educators working in higher education institutions, these feelings will be exacerbated as they juggle the competing demands associated with their many roles and the often complex relationships between higher education institutions and schools. These demands include teacher educators' attempts to service school partnerships while trying to ensure they can meet their own institution's expectations to publish academic articles (Ellis et al., 2013; Guberman & Mcdossi, 2019). In view of the three career paths mentioned above and the multitude of roles, knowledge and skills each of these requires, the current chapter describes how higher education-based teacher educators perceive their professional learning needs. This information will enrich our limited knowledge about teacher educators' professionalism (Goodwin et al., 2014) and will be useful to policy makers and leaders of teacher education programmes who wish to provide teacher educators with the professional learning opportunities they need.

Methodology

The study

At present, there are few systemic routes for teacher educators' ongoing learning and little research documentation of these (Berry, 2013; Murray et al., 2011; Smith, 2012). Given the unique occupational position of teacher educators and the lack of formal focus on their professional learning, our starting point lies in their practice positioned within local, national, regional and global policy contexts. According to the European Commission (2012), 'if teachers are the most important in-school factor influencing the quality of students' learning, the competences of those who educate and support teachers [teacher educators] must be of the highest order' (p. 52). Building on the recommendations of two European Commission reports that promote and support a shared vision and common understanding of what is meant by quality in educating teachers and access to high-quality opportunities for continuing professional development (European Commission, 2012, 2013), this two-part sequential mixed study comprises a large-scale quantitative survey followed by in-depth exploratory semi-structured interviews. Both parts of the study address two main research questions:

1 What professional learning activities do higher education-based teacher educators value?
2 How best can these professional learning activities be realized?

The research questions for this study are significant when considering that many teacher educators acquire their expertise *after* taking on the position of teacher educator, especially if their background lies solely in either school teaching or research (Murray & Male, 2005; Smith, 2012).

Participants

Participants were recruited through the institutions in which they worked and through professional networks. The participants were 1,158 teacher educators working in higher education institutions from six countries: Belgium (176, 16.6%), Ireland (54, 5.1%), Israel (101, 9.5%), the Netherlands (358, 33.8%), Norway (76, 7.2%), and the United Kingdom (294, 27.8%). There were 61 higher education teacher educators who took part in the survey (15 from England; 11 from Scotland; 10 from Ireland; 10 from Israel; 10 from Norway; five from The Netherlands)[3] and voluntarily took part in follow-up interviews.

Background variables are presented both in raw numbers and as valid percentages, excluding participants with missing data. The median age group was 45–54 years old. The number of years' experience as teacher educators ranged from 0 to 47, with a mean of 11.99 years (SD = 8.77). In total, 908 (78.5%) indicated they had experienced teaching before being recruited as teacher educators. There were 341 (34.0%) participants with doctorates; 599 (59.6%) with a master's degree; 61 (6.1%) with BA/BSc; and three (0.03%) with non-academic qualifications.

As for the 61 interviewees, similar to the survey sample, there were 17 (28%) males and 44 females (72%). The median age group was 45–54 years old. The number of years of experience as teacher educators ranged from six months to 33 years. Moreover, 40 (66%) were university based, whereas 21 (34%) worked in teacher education colleges.

The questionnaire

Professional learning needs were assessed by a questionnaire that had four sections: professional learning preferences (31 items); factors considered before a professional learning activity is engaged in (eight items); research dispositions and experience (four multi-item questions that will not be dealt with here); and role description and background information (28 items).

Participants rated on a Likert response scale, ranging from 1 (*not at all*) to 6 (*very much*), their level of satisfaction with the professional learning opportunities they have had (one item), their degree of interest in further professional learning (one item) and their degree of interest in specific professional learning options (27 items). Participants also provided qualitative responses to two survey questions: 'What are your two most important professional learning needs?' and 'What professional learning opportunities would best meet these needs?' The qualitative data for each question was analysed separately for the 624 participants who provided responses in English. The results of this analysis were combined with insights gained from the interviews (see below).

Responses to the specific professional development options were subjected to principal component factor analysis with Kaiser Varimax (orthogonal) rotation yielding two main factors. The first factor, 'Academic Interest' (13 questionnaire items), comprises activities characteristic of research universities (e.g., reviewing papers and presenting at conferences), whereas the second factor, 'Educational Interest' (12 items), comprises activities and content areas specific to teaching and teacher education (e.g., curriculum development and assessment). Together, these two factors account for 37.80% of the variance. Two items did not load on any of these factors (i.e., were not correlated with any of them): 'interest in online learning' and 'specialisation in academic administration'.

The interview

To gain a deeper understanding of the professional learning needs raised in the survey findings, semi-structured interviews were carried out with participants volunteering to take part in this part of the study. The interview questions closely mapped the sections of the previously completed survey and constituted questions on (a) background and demographics, (b) professional learning opportunities and (c) teacher education and research. Interviews were conducted in each participant's native language in a setting of their choosing, with interviewees providing informed consent for the interviews. The interview data were analysed thematically. A coding process used in identifying similar text units, followed by linking and retrieval of similarly coded segments (Mason, 1996), were standardised across the six jurisdictions[4].

Findings

Developing teaching and learning

Most teacher educators wished to learn more ways to improve teaching and learning without compromising their responsibility for delivering all areas of the curriculum. There was an implication for many that insufficient affordances were offered in developing their teaching. As one Norwegian interviewee stated:

I still feel they're [teacher education practices] kind of traditional, the ways of doing it, the lecturing … and lack of resources, always … and we don't have the opportunities to develop our own teaching in the teacher education as much as I'd like to.

Professional learning needs included up-skilling in new pedagogies associated with particular subject disciplines, developing more generic teaching and learning strategies (e.g., active teaching approaches, integrating theory and practice, self-directed learning, feedback, flipping the classroom) and consideration of class management (e.g., managing large class sizes, managing different learning needs, managing different populations such as disadvantaged students). For some, this need to generate or rekindle classroom expertise and currency of knowing what teaching is in schools could be addressed by returning to school for a period of time to experience the reality of practice as a teacher: 'every day that I work at university, it's one day longer since I worked in schools. The gap between "walking the walk" and "talking the talk" is getting bigger' (England).

However, the opportunity for teacher educators to visit schools to observe student teachers on school placement had been removed for some participants, resulting not just in feeling removed from the reality of teaching and the fostering of collaboration between different communities, but in some cases, also losing out research capacity: 'it's [school placement] shared knowledge, it's new knowledge, it's a dialogue space you know and there are opportunities for joint research as well and that has been removed now' (Scotland).

The most valued opportunities to improve teaching and learning involved informal learning conversations with other colleagues, visits to other schools or teacher education institutions, and learning about current developments in teacher education. All of these rated above 4.5 out of 6 in the survey. University courses, workshops, seminars and conferences were all mentioned as sites where upskilling could take place. Many teacher educators expressed a desire for in-house courses tailored to their specific teaching needs. Many teacher educators also sought opportunities to observe and be observed by colleagues to share professional experiences and develop ideas.

The *Educational Interest* scale was correlated with participants' academic qualifications and experience: master's degree holders were more interested in educational activities than doctorate holders, and teacher educators with up to 10 years of experience were more interested in educational activities than those with longer experience (see Table 3.1).

Developing research and writing

Participants were seemingly more interested in professional learning activities addressing teaching and learning ($M = 4.80$, $SD = 1.12$) than in those addressing research and writing skills ($M = 3.84$, $SD = 1.38$, $t_{(999)} = 20.40$, $p < .001$).

Table 3.1 Simultaneous regression analysis predicting interest in professional development

	Academic Interest			Educational Interest		
Variable	B	SE B	β	B	SE B	β
Gender	.24	.06	.14***	.26	.05	.16***
Degree	.24	.05	.14***	−.26	.05	−.17***
Employment	.29	.05	.17***	.03	.05	.02
Experience	−.10	−.06	−.06	−.20	.05	−.13***
Intercept	3.60	.07		4.33	.12	
R²	**.07**			**.08**		

*p < .05, **p < .01, ***p < .001.

Gender: 0 = male, 1 = female

Degree: 0 = up to 2nd degree, 1 = doctorate

Employment: 0 = part time, 1 = full time

Experience: 0 = up to 10 years, 1 = more than 10 years

Opinions in follow-up interviews diverged on whether teacher educators need to be active researchers. Echoing much of the literature discussed above, some teacher educators in this study were recruited from the research field and valued research related activities. There was consensus from those interviewed[5] that contractual obligations as a teacher educator in a university, in many cases, resulted in research being part of teacher educators' remit as well as legitimacy: 'research is very important in teacher education. It has to do with legitimacy' (Israel); and 'it's in my job descriptor and it is fundamental. I mean, it is there in black and white that I have a responsibility to carry out research and to write up that research as part of what I do' (Scotland).

However, a significant number of participants had begun their careers as teacher educators without a doctorate. Increasing pressure from institutions to employ teacher educators with doctorates led many to undertake doctoral studies once in post. Subsequently, many were able to articulate the benefits of being research literate:

> Research is very important, and more and more, of course. When I started as a teacher educator, it wasn't that way. I discovered this along the way, and also when I started doing my own research and my PhD, of course.
>
> (Norway)

Other teacher educators were more ambivalent towards imposed research foci with some doubting its relevance to the education of teachers:

> I think you should engage with the research but it is not essential to be a good researcher in your own right, presumably we are teaching our trainees to engage and act on research and critical thinking, but my feeling is that doing your own research is not essential for a good teacher/educator.
>
> (England)

The influence of teacher educators' background and work context was evident in the quantitative data too; doctorate holders appeared to be more interested in activities related to their academic interests than master's degree holders. Full-time employees were more interested than part-time employees (see Appendix 1).

Participants' need to publish research and/or write for publication *was* noted in our findings at two distinct levels. First, many participants conveyed the need to begin writing for publication, seeking direction on how best to develop ideas, and subsequently transform ideas into a publication, as well as understanding more about the publishing process. Second, many appeared to have some level of experience in publishing and expressed the need to increase their publication rate, develop a higher quality of publication and consider how to write for different audiences.

The research related activities that attracted a high level of interest (above 4.5 on the 6-level Likert response scale) were personal reading and performing practitioner-based research, such as action research.

The importance of collaboration

In addressing how the above activities might be realised, having other teacher educator colleagues as mentors as a beginning teacher educator was, in interviews, commonly depicted as a valuable learning experience:

> When I arrived at the college it was after the academic year had already started and I didn't know anything, really – nothing at all. But there were two adjacent instructors that supported me tremendously, all along the way, and that's how I reached my current position.
>
> (Israel)

Having access to a community of teacher educators was consistently reported as an effective and preferred means of experiencing professional development: 'a community of people with whom you can discuss current affairs, where you can discuss things and where you can compare your practices to others' (The Netherlands).

However, participants identified little by way of any formalised provision mentoring, and teacher educators were cautious in their expectations of what colleagues with demanding job remits could feasibly contribute, often informally, with respect to collaborative community support: 'it feels too difficult to carve out staff time or resources for it or to ask other people to collaborate because you know that they will be collaborating over and above their normal responsibility' (Scotland). Consequently, even if informal support in a learning community is valued, it has its challenges. Within the sample of those interviewed, very few teacher educators mentored other teacher educators. Those who did found the experience rewarding and enriching:

> I guide an amazing researcher. We conduct inter-cultural research. Intercultural research allows me to learn, to know the other … We are currently working on the first paper. It is very important for him to publish, and it is very important for me that he will publish … I also learn from my post-doctoral student. Very much.
>
> (Israel)

A desire to collaborate with experienced colleagues in relation to research capability (including doctoral supervisors) was portrayed as an opportunity to discuss research papers, share how best to engage with research and writing, and access colleagues across a range of higher education institutions. With respect to coaching and mentoring, one teacher educator echoed the request of others when proposing 'allocation of a mentor to help support and advice from a research background'. With respect to collaborating with (experienced) colleagues, related activities included peer learning, working on specific publications with colleagues and working in a writing group.

Discussion

If the quality of teaching is affected by the quality of teachers, and by inference the quality of their teacher educators, as suggested by this book and based on the European Commission (2012, 2013), then politicians and policy makers must take account of the support needed for teacher educators' professional development. As professional learners themselves, only teacher educators can ensure such quality is nurtured, maintained, developed and perfected. Professional contexts vary and teacher educators, as stated earlier, are far from being a homogenised professional group. With respect to the 'traditional group' of higher education based teacher educators, not all institutions of higher education are universities and not all universities place the same emphases on research-related activities. Our findings question the extent to which all higher education-based teacher educators can currently access sufficient professional learning opportunities that help them develop an integrated professional profile that, where applicable, can embrace the three interrelated cognitive, community and organisational careers (Guberman & Mcdossi, 2019; Laudel & Glaser, 2008) and discussed earlier in this chapter.

Several factors impede the development of that profile, not least the bifurcation identified by many in this study between teacher/teacher educator as practitioner and researcher. It is clear from both the quantitative and qualitative data that, while teacher educators consistently appear to value professional learning, divergence exists in their priorities and needs, and are contextualised in many cases by the sorts of institution in which they are employed. Two types of teacher educators' professional learning needs arise from the data: (a) those involving the development of educational capacities related to organisational careers, that is, their day-to-day remit as a teacher educator (e.g., in the delivery of taught programmes); and (b) those required for progressing both their cognitive and community careers, with research and writing skills being the most salient.

It is also clear that many teacher educators strive to improve their current strengths rather than seek further professional development in areas in which they have limited or no experience. A difference exists, for example, in the type of professional needs identified by those with a master's degree (which were more aligned to teacher educators' educational capacities) and those with doctorates (more aligned to scholarly activities to progress their academic career). These divisions can, in part, be explained by the two distinct policies for recruiting teacher educators referred to earlier, namely the recruitment of teachers from schools and/or the recruitment of teachers from a predominantly research background. Although, as we have seen, this distinction is, itself, problematic.

A tension revealed in the interviews in relation to teaching, was the elapsed time between being a teacher in a school and operating as a teacher educator. Our findings support the notion that teacher educators want to retain proximity to the practice field and to be updated on the realities of teaching (MacPhail & O'Sullivan, 2019; Van der Klink et al., 2017). Many of the more experienced teacher educators who took part in this study had entered the teacher education profession as practicing schoolteachers with no higher research degree. It was evident that for this specific subset of teacher educators, the terms of their initial appointment were shifting in an institutional climate that had changed, in some instances quite aggressively, towards research activity and research output (the 'university turn' described in chapter 1).

Many of the same teacher educators noted the inextricable link between teaching and research, and specifically that teaching is research-informed. However, there was less consensus on the contribution of active participation in research to educating teachers. Some teacher educators implied it was sufficient to infuse research through teaching, while others believed that there was no other option than to undertake a doctorate (if not already done so) and contribute to the institute's research metrics. A different mind-set was evident from those who had been employed more recently and had contractual obligations to be research active, with many already having a doctorate and a developing research profile.

The need for opportunities to generate critical and collaborative professional learning conversations has previously been supported in the literature (Loughran, 2006), with research beginning to explore specifically professional learning communities for teacher educators (Hadar & Brody, 2010; MacPhail et al., 2014). This study builds on this literature emphasizing the ways in which teacher educators, as both teachers and researchers, want to be part of a collaborative community where they can feel supported, listened to and share their practices and experiences. However, those practices and experiences vary depending on the professional identity and trajectory of the teacher educator.

The extent to which collaborative communities can operate successfully is dependent on the human and material resources available to those seeking professional development opportunities. For example, numerous requests were made by both full-time and part-time teacher educators to reconfigure current workloads to allow them space and time to engage in professional learning. While some admitted managing their time efficiently, many comments called for management of higher-education institutions to acknowledge high (predominantly teaching) workloads and subsequently find ways to incorporate time for professional learning.

Regardless of the type of development need, or whether teacher educators came from a school-teaching or academic background, participants in this study expressed a strong preference for professional learning opportunities that are continuous and based around experiential learning (e.g., working collaboratively with, and observing colleagues/experienced researchers; being mentored; being part of a team). However, for both groups to effectively share their practices and experiences in future, there is much work to be done in the 'siloed' organisational cultures that are currently found in many higher educational institutions (Anderson et al., 2015).

A level of frustration was evident when teacher educators reported that there had been an expectation on entering the teacher education profession that they had already acquired the necessary skill set to be an effective teacher educator. The infrastructure of institutes appeared not to provide time to support or mentor beginning teacher educators, with many teacher educators reporting that they were expected to 'hit the ground running' from day one of their appointment. This finding is consistent with other reports claiming that beginning teacher educators experience a period of 'de-skilling' as they try to adapt to their new roles as higher education-based teacher educators (e.g., Murray & Male, 2005, Zeichner, 2005). With the ever increasing diversification of routes to teaching, allocating designated time for proper induction and professional learning would enable policy makers and higher education institutions to encourage teacher educators to acquire and develop a more diversified and balanced, integrated professional profile rather than expect them to achieve this on their own.

Conclusion

The authors acknowledge the limitations of a chapter of this nature, not least, the extent to which such a chapter is able to address the in-depth specificities of teacher educators' professional learning on a country-by-country basis. However, other papers published from this study have attempted to do this (e.g., England: Czerniawski et al., 2018; Ireland: MacPhail & O'Sullivan, 2019; Norway: Ulvik & Smith, 2018).

The authors also acknowledge that this study focuses solely on teacher educators who work in higher education institutions and does not cover the professional learning needs of teachers in schools (e.g., when supporting student teachers and more experienced colleagues). This omission is (at the time of writing) being addressed by the authors with the launch at the end of 2019 of a second pan-European InFo-TED survey that focuses on school-based teacher educators' professional learning needs.

The findings from the research described in this chapter have indicated that much more needs to be done to foster the professional learning needs of higher education-based educators. This study begins to address the lack of research into the professional learning of teacher educators and, moreover, to determine what is effective in supporting them in their professional growth (Lunenberg et al., 2014). When professional development is narrowly and instrumentally conceived as an external activity 'done to' recipients, then opportunities for authentic teacher educators' professional learning is limited. If, however, a wider interpretation of professional development is used that embraces both formal and informal activities that enable critical professional reflection, then professional development, as a term, has validity. This chapter emphasises that professional learning is deemed more valuable, authentic and visceral when constructed as a duality through both the formal provision of professional learning activities and informal work-placed learning.

Acknowledging the significance of this duality by those with educational leadership responsibilities is important when we consider the integral role that teacher educators, in all their forms, play in the development of future generations of learners. As teacher educators in the 21st century, we are not just 'teachers of teachers' (Lunenberg et al., 2014). Depending on where we work, we are often involved in coaching, mentoring, researching, assessing, marketing, bid writing and designing curricula amongst many other activities. We are the gate-keepers and emotional carers of a future generation of classroom practitioners. But we must not lose sight of what our primary focus should be – the preparation of future professional teachers who are equipped to develop young people to play their part in the formation of a socially, economically and environmentally just and viable society. Working collectively, we must ensure this duality in formal provision and informal work-placed learning mentioned above is 'fit-for-purpose' for teacher educators preparing teachers to teach young people who may be alive at the turn of the next (22nd) century.

Notes

1 Acknowledging the contested and fuzzy nature of both 'professional development' and 'professional learning', and the assertion that one 'should become the best

professional one can possibly be' (Smith, 2003, p. 203), we define teacher educators' professional learning as both the formal and informal processes that enable them to improve their professional practice throughout their careers with a commitment to transform education for the better.

2 However even the use of this distinction internationally can be problematic when, for example, universities in England vary greatly in the extent to which research related activity and the demands placed on individual academics are often dependent on the type of university, its status, age and levels of funding.

3 After completion of the primary analysis of these interview data, six additional interviews were conducted in The Netherlands. Exploratory analysis of these additional interview data confirmed the findings reported here (Guberman et al., 2020)

4 For more methodological details of the interviews carried out for this part of the study, see MacPhail et al. (2018).

5 However, the authors acknowledge that many higher education institutions are not universities and, as such, may not impose the same expectations on academic employees to be researchers.

Acknowledgements

This chapter draws, in part, from three articles (Czerniawski et al., 2017; Czerniawski et al., 2018; MacPhail et al., 2018) that were associated with the publication of both the survey and interview findings that this chapter has presented.

European Journal of Teacher Education, published online on 2 November 2016, copyright Association for Teacher Education in Europe, published by Routledge, Taylor & Francis Group, Informa Group Plc, available online: https://doi.org/10.1080/02619768.2016.1246528.

Journal of Education for Teaching, published online on 5 January 2018, copyright Routledge, Taylor & Francis Group, Informa Group Plc, available online: https://doi.org/10.1080/02607476.2017.1422590.

Professional Development in Education, published online on 4 October 2018, copyright International Professional Development Association, published by Routledge, Taylor & Francis Group, Informa Group Plc, available online: https://doi.org/10.1080/19415257.2018.1529610

References

Anderson, C., Foley, Y., & Sangster, P. (2015, December). Seminar series on teacher education for the changing demographics of schooling: Policy, practice and research. Economic & Social Research Council. http://www.ed.ac.uk/files/atoms/files/briefing_paper_-_seminar_6.pdf.

Berry, M. (2013, July 2–7). *Teacher educators' professional learning: 'You're more or less on your own'*[Conference presentation]. 16th Biennial Conference of International Study Association on Teachers and Teaching, Ghent, Belgium.

Boyd, P., Harris, K., & Murray, J. (2011). *Becoming a teacher educator: Guidelines for induction*. Higher Education Academy, Subject Centre for Education (ESCalate).

Czerniawski, G., Gray, D., MacPhail, A., Bain, Y., Conroy, P., & Guberman, A. (2018). The professional learning needs and priorities of higher-education-based teacher educators in England, Ireland and Scotland. *Journal of Education for Teaching*, 44 (2), 133–148.

Czerniawski, G., Guberman, A., & MacPhail, A. (2017). The professional developmental needs of higher education-based teacher educators: An international comparative needs analysis. *European Journal of Teacher Education*, 40(1), 127–140.

Ellis, V., Glackin, G., Heighes, D., Norman, M., Nicol, S., & Norris, K. (2013). A difficult realization: The proletarianisation of higher education-based teacher educators. *Journal of Education for Teaching: International Research and Pedagogy*, 39(3), 266–280.

European Commission. (2012). Supporting the teaching professions for better learning outcomes. https://eur-lex.europa.eu/LexUriServ/LexUriServ.do?uri=SWD:2012: 0374:FIN:EN:PDF.

European Commission. (2013). Supporting teacher educators for better learning outcomes. https://ec.europa.eu/assets/eac/education/policy/school/doc/support-teacher-educators_en.pdf.

Goodwin, L., Smith, L., Souto-Manning, M., Cheruvu, R., Tan, M. Y., Reed, R., & Taveras, L. (2014). What should teacher educators know and be able to do? Perspectives from practicing teacher educators. *Journal of Teacher Education*, 65(4), 284–302.

Griffiths, V., Thompson, S., & Hryniewicz, L. (2014). Landmarks in the professional and academic development of mid-career teacher educators. *European Journal of Teacher Education*, 37(1), 74–90.

Guberman, A., & Mcdossi, O. (2019). Israeli teacher educators' perceptions of their professional development paths in teaching, research and institutional leadership. *European Journal of Teacher Education*, 42(4), 507–522.

Guberman, A., Ulvik, M., MacPhail, A., & Oolbekkink-Marchand, H. (2020). Teacher educators' professional trajectories: Evidence from Ireland, Israel, Norway and the Netherlands. *European Journal of Teacher Education*, (7).

Hadar, L., & Brody, L. D. (2017). *Teacher educators' professional learning*. Routledge.

Labaree, D. F. (2003). The peculiar problem of preparing educational researchers. *Educational Researcher*, 32(4), 13–22.

Laudel, G., & Glaser, J. (2008). From apprentice to colleague: The metamorphosis of early career researchers. *Higher Education*, 55, 387–406.

Loughran, J. (2006). *Developing a pedagogy of teacher education: Understanding teaching and learning about teaching*. Routledge.

Lunenberg, M., Dengerink, J., & Korthagen, F. (2014). *The professional teacher educator: Roles, behaviour, and professional development of teacher educators*. Sense Publishers.

MacPhail, A., & O'Sullivan, M. (2019). Challenges for Irish teacher educators in being active users and producers of research. *European Journal of Teacher Education*, 42(4), 492–506.

MacPhail, A., Patton, K., Parker, M., & Tannehill, D. (2014). Leading by example: Teacher educators' professional learning through communities of practice. *Quest*, 66 (1), 39–56.

MacPhail, A., Ulvik, M., Guberman, A., Czerniawski, G., Oolbekkink-Marchand, H., & Bain, Y. (2018). The professional development of higher education-based teacher educators: Needs and realities. *Professional Development in Education*, 45(5), 848–861.

Mason, J. (1996). *Qualitative researching*. SAGE Publications.

Murray, J., Czerniawski, G., & Barber, P. (2011). Teacher educators' identities and work in England at the beginning of the second decade of the twenty-first century. *Journal of Education for Teaching: International Research and Pedagogy*, 37(3), 261–277.

Murray, J., Lunenberg, M., & Smith, K. (2017). Educating the educators: Policies and initiatives in European teacher education. In M. A. Peters, B. Cowie, & I. Mentor (Eds.), *A companion to research in teacher education* (pp. 651–666). Springer.

Murray, J., & Male, T. (2005). Becoming a teacher educator: Evidence from the field. *Teaching and Teacher Education*, 21(2), 125–142.

Smith, K. (2003). So, what about the professional development of teacher educators? *European Journal of Teacher Education*, 26(2), 201–215.

Smith, K. (2012). The multi-faceted teacher educator: A Norwegian perspective. *Journal of Education for Teaching: International Research and Pedagogy*, 37(3), 337–349.

Swennen, A., Jones, K., & Volman, M. (2010). Teacher educators: Their identities, sub-identities and implications for professional development. *Professional Development in Education*, 36(1–2),131–148.

Ulvik, M., & Smith, K. (2018). Lærerutdanneres profesjonelle utvikling [Teacher educators' professional development]. *UniPed*, 41(4), 425–440.

Van der Klink, M., Kools, Q., Avissar, G., White, S., & Sakata, T. (2017). Professional development of teacher educators: What do they do? Findings from an explorative international study. *Professional Development in Education*, 43(2), 163–178.

Van Velzen, C., van der Klink, M., Swennen, A., & Yaffe, E. (2010). The induction and needs of beginning teacher educators. *Professional Development in Education*, 36(1–2),61–75.

Zeichner, K. (2005). Becoming a teacher educator: A personal perspective. *Teaching and Teacher Education*, 21(2), 117–124.

Chapter 4

Interlude: Teacher educators' professional development in Australia

Context and challenges

Amanda Berry

Introduction

This chapter reflects on the work of the International Forum for Teacher Educator Development (InFo-TED) group in supporting the professional learning and development of teacher educators, and connects these reflections with the professional development of teacher educators in Australia. Over the past two decades, and across the globe, acknowledgement of the significant role of teacher educators in the improvement of educational outcomes has been growing steadily. Teacher educators have been identified as the 'linchpins of reform' (Cochran-Smith, 2005, p. 3), who are 'crucial players' in building and maintaining a high-quality teaching workforce (European Commission, 2013, p. 5) with the need for knowledge and skills 'of the highest order' (p. 54).

Despite this emphasis on the important role of teacher educators, knowledge about how they learn and develop, and what constitutes their specific professional knowledge has not gained the same level of importance or attention. Partly, this appears to be a definitional issue. The question of who is a teacher educator and what a teacher educator does remains fuzzy, with a corresponding fuzziness about their professional learning needs and pathways. Partly, this is also an issue of how teacher educators are increasingly positioned within the education policy landscape as deliverers of a predetermined curriculum, rather than agentic professionals with a career trajectory. In this chapter, I explore these issues of teacher educator professional status, and their learning and development through the lens of my experiences and knowledge of the Australian teacher education landscape, and reflect on the work of the InFo-TED group.

This chapter is presented in three parts. I begin by looking at definitions, specifically two definitional confusions that lie at the heart of the issues confronting teacher educators and their professional development. Next, I consider issues regarding the preparation and ongoing learning of teacher educators in my local context of Australia, and finally, I consider ways in which the InFo-TED agenda might be taken up to support and strengthen the professional learning of teacher educators in Australia.

Teacher educator

Murray et al. (see chapter 1) acknowledge the well-known 'problem of definition' (Ducharme, 1993, p. 2) regarding the term 'teacher educator' and its associated descriptors. Over the years, the meaning of the label teacher educator has become increasingly broadened to include a range of different groups and sub-groups, such as school-based or field-based, university-based and more recently, community-based teacher educators (White, 2019).

In Australia, the label of teacher educator includes those who teach pre-service teachers in universities, those who mentor and supervise pre-service and newly graduated teachers in schools, school-based teachers who facilitate the professional learning of their colleagues, and external professional development providers. While the profusion of roles and associated terms may appear to be a minor issue, labels matter, as they carry hidden meanings that shape our thinking and expectations. If we don't have a reasonable consensus about who is a teacher educator or what the work of teacher educators involves, how can we argue for their status as professionals, or for that matter, understand their professional learning needs? White (2019) points out the need for all types of teacher educators to 'name and claim their identity' (p. 215) as a means of collectively enhancing the status of teacher educators' work, and so that they can 'have a more pro-active role and voice in responding to and critiquing teacher education reform policies' (p. 215).

One of the prevailing difficulties in defining the role of teacher educator has been the long-held assumption that teaching teachers does not require any specific expertise that is different from teaching children, so that 'if one is a good teacher of primary or secondary school students, this expertise will automatically carry over to one's work with novice teachers' (Zeichner, 2005, p. 118). Yet the work of teacher educators has been revealed as more complex than commonly assumed. Teaching about teaching, while modelling the practices being advocated, requires particular knowledge, skills and capabilities beyond knowing what to teach (Russell, 2010). Teacher educator scholars have long argued for a distinct and specialised pedagogy of teacher education to be recognised, developed and refined by teacher educators as they become more expert at teaching about teaching (Loughran, 2006).

Professional development and professional learning

Another 'problem of definition' relates to the terms 'professional learning' and 'professional development'. While these terms are often used interchangeably, there is an important distinction to be made between notions of professional development (PD) and professional learning (PL). PD has been traditionally associated with a 'banking model' (Freire, 1963) of education, focusing on the delivery of information through organised programs and content in 'bite-sized pieces' (Lieberman, 1995, p. 591) for participants to 'digest'. Viewed through this lens, PD implies a passive participant, with learning seen as 'filling up a reservoir of knowledge in a professional's mind that will run dry if left too long' (Webster-Wright, 2009, p. 712). This discourse runs counter to current views of learning as 'situated, social, and constructed' (Putnam & Bork, 2000, p. 5) and of professionals as engaged and agentic individuals who are capable of directing their own learning. While PD experiences may lead to PL, they are not the same.

In chapter 3 of this book, Czerniawski et al. take up this issue in relation to teacher educators as follows: 'When professional development is narrowly and instrumentally conceived as an external activity "done to" recipients then opportunities for authentic teacher educators' professional learning is limited.' (INSERT PAGE REFERENCE). These authors argue that PD may be considered valid if it encompasses informal as well as formal activities and that these activities 'enable critical professional reflection' (INSERT PAGE REFERENCE).

Expanding on this idea, I propose an explicit shift from the term 'professional development' with its associations of training or upskilling, to 'professional learning', as a process of professional growth whereby learning is ongoing, situated and constitutes the processes that teacher educators engage in when they expand, refine and change their practice (Clemans et al., 2010). PL then becomes authentically embedded in professional life and constitutes a 'professional-way-of-being' (Dall'Alba, 2004, p. 680). Even more than a change in terminology, this shift implies a different conceptualisation of knowledge and a more active positioning of teacher educators in their own learning processes.

Addressing the issues associated with the PL and PD of teacher educators is therefore a dual challenge that requires both an understanding of the nature of the professional domain of 'teacher educator', and an understanding of what is meant by 'learning and development'. I now turn to consider work and learning of teacher educators in the Australian context.

The Australian landscape: teacher educators' professional learning in Australia higher education

Over the past five decades, initial teacher education in Australia has shifted from being located in stand-alone teachers' colleges (with a few universities offering a post graduate qualification in secondary teacher education) to a predominantly university-based model, emerging in the late 1980s. This shift, similar to that noted by Murray et al. in chapter 1, has brought with it an increased emphasis on research-informed program design and a corresponding expectation regarding the academic requirements and associated career pathways of teacher educators.

Under the current Australian system, teacher educators (as with all university teaching staff) must be qualified to at least one level higher than the course of study being taught (Australian Tertiary Education Quality and Standards Agency [TEQSA]). University-based teacher educators require at least a master's level of qualification for teaching Bachelor of Education students, and a

PhD for teaching Master of Teaching students[1], and their career advancement is associated with traditional university requirements including research production and service.

Interestingly, while research requirements for university-based teacher educators have increased, there has been no corresponding increase in the requirement for a specialist knowledge of teaching teachers, beyond a university recognised teaching qualification and familiarity with the Australian Professional Standards for teaching (Australian Institute for Teaching and School Leadership [AITSL], 2011). In fact, recent changes to Australian teacher education policy, through the introduction of externally predetermined and assessed outcomes, have effectively limited teacher educators' role to that of technicians.

In other publications (see, e.g., Berry & Forgasz, 2015, 2018), I have argued that the current Australian teacher education policy environment de-professionalises teacher educators' work, allowing them few opportunities to exercise their autonomy or professional judgment. Similarly, Green et al. (2017) characterise the situation currently facing Australian teacher education in a similar way: 'Abstracted, reified, denatured and increasingly devalued in policy, teacher education is indeed struggling to thrive as an intellectual and practical endeavour in a policy context that increasingly seeks to render it as an instrumental field' (p. 39).

In terms of national support for teacher educators, the Australian Teacher Education Association (ATEA) is the major professional association for teacher educators in Australia. Their mission includes 'improve[ing] the nature, quality, and availability of professional development for teacher educators' (ATEA, 2020); however, the organisation itself does not offer any formal professional learning opportunities beyond its biennial conference. This means that for the most part, the professional learning of teacher educators in higher education tends to be conducted in ad hoc, haphazard ways that are largely left up to each individual. This situation is consistent with that described by Murray et al. in chapter 1, who state that the 'currently provision is still too dependent on small-scale, ad hoc, intermittently funded and local initiatives' (INSERT PAGE REFERENCE).

School-based teacher educators

A similar absence of formal learning opportunities exists for school-based teacher educators (also known as mentors or supervising teachers). In Victoria (the state where the author resides), there is no formal accreditation requirement for school-based teacher educators who support the learning of new teachers and few, if any, professional learning opportunities specifically focused on learning about teaching about teaching. The Victorian Institute of Teaching (VIT) runs a two-day workshop for school-based teacher educators to learn how to mentor newly graduated teachers so that they can successfully complete their formal teacher accreditation. In this case, the learning focuses on how to understand and apply the Australian Professional Standards, which seems more akin to information delivery than genuine professional learning.

A new and growing group of school-based teacher educators are those charged with the responsibility of supporting the learning of their peers. These teachers are typically appointed on the basis of their excellent reputation as classroom teachers. Yet, here again, there is a conspicuous absence of organised professional learning in terms of understanding how teachers learn and develop. It is an interesting anomaly that, while research into the learning needs school-based teacher educators is growing (see chapter 1), the needs of school-based teacher educators seem to have attracted little attention in the Australian context.

While the situation I have described thus far presents a rather gloomy picture of the systemic recognition and formal learning opportunities for Australian teacher educators, there are a number of local initiatives that have emerged over the years to build a collective professional identity of teacher educators and to support their learning. For example, the Victorian government funded Teaching Academies of Professional Practice (TAPP) was set up to encourage partnerships between schools and university-based teacher education for the purpose of improving initial teacher education. Grimmett et al. (2018) worked with a local TAPP over several years to reposition school-based mentor teachers as fellow teacher educators so as to promote expansion in their understanding and enactment of their role.

Findings from a study of this TAPP showed that partnerships between schools and universities can enhance learning opportunities for all when commitments are made to creating collaborative and dialogical spaces to support new approaches to teacher education. Similar initiatives include co-teaching situations whereby highly accomplished teachers from local schools work with university teacher educators in the design and teaching of their programs. Such programs benefit not only the learning of the pre-service teachers but also, when carefully organised, enable teacher educators to reflect on their own knowledge and understanding, and can contribute to authentic professional learning through their experiences of planning and teaching together (Marangio et al., 2019).

Beyond these local examples, the self-study of the teaching and teacher education (S-STEP) community has been an important and longstanding professional network for teacher educators in Australia, also linking them with their international colleagues. S-STEP emerged in the early 1990s led by teacher educators concerned to better understand, value and advance knowledge of teaching about teaching. S-STEP is now a global movement that includes a special interest group of the American Education Research Association, a dedicated journal, *Studying Teacher Education*, and a biennial conference, the Castle Conference[2]. The accumulation of research produced through self-study has led to the production of two international handbooks (Kitchen et al., 2020;

Loughran et al., 2004) that clearly signal this methodology as a well-established field of research into the specialised knowledge of teacher educators.

As a stance, a methodology and a form of scholarship, S-STEP has significant potential to impact the professional learning of teacher educators. First, as a stance, self-study values the nature of teacher educator professional knowledge as contextualised, enacted and contingent. Second, as a methodology, self-study enables teacher educators to discover, develop and refine their individual knowledge of practice. Third, through impactful public dissemination, self-study scholarship has the potential to reposition teacher educators' knowledge in powerful counterpoint to the instrumentalist-technicist discourses that currently dominate teacher education (Berry & Forgasz, 2018).

Re-imagining the professional learning of teacher educators

In previous publications, I have argued that while the relative absence of organised professional learning opportunities for teacher educators is cause for concern, it also can be seen as a 'double edged sword', since teacher educators themselves learn to build their own professional learning pathways (Berry, 2016; Vanassche & Berry, 2019). In fact, being 'left alone' can be a necessary condition for promoting teacher educators' professional learning. When teacher educators take ownership of their professional learning, formal and informal opportunities and workplace learning can offer rich and contextualised opportunities for learning about being and becoming a teacher educator. Ultimately an essential professional task of each teacher educator is in learning how to draw from and restructure their existing knowledge in ways that enable them to facilitate learning about the teaching of others, and to be able to articulate this knowledge and its process of development. This is necessary so it can be made clear to themselves, other teacher educators, the public and most importantly, to the prospective teachers with whom they work.

Contribution of InFo-TED

Through the nature and scope of its work, the InFo-TED group has made a substantial contribution to supporting and valuing teacher educators' status and work. The conceptual model (see chapter 2) offers a framework for understanding teacher educator learning that recognises its complexity and is sufficiently expansive to account for the range of contexts and roles in which teacher educators work and learn. The model also offers a useful language of teacher educator knowledge and practice, which is essential to establishing a shared knowledge base. Through connecting with teacher educators across a range of European countries and Israel, opportunities are opened up to build collective recognition of the teacher educator role as well as collective capacity in responding to education policy initiatives. Bringing together teacher educators into an international community of practice in this way emphasises teachers' collective agency and communal effort, and contributes to what Goodwin (2020) calls a 'global mind-set'.

Value of InFo-TED

The InFo-TED project marks an important step forward in bringing together those concerned with the preparation and ongoing learning of teacher educators of all kinds, and building a shared conception and language of teacher education as a profession and of the learning needs of those who participate in it. Coming together in these organised ways to both investigate the scope and nature of teacher educators' learning, and to support teacher educators along their career trajectories creates significant value for the profession both now and into the future. Extending the network of teacher educators involved in InFo-TED beyond its current borders would be a welcome next step for this group. The Covid-19 pandemic situation has shown us even more so than before that when travel is not possible, we can successfully link into the world through virtual means. I look forward to a virtual Summer Academy that can include an Australian cohort!

Notes

1 There are two main pathways to becoming a teacher in Australia.
2 Visit the Castle Conference website for more information: https://www.castle conference.com.

References

Australian Institute for Teaching and School Leadership. (2011). Australian professional standards for teachers. https://www.aitsl.edu.au/docs/default-source/national-policy-framework/australian-professional-standards-for-teachers.pdf.

Australian Teacher Education Association. (2020, September). About ATEA. https://atea.edu.au/about-atea/.

Berry, A. (2016). Teacher educators' professional learning: A necessary case of 'on your own'? In B. De Wever, R. Vanderlinde, M. Tuytens, & A. Aelsterman (Eds.), *Professional learning in education: Challenges for teacher educators, teachers and student teachers* (pp. 39–56). Academia Press.

Berry, A., & Forgasz, R. (2015). Becoming ourselves as teacher educators: Trespassing, transgressing and transformation. In M. Hayler, & J. Williams (Eds.), *Transitions and transformations: Teacher educators' journeys of becoming* (pp. 95–106). Springer.

Berry, A., & Forgasz, R. (2018). Disseminating secret-story-knowledge through the self-study of teacher education practice. *Studying Teacher Education*, 14(3), 235–245.

Clemans, A., Berry, A., & Loughran, J. (2010). Lost and found in transition: The professional journey of teacher educators. *Professional Development in Education*, 36(1–2), 211–228.

Cochran-Smith, M. (2005). The new teacher education: For better or for worse? *Educational Researcher*, 34(7), 3–17.

Dall'Alba, G. (2004). Understanding professional practice: Investigations before and after an educational programme. *Studies in Higher Education, 29*(6), 679–692.

Ducharme, E. R. (1993). *The lives of teacher educators.* Teachers College Press.

European Commission. (2013). Supporting teacher educators for better learning outcomes. https://ec.europa.eu/assets/eac/education/policy/school/doc/support-teacher-educators_en.pdf.

Freire, P. (1963). *Pedagogy of the oppressed.* Herder and Herder.

Goodwin, A. L. (2020). Globalization, global mindsets and teacher education. *Action in Teacher Education, 42*(1), 6–18.

Green, W., Reid, J-A., & Brennan, M. (2017). Challenging policy, rethinking practice; Or, struggling for the soul of teacher education. In T. A. Trippestad, A. Swennen, & T. Werler (Eds.), *The struggle for teacher education: International perspectives on governance and reforms* (1st ed., pp. 39–55). Bloomsbury Academic.

Grimmett, H., Forgasz, R., Williams, J., & White, S. (2018). Reimagining the role of mentor teachers in professional experience: Moving to I as fellow teacher educator. *Asia Pacific Journal of Teacher Education, 46*(4), 340–353.

Kitchen, J., Berry, A., Bullock, S., Crowe, A., Taylor, M., Guðjónsdóttir, H., & Thomas, L. (Eds.). (2020). *2nd international handbook of self-study of teaching and teacher education practices.* Springer.

Lieberman, A. (1995). Practices that support teacher development: Transforming conceptions of professional learning. *Phi Delta Kappan, 76*(8), 591–596.

Loughran, J. (2006). *Developing a pedagogy of teacher education: Understanding teaching and learning about teaching.* Routledge.

Loughran, J., Hamilton, M. L., LaBoskey, V. K., & Russell, T. (Eds.). (2004). *International handbook of self-study of teaching and teacher education practices.* Springer.

Marangio, K., Cooper, R., & Berry, A. (2019, August 26–30). *Science teachers' views on co-teaching with science teacher educators in preservice teacher education* [Conference presentation abstract]. Conference of the European Science Education Research Association, 2019, Bologna, Italy. https://www.esera2019.org/programme/.

Putnam, R., & Borko, H. (2000). What do new views of knowledge and thinking have to say about research on teacher learning? *Educational Researcher, 29*(1), 4–15.

Russell, T. (2010, July 4–7). *Improving the quality of teaching and learning: Lessons learned as a teacher educator* [Conference presentation]. Annual Conference of the Australian Teacher Education Association, Townsville, Australia.

Vanassche, E., & Berry, A. (2019). Teacher educator knowledge, practice, and S-STTEP research. In J. Kitchen, A. Berry, S. Bullock, A. Crowe, M. Taylor, H. Guðjónsdóttir, & L. Thomas (Eds.), *2nd international handbook of self-study of teaching and teacher education practices* (pp. 1–38). Springer.

Webster-Wright, A. (2009). Reframing professional development through understanding authentic professional learning. *Review of Educational Research, 79*(2), 702–739.

White, S. (2019). Teacher educators for new times? Redefining an important occupational group. *Journal for Education and Training, 45*(2), 200–213.

Zeichner, K. (2005). Becoming a teacher educator: A personal perspective. *Teaching and Teacher Education, 21*(2), 117–124.

Chapter 5

Learning and design principle for teacher educators' professional development

Hanne Tack, Ruben Vanderlinde, Yvonne Bain, Warren Kidd, Mary O'Sullivan and Amber Walraven

Introduction

Worldwide, a friction is noted between the rather limited attention given to teacher educators' preparation, induction and on-going professional development, and the growing need expressed by teacher educators themselves to engage in meaningful professional development initiatives related to their role as a teacher educator (Czerniawski et al., 2017; Tack et al., 2018). This discrepancy is noted in diverse countries worldwide (see Bain & Gray, 2018; Czerniawski et al., 2017; Lunenberg et al., 2014). Based on an international comparative study with 1,158 higher education-based teacher educators from six different countries, Czerniawski et al. (2017) concluded that teacher educators are only moderately satisfied with their current professional development experiences and strongly desire further professional development opportunities (see chapter 3).

These studies mirror the wider call for a systematic approach to teacher educators' professional development (see Kelchtermans et al., 2018; Smith, 2015; Tack et al., 2018). Teacher educators need to be able to develop the complex competencies required to prepare future teachers, rendering essential continuous professional development of the highest quality as well as access to support throughout their careers (European Commission, 2013). Yet, similar to the lack of sufficient professional training in the induction period, their need for on-going professional development has not been addressed systematically (Cochran-Smith, 2003). On the contrary, teacher educators' professional development has been described as 'ad hoc' (Berry, 2007). Nevertheless, recent international awareness of the importance of teacher educators' professional learning and development has led to the initiation of diverse professional learning and development initiatives on local, national and international levels (Smith, 2015). Up until now, no clear sets of design principles yet exist to guide the design, organisation and implementation of such initiatives. If we consider the poly-contextual and 'boundary crossing' nature of this professional group, as recognised in much of the literature, we need to recognise the relevance of establishing such design principles (Czerniawski et al., 2018; Kidd et al., 2020; Vanassche et al., 2019).

As such, in line with the conceptual model of teacher educators' professional development (see chapter 2), this chapter presents 12 design principles that seem crucial for the design of professional learning development activities for teacher educators. The formulation of these design principles is based on research literature related to teacher educators' professional development on the one hand, and the principles are reflected in several existing national and international initiatives on the other hand. In particular, despite differences in national and local contexts, a strong overlap is noted between existing initiatives focusing on teacher educators' professional development. By comparing these initiatives in combination with evidence from the research literature, 12 design principles could be formulated.

12 principles for teacher educators' professional development and learning activities

Twelve core design principles are distinguished as essential in designing teacher educators' professional development and learning principles: (1) ownership of content and process; (2) working in professional learning communities; (3) knowing each other and sharing; (4) creating opportunities for informal and formal learning at the workplace; (5) attention for teacher educators' multiple roles and multi-layered identities; (6) acknowledging that changing practices takes time; (7) considering the pressures on teacher educators' time; (8) focusing on forming networks; (9) striving for integration; (10) ICT is never an end in itself; (11) the need for asynchronous group discussions with information resources; and (12) (virtual) space with sharing opportunities.

The final three design principles (DP10–12) are related to how blended learning can be implemented in professional development activities for teacher educators. A blended learning approach offers the flexibility needed as teacher educators are working in diverse professional contexts at local, national and European levels. Its potential should be considered for teacher educators in particular, since blended learning provides learning and educational opportunities available for those who cannot attend face-to-face education, and it offers the opportunities to make both instructors and teacher educators available in places where they would otherwise have not been available (Bakker, 2018).

All design principles are evidenced in research literature on teacher (educators') professional development in this section; and existing local and national initiatives on teacher educators' professional development are evidenced in the next section. The evidence for the relevance of these design principles is thus twofold, that is, in both research literature and existing successful national and local initiatives.

1) Ownership of content and process

Based on the notion that professional development is more meaningful to professionals when they exercise ownership of its content and process (Borko,

2004; Loughran, 2014), professional learning activities should respond to teacher educators' self-identified needs and interests. Having ownership of the
learning content and process means that teacher educators have full ownership *this was mentioned in week 1 study*
of their own learning pathway; the teacher educator designs and leads his or her
learning process including what and how to learn, not the facilitator. An
important side note on this first design principle, however, is that research
shows that participants in any learning environment have a different sense of
self-efficacy, confidence, belief in their own agency and willingness to take
ownership, whether this is based on personality, past experience, power or
identity (Bali & Caines, 2018). These differences in participants' will are likely
to affect one's level of perceived and exercised ownership.

2) Working in professional learning communities

Professional learning activities should be organised in professional learning
communities (Borko, 2004). A professional learning community is a type of
'community of practice' (Lave & Wenger, 1991) and broadly refers to a group
of practitioners that share a common interest in a particular topic and work
together towards a common goal. In professional learning communities, practitioners share a common concern, set of problems or passion about a topic, and
the communities are characterised by a deepening of knowledge and expertise
by means of on-going interaction (Lave & Wenger, 1991). In such communities
professional learning is assumed to occur through social interaction. However,
considering a community of practice as a single entity underplays the complex
reality that there are different communities of practice that come together to
dynamically shape and inform a professional grouping (Wenger-Trayner &
Wenger-Trayner, 2015).

Because of its dynamic, dialogic, situated and complex nature, learning in
professional learning communities is considered more significant than traditional forms of professional development, such as one-time workshops
(Cochran-Smith, 2003). Previous research shows that communities also provide
safe spaces that facilitate learning through action-based discourse and reflection
(Zellermayer & Margolin, 2005; Valckx et al., 2020). Inspired by the benefits
of learning in communities, researchers have used the term professional learning
community to describe a broad range of collaborative professional development
activities (see, e.g., Hadar & Brody, 2016). Stoll et al. (2006, p. 223) define a
professional learning community as 'a group of people sharing and critically
interrogating their practice in an on-going, reflective, collaborative, inclusive,
research-oriented, growth-promoting way operating as a collective enterprise'.

Professional learning communities are characterised by a culture of collaboration
with a focus on questioning and learning. As such, professional learning communities serve multiple purposes, as for instance, on-going professional development,
enhancement of instructional practice and promotion of continued institutional
improvement (Hadar & Brody, 2016).

3) Knowing each other and sharing practices

Professional learning activities are assumed to be more successful when the participants trust each other to share their own practice. As such, the third design principle focuses on the social aspect and the conditions under which people are willing to share and discuss their practice. Learning collectively requires a considerable amount of vulnerability and openness (Lunenberg et al., 2014). Creating an open and safe climate where participants can build relationships and which respects individuality, honesty, openness and values is vital (Stoll et al., 2006).

Rusman et al. (2013) specify ten antecedents that are important when assessing trustworthiness: communality (have something in common), responsibility, skills, sharing, persistence, caring, discretion, competence, commitment and availability. Skills, sharing, persistence, caring and discretion can only influence trustworthiness after extensive collaboration. This means that professional development and learning activities for teacher educators should first focus on dialogue between people, starting from sharing who you are and the context in which you work towards collaboratively developing professional practice (as teacher educators of teacher educators). It enables coming to a shared knowledge base about practice, but doing so in a way that is open to critique and challenge to further shape the collective and shared knowledge base.

4) Informal and formal learning at the workplace

The fourth design principle relates to the idea that professional learning opportunities can be found in both formal and informal learning opportunities. Formal learning opportunities are institutional workshops, seminars, professional development programs and so on.

Informal learning opportunities often occur in and through teacher educators' professional practice and refer, for instance, to informal collegial support (Lunenberg et al., 2014). Drawing on the situated learning theory (Lave & Wenger, 1991), studies of teacher educator learning indicate how important informal learning is in the workplace (Murray & Male, 2005). For such informal learning to occur, an 'expansive learning environment' (Fuller & Unwin, 2003, p. 78) is required, that is, one which will enable a community of practice to analyse and transform its practice. Such an environment presents wide-ranging opportunities for learning in the workplace and a culture that promotes both individual and communal learning. Within such an approach, professional learning is viewed as an essential and integrated aspect of day-to-day work, rather than the achievements of short-term, easily measurable outcomes.

Up until now, professional learning of teacher educators has been based to a large extent on informal and self-initiated activities (Lunenberg et al., 2014; Tack et al., 2018). In recent years, more formal and intentional initiatives have been established (Hadar & Brody, 2016). The collaborative model for both

formal learning helps to build
professional learning communities.

formal and informal initiatives has gained favour and is especially relevant to supporting the professional learning of teacher educators coming from multiple communities of practice to develop shared collective knowledge about their practice.

5) Multiple roles and multi-layered identities

The constellation of teacher educators' multiple roles and multi-layered identities (Lunenberg et al., 2014), whether or not they conflict with another, forms the fifth design principle that needs careful consideration when designing teacher educators' professional development activities. The importance of the teacher educator as a role model for the next generation of teachers cannot be understated (Lunenberg et al., 2014; Smith, 2003). Until recently, however, a focus was lacking within higher education institutions on the identities and roles of teacher educators themselves (Tack et al., 2018).

Several authors (e.g., Zeichner, 2005) argue that good teachers do not necessarily become effective teacher educators; they need appropriate training and induction into several roles specifically related to becoming a teacher educator. In this respect, teacher educators, are not only teachers of teachers, they also fulfil other roles, such as curriculum developer, gatekeeper, broker, coach and researcher (Lunenberg et al., 2014). While these multiple professional roles have been identified through a literature review (Lunenberg et al., 2014), it must be stated that not all teacher educators experience each of these roles. In this respect, the particular circumstances of teacher educators in different contexts will determine which subset of these roles constitutes their professional practice. In many cases, teacher educators have to transform themselves in order to take on certain identities, especially the researcher role (Lunenberg et al., 2014).   *teacher educators come from many different*

Finally, even when teacher educators themselves talk about their job *educational* responsibilities, they often express confusion and perceive their professional role *contexts* to be far from simple (Davey, 2013). These complexities motivate the need for *and that* a careful consideration of the multiple roles and multi-layered identities of *must* teacher educators as determining factors in teacher educators' professional *be considered* learning (Hadar & Brody, 2016).

6) Changing practice takes time

Another design principle is based upon the notion that changing teaching and assessment practices takes time and demands extended and intensive processes (Desimone, 2009; Lawless & Pellegrino, 2007; Merchie et al., 2016). Therefore, formal professional learning activities should last long enough with sufficient autonomy and freedom for teacher educators to learn and reflect at a time of their convenience. Although no exact tipping point exists, research supports activities that are spread out over the year, including a contact time of 20 hours or more (Desimone, 2009; Merchie et al., 2016). Enabling engagement over an extended period of time requires a carefully designed environment to sustain the engagement and learning of the community.

7) Considering the pressures on teacher educators' time

The seventh design principle refers to the idea that formally organised professional learning activities should be structured enough. In this respect, previous research strongly indicates the high pressures on teacher educators' time and opportunities to engage in research (Tack & Vanderlinde, 2019). Designated days for face-to-face meetings should be identified and protected, and follow-up activities should be planned in the knowledge that there are many competing demands being made of teacher educators.

8) Forming networks

Professional development activities for teacher educators should focus on creating networks. Working in isolation seems to be typical of the nature of teacher education and is described as one of the major challenges teacher educators struggle with (Smith & Vattøy, 2015). Colleges and universities, often teacher educators' work contexts, are organised by departments, a phenomenon that discourages interdisciplinary discourse (Hadar & Brody, 2016). Further, within these departments often only one or two experts for each subject are available (Trower & Ghallagher, 2008) resulting in limited opportunities to discuss student learning and share work related problems, successes and doubts. Often, teacher educators take sole responsibility for content (Smith & Vattøy, 2015). Interaction among faculty can be limited to cordial everyday talk instead of robust issues about student learning (Hadar & Brody, 2016).

As such, attention should be paid to creating networks across institutions and nations. With regard to teacher educators' engagement in research activities, for instance, institutions could cooperate in applying for research grants. In this respect, teacher educator mobility is a keyword in numerous European policy documents (European Commission, 2013). Today there are multiple possibilities for virtual networking; however, there is also a need to meet face-to-face and get to know each other. There is a need to create physical meeting places so people can meet, learn to trust each other and embrace new initiatives from ideas emerging from lunchtime conversations, etc. These physical meeting places can be the starting point and anchor points for establishing and nourishing (inter)national networks among teacher educators.

need people in their corner to bounce ideas off

9) Striving for integration

The ninth design principle refers to the need for professional learning activities to strive for integration. Teacher education curriculum is often criticised for being 'fragmented'. In too many places, teacher education curriculum consists of courses that are only loosely connected with each other, students are not exposed to the pedagogy they are called to embrace, and field experience is detached from relevant theories (Kitchen & Petrarca, 2016). The study by Czerniawski et al. (2017, 2018) revealed that teacher educators distinguish 'academic' and 'pedagogic' professional development needs. It is therefore suggested that professional development activities build upon the diverse participants' viewpoints, professional experience and professional development needs to create an integrated learning experience.

10) ICT is never an end in itself

Important in implementing blended learning in teacher educators' professional development activities is that an information and communication technology (ICT)-based (online) environment supporting teacher educators' professional development can never be an end in itself (Kosnik et al., 2016). Research (Kosnik et al., 2016) shows that teachers and teacher educators ask for face-to-face contact in the context of professional development activities. The use of virtual learning environments thus has merely a supportive function. Nevertheless, by using advanced ICT-based tools, teacher educators may experience the advantages these tools contributed to their learning, and as a consequence, be motivated to implement ICT-based tools in their own teaching. Beyond that however, the use of online technology extends engagement beyond the place and time of coming together.

11) Asynchronous group discussions with information resources

Professional learning activities that implement blended learning should also consider the opportunity to keep contact before, during and after professional development activities. In this respect, it is important that teacher educators are able to discuss their experiences in asynchronous discussions, similar to those described by Prestridge (2010). These asynchronous discussions enable multiple users to engage in discussions with each other online, at their own time of convenience.

allows for group reflection to decide effectiveness

These asynchronous discussions lead to both collegial and critical forms of discussion. Collegial discussion is important in developing and maintaining community, while critical discussion is vital for its role in transforming practitioners' beliefs (Prestridge, 2010). Moreover, the virtual learning platform should provide storage and access to relevant resources and research literature (wiki-environment). In this way, teacher educators are able to learn from each other's experience, but at a time and place that is chosen by them, which allows for greater flexibility (Murray, 2008; Tack, 2017).

this would be more motivating to continue convo.

12) (Virtual) space with sharing opportunities

Since the starting point for teacher educators' professional development lies in teacher educators' actual practices (see chapter 1 and chapter 2), an ICT-based learning environment can support teacher educators to share practices with each other. As said previously, sharing practices and being involved in professional learning communities requires being vulnerable, being open to others, and having trust. With online collaboration, it is important then to consider when this online collaboration takes place (before or after people may have met face to face) in order to nurture a social connection and development of relationships to grow the trust, respect and collegiality needed for sharing and engaging with others.

Which information has already been shared, or which information needs to be shared online before learning and working together can take place? Information on a person's competence, commitment and availability are considered important aspects to foster a sense of trust between participants, as well as communality, and responsibility (Murray, 2008; Prestridge, 2010). To put it differently, when implementing professional learning activities for teacher educators, the implementation of a (virtual) space with sharing opportunities needs planned consideration.

Similarities between design principles and diverse national and local initiatives

Strong similarities between the formulated design principles and diverse national and local initiatives on teacher educators' professional development are noted. As such, apart from the evidence of these design principles in the research literature (see section 2), the design principles are also visible in diverse professional development initiatives at local and national levels. This section discusses how these design principles are reflected in the InFo-TED Summer Academy (SA; see chapter 8), the Flemish-wide educational programme for teacher educators in Belgium, a local initiative at the University of Nijmegen in the Netherlands, and in initiatives in Scotland, Ireland and the United Kingdom.

The presented design principles are visible in diverse professional development initiatives at local and national levels. Before moving to the national and regional contexts (i.e., Flanders, the Netherlands, Scotland, Ireland and the United Kingdom), a connection is made to the InFo-TED SA, in which the design principles were reflected as well. The core didactical focus of the InFo-TED SA was on exchanging practices among teacher educators in order to establish a network and realise communities of practice for teacher educators.

The design of the InFo-TED SA foresaw 25 teacher educators from different countries working in small groups to discuss, share ideas and socialise for the purpose of establishing national and international networks beyond the Academy. The InFo-TED SA was scheduled and pre-structured in a five-day-program during the summer holiday period. As such, teacher educators were free of teaching restrictions and other restrictions bound to the academic year. Even though the InFo-TED SA was pre-structured and formally organised, there was a strong focus on self-directed learning with scheduled time for informal collegial discussions.

Before the collective learning process started, the programme of the InFo-TED SA first focused on getting to know each other and each other's practices in small groups by means of storytelling. A heterogeneous selection of the participants guaranteed exposure to diverse and complex profiles of teacher educators' identities. These tensions were linked to theoretical frameworks, making tensions in participants' own identities and roles visible as well. Throughout the week, several moments were scheduled for teacher educators to link the provided theoretical frameworks to their own professional learning by means of, for instance, storytelling.

In order to obtain integration of the teacher educator curriculum, theorizing (e.g., by means of the building blocks) and application of knowledge (e.g., by means of the blogs with experiences of teacher educators) alternated during the InFo-TED SA. Realising that changing practices takes time, the InFo-TED SA served as a starting point for professional learning. Afterwards, follow-up was planned by means of the virtual platform and email conversations.

[handwritten margin note: lots of opportunity for reflection and communication]

In the design of the InFo-TED SA, careful thought was given to when ICT could be implemented and for what purpose. As such, a private forum was installed a few months before the InFo-TED SA so participants could get to know each other. During and after the InFo-TED SA, this forum served as a virtual space for participants to share their developed 'products' and have discussions. Moreover, the InFo-TED website with its building blocks and blogs also served as an essential tool in striving for integration and provided freedom for participants to learn and reflect at a time of their convenience. Finally, apart from the private forum, asynchronous group discussions were organised by means of the forum blogs and the online building blocks from the knowledge base served as information resources.

In Flanders, the Flemish-wide educational programme for teacher educators with five course units that can be spread over one or two academic years embodies most of the design principles. The educational programme starts from teacher educators' own practice, combines theoretical frameworks with transfer to practice, is attended by a heterogeneous group of teacher educators from different institutions, and puts blended learning high on the agenda. With a focus on sharing practices, participants are challenged to share their practice not only within the educational programme, but also within their own institution, at international conferences, and in research journals for teacher educators (Katholieke Universiteit Leuven, n.d.). Moreover, there is a strong link with InFo-TED and graduates are yearly invited to attend the InFo-TED SA.

In the Netherlands, a local initiative at the University of Nijmegen involves teacher educators taking literature seminars, masterclasses and a professional development programme on teacher education pedagogies. In all of these initiatives, teacher educators' own practices are central. Furthermore, they can be seen as a learning community, and time is allocated for these activities. The activities are open to both subject (e.g., maths, French, history) and general didactics teacher educators, thus combining different viewpoints and creating opportunities to share and combine practices.

In Scotland, however, like many other countries, there is no formal professional learning for teacher educators beyond what their own institutions might offer for induction, although there is a recognised need for supporting their development (Bain & Gray, 2018). Scottish participants of the InFo-TED SA welcomed the opportunity and developed their collaborative networks through the experience.

In Ireland, the teacher educators who attended the InFo-TED SA have collaborated with a cohort of teacher educators from Israel in sharing best practice around school placements, assessments and mentoring. The establishment of an Irish Teacher Education Forum has been inspired and supported by Irish and international colleagues engaged with InFo-TED. One outcome of this engagement has been studies on needs of Irish teacher educators (MacPhail & O'Sullivan, 2019).

In the United Kingdom, InFo-TED SA participants are now undertaking a variety of local and national projects aimed to extend and continue the momentum of the professional learning and development from the InFo-TED SA experience (see Kidd et al. 2020). In particular, this involves the mentoring and coaching of other new, boundary-crossing professionals as they enter the teacher education community. These observations show that the design principles have gained widespread support in several countries and are applicable in very diverse professional development contexts.

Conclusions

More and more professional development initiatives for teacher educators are being designed, developed and organised by local teacher education institutions, national organisations and international networks. As professional development for teacher educators is only recently described in the literature, no clear sets of design principles yet existed. This chapter presented 12 design principles, focusing on transformative community learning in teacher educators' professional development and on how blended learning can be implemented. Afterwards, connections were drawn to existing local and national initiatives.

The young research field on teacher educators' professional learning and development has increasingly evolved over the past 20 years (e.g., Loughran, 2014; Lunenberg et al., 2014; Smith, 2015; Tack, 2017). Studies have gained insight in the multiple roles and multi-layered identities of teacher educators (e.g., Lunenberg et al., 2014), the professional development needs of teacher educators (e.g., Czerniawski et al., 2018; Tack et al., 2018), the professional learning processes and experiences of teacher educators (e.g., Smith, 2015;

Tack, 2017), reported on local professional development initiatives (e.g., Murray, 2008; Smith, 2015), and studied hindering and facilitating factors (e.g., Hadar & Brody, 2016). As a consequence, researchers have also increasingly started to think of and conceptualise teacher educators' professional development (see, e.g., chapter 2; Kelchtermans et al., 2018; Loughran, 2014).

It may be clear that all these studies have yielded valuable results in advancing the field of teacher educators' professional development. However, in order to further mature research in this field, this chapter concludes with a plea for more design-based research on teacher educators' professional development. Design-based research refers to 'a series of approaches, with the intent of producing new theories, artefacts, and practices that account for and potentially impact learning and teaching in naturalistic settings' (Barab & Squire, 2004, p. 2). Design-based research (re)designs the learning context, based on theory, in collaboration with stakeholders (e.g., teacher educators, student teachers, educational designers, researchers) and uses mixed methods in iterative cycles of analysis, design and evaluation (Bakker, 2018; McKenney & Reeves, 2013). We are strongly convinced that such design-based research is needed to explicitly make a connection between the formulated design principles of professional development initiatives and the resulting learning processes of teacher educators. Such research is currently lacking. *not enough design-based research to know success*

This chapter offers the first step by providing some general design principles that are reflected in several existing national and international initiatives. Since design-based studies are conducted in a real environment, they are locally relevant and provide useful insights for practice. However, because the intervention or design principles are connected to theoretical claims that go beyond the local context, they also offer a promising approach to advance our theoretical understanding.

Finally, we should keep in mind that there is no one-size-fits-all solution to address teacher educators' professional development. We should be very careful in drawing conclusions about which professional development approach works best. No single solution works optimally under all conditions, and blueprint approaches need to be avoided (see also chapter 2). At most, design-based research can help us gain better insight into why certain initiatives with certain characteristics, preferably based on theory, might work in a specific context with specific goals in mind. Given the highly context-specific character of teacher educators' professional development, it needs to be reinvented again and again. This chapter offers an inspiring guide and starting point for navigating, designing and developing teacher educators' professional learning and development activities. *this is why we need the research (kind of a frustrating end, but true)*

References

Bain. Y., & Gray, D. (2018). The professional development of teacher educators in Scotland: Researcherly dispositions and tensions. *Scottish Educational Review*, 50(2), 54–72.

Bakker, A. (2018). *Design research in education: A practical guide for early career researchers.* Routledge.

Bali, M., & Caines, A. (2018). A call for promoting ownership, equity, and agency in faculty development via connected learning. *International Journal of Educational Technology in Higher Education*, 46, 15–46.

Barab, S., & Squire, K. (2004). Design-based research: Putting a stake in the ground. *Journal of the Learning Sciences*, 13(1), 1–14.

Berry, A. (2007). *Tensions in teaching about teaching: Developing practice as a teacher educator.* Springer.

Borko, H. (2004) Professional development and teacher learning: Mapping the terrain. *Educational Researcher*, 33(3), 3–15.

Cochran-Smith, M. (2003). Learning and unlearning: The education of teacher educators. *Teaching and Teacher Education*, 19(1), 5–28.

Czerniawski, G., Guberman, A., & MacPhail, A. (2017). The professional developmental needs of higher education-based teacher educators: An international comparative needs analysis. *European Journal of Teacher Education*, 40(1), 127–140.

Czerniawski, G., Gray, D., MacPhail, A., Bain, Y., Conroy, P., & Guberman, A. (2018), The professional learning needs and priorities of higher-education-based teacher educators in England, Ireland and Scotland. *Journal of Education for Teaching*, 44(2), 133–148.

Davey, R. (2013). *The professional identity of teacher educators: Career on the cusp?* Routledge.

Desimone, L. M. (2009). Improving impact studies of teachers' professional development: Toward better conceptualizations and measures. *Educational Researcher*, 38(3), 181–199.

European Commission. (2013). Supporting teacher educators for better learning outcomes. https://ec.europa.eu/assets/eac/education/policy/school/doc/support-teacher-educators_en.pdf.

Fuller, A., & Unwin, L. (2004). Expansive learning environments: Integrating organizational and personal development. In H. Rainbird, A. Fuller, & A. Munro (Eds.), *Workplace learning in context* (pp. 126–144). Routledge.

Hadar, L., & Brody, D. (2016). Professional development for teacher educators in the communal context: Factors which promote and hinder learning. In B. De Wever, R. Vanderlinde, M. Tuytens, & A. Aelterman (Eds.), *Professional learning in education: Challenges for teacher educators, teachers and student teachers* (pp. 57–78). Academia Press.

Katholieke Universiteit Leuven. (n.d.). Opleiding voor lerarenopleiders: Visie [Training for teacher educators: Vision]. https://ppw.kuleuven.be/opleiding-lerarenopleiders/visie.

Kelchtermans, G., Vanderlinde, R., & Smith, K. (2018). Towards an 'international forum for teacher educator development': An agenda for research and action. *European Journal of Teacher Education*, 41(1), 120–134.

Kidd, W., McMahon, A., & Viswarajan, S. (2020). Developing a pan-European approach to teacher educators' collaborative learning: Learning about, learning how and learning from. *Research in Teacher Education*, 9(2), 39–45.

Kitchen, J., & Petrarca, D. (2016). Approaches to teacher education. In J. Loughran, & M. L. Hamilton (Eds.), *International Handbook of Teacher Education* (pp. 137–186). Springer.

Kosnik, C., Beck, C., & Goodwin, L. (2016). Reform efforts in teacher education. In J. Loughran, & M. L. Hamilton (Eds.), *Handbook on teacher education* (pp. 207–224). Springer.

Lave, J., & Wenger. E. (1991). *Situated learning: Legitimate peripheral participation.* Cambridge University Press.

Lawless, K. A., & Pellegrino, J. W. (2007). Professional development in integrating technology into teaching and learning: Knows, unknowns, and ways to pursue better questions and answers. *Reviews of Educational Research, 77*(4), 575–614.

Loughran, J. (2014). Professionally developing as a teacher educator. *Journal of Teacher Education, 65*(4), 1–13.

Lunenberg, M., Dengerink, J., & Korthagen, F. (2014). *The professional teacher educator: Roles, behaviour, and professional development of teacher educators.* Sense Publishers.

MacPhail, A., & O'Sullivan, M. (2019). Challenges for Irish teacher educators in being active users and producers of research. *European Journal of Teacher Education, 42*(4), 492–506.

McKenney, S., & Reeves, T. (2012). *Conducting educational design research: What it is, how we do it, and why.* Routledge.

Merchie, E., Tuytens, M., Devos, G., & Vanderlinde, R. (2016). Evaluating teachers' professional development initiatives: Towards an extended evaluative framework. *Research Papers in Education, 33*(2), 1–26.

Murray, J. (2008). Teacher educators' induction into higher education: Work-based learning in the micro communities of teacher education. *European Journal of Teacher Education, 31*(2), 117–133.

Murray, J., & Male, T. (2005) Becoming a teacher educator: Evidence from the field. *Teaching and Teacher Education, 21*(2), 107–115.

Prestridge, S. (2010). ICT professional development for teachers in online forums: Analysing the role of discussion. *Teaching and Teacher Education, 26*(2), 252–258.

Rusman, E., van Bruggen, J., Sloep, P., Valcke, M., & Koper, R. (2013). Can I trust you? Profile elements that inform first impressions of trustworthiness in virtual project teams. *International Journal of Information Technology Project Management, 3*(1), 15–35.

Smith, K. (2003). So, what about the professional development of teacher educators? *European Journal of Teacher Education, 26*(2), 201–215.

Smith, K. (2015). The role of research in teacher education. *Research in Teacher Education, 5*(2), 43–46.

Smith, K., & Vattøy, K. (2015). *NAFOL- Evaluering av den første prosjektperioden, 2010–2015* [*NAFOL- Evaluation of the first project period, 2010–2015*]. Nasjonal forskerskole for lærerutdanning.

Stoll, L., Bolam, R., McMahon, A., Wallace, M., & Thomas, S. (2006). Professional learning communities: A review of the literature. *Journal of Educational Change, 7*(4), 221–258.

Tack, H. (2017). Towards a better understanding of teacher educators' professional development: Theoretical and empirical insight into their researcherly disposition. [Doctoral dissertation, Ghent University]. https://biblio.ugent.be/publication/8532727/file/8533022.

Tack, H., Valcke, M., Rots, I., Struyven, K., & Vanderlinde, R. (2018). Uncovering a hidden professional agenda for teacher educators: A mixed method study on Flemish teacher educators and their professional development. *European Journal of Teacher Education, 41*(1), 86–104.

Tack, H., & Vanderlinde, R. (2019). Capturing the relations between teacher educators' opportunities for professional growth, work pressure, work related basic needs satisfaction, and teacher educators' researcherly disposition. *European Journal of Teacher Education*, 42(4), 459–477.

Trower, C. A., & Gallagher, A. S. (2008). Why collegiality matters. *Chronicle of Higher Education*, 55(11), 50–51.

Valckx, J., Vanderlinde, R., & Devos, G. (2020). Departmental PLCs in secondary schools: The importance of transformational leadership, teacher autonomy, and teachers' self-efficacy. *Educational Studies*, 46(3), 282–301.

Vanassche, E., Kidd, W., & Murray, J. (2019). Articulating, reclaiming and celebrating the professionalism of teacher educators in England. *European Journal of Teacher Education*, 42(4), 478–491.

Wenger-Trayner, E., & Wenger-Trayner, B. (2015). Learning in a landscape of practice: A framework. In E. Wenger-Trayner, M. Fenton-O'Creevy, S. Hutchinson, C. Kubial, & B. Wenger-Trayner (Eds.), *Learning in landscapes of practice*. Routledge.

Zeichner, K. (2005). Becoming a teacher educator: A personal perspective. *Teaching and Teacher Education*, 21(2), 117–224.

Zellermayer, M., & Margolin, I. (2005). Teacher educators' professional learning described through the lens of complexity theory. *Teachers College Record*, 107(6), 1275–1304.

Chapter 6

Designing knowledge bases for teacher educators

Challenges and recommendations

Mieke Lunenberg and Jurriën Dengerink

Introduction

Since the 1990s, there is a growing awareness that the work of teachers and of teacher educators is significantly different in important ways (Dinkelman et al., 2006). Teacher educators are crucial in maintaining and developing the quality of teachers as gatekeepers to the teaching profession. It is their responsibility to 'embody the professional standards and values they considered should underpin school teaching and to practise what they preached' (Hall & Schulz, 2003, p. 370). Loughran (2014) emphasises that becoming a teacher educator is not about 'upskilling' consisting qualities, but about an ongoing process 'of learning, development, and change' (p. 273), that is, about developing a pedagogy of teacher education.

As a consequence of this growing awareness, the specific knowledge and practice teacher educators need have been more and more distinguished from the knowledge and practice needed for the teaching profession. Loughran (2014) stated:

ultimate goal

> a teacher educator needs to be, or at least seek to be, well informed ... If students of teaching are to move beyond their own personal opinions about what they need to do to develop their teaching...then teacher educators need to be informed about the research that can assist in cata-lysing that shift.
>
> (p. 277)

This was confirmed in an extensive review study on the professional development of teacher educators (Lunenberg et al., 2014). This study also showed that teacher educators often feel they lack a frame of reference and a solid theoretical basis for their practice. Hence, building solid knowledge bases for teacher educators is important. How to do that, however, is still under study.

The idea that teacher educators should be able to draw on a body of structured knowledge is not just an abstract criterion. In 1996, the Association of Teacher Educators (ATE; USA) presented standards for teacher educators, and in 1999 the Dutch Association of Teacher Educators (VELON) initiated the project *Professional Quality of Teacher Educators*, in which a professional standard and a procedure for (self-assessment and) professional development were developed for teacher educators to obtain certification. In 2012 the Flemish Association of Teacher Educators (VELOV) presented a development profile for teacher educators, and in 2016–2019 the International Forum of Teacher Educator Development (InFo-TED) developed knowledge bases. These initiatives show a variety of interpretations of the concept of knowledge bases. While, for example, the ATE standards focus on behaviour and skills of teacher educators, InFo-TED offers teacher educators building blocks to underpin their practices.

In this chapter we focus on the Dutch knowledge base and the international knowledge bases developed by InFo-TED. Both initiatives are web-based. The designs and the development processes of these knowledge bases were different, and so are the results. We analyse and compare both initiatives, and conclude this chapter with an overview of challenges developers of knowledge bases face, and formulate some recommendations for the future.

Knowledge bases

There are various conceptions and definitions about what a knowledge base is and how it can be constructed. In their study on the knowledge base of teachers Verloop et al. (2001) made the distinction between personal practical knowledge that individual practitioners collect for their own work (knowledge of teachers) and teacher knowledge, mostly collected by experts or researchers, which is relevant for a whole group of teachers (knowledge for teachers). The problem with the first kind of knowledge is that it is 'highly determined and "colored" by ... individual experiences, personal history... personality variables, subject matter knowledge, and so on' (p. 443), while the latter has the risk of disregarding all these aspects and the complexity of teaching.

To overcome this gap researchers like Hiebert et al. (2002) studied what a random group of practitioners consider relevant knowledge, which resulted in a knowledge base as a collection of local practical knowledge. But also, they stress, that 'local knowledge is immediate and concrete but always incomplete and sometimes blind and insular' (Hiebert et al., 2002, p. 8). Another approach regards a group of experienced practitioners who explore, articulate and document the development of their knowledge of practice (Berry, 2007) to come to conclusions for the knowledge base of the professional community at large (Goodwin & Kosnik, 2013; Selmer et al., 2016). Achinstein and Davis' (2014) approach focusses on narrowing the purpose of a 'general' knowledge base: a group of experienced practitioners and researchers structures the knowledge, collects resources or builds a resource portal (possibly as part of a more extensive learning platform) for a specific professional development programme (e.g., content-focused mentoring of new teachers).

A final approach is developed by Shulman (1987; see also Achinstein & Athansases, 2005), who defines a knowledge base as knowledge structured by larger groups of experts in interaction with the community of professionals to which they belong, and relevant for the professional community at large. In this kind of knowledge base is knowledge of teachers and knowledge for teachers combined.

Hence, according to the authors mentioned above knowledge bases may be constructed by (local) practitioners, researchers or a larger professional community, in which practitioners and researchers cooperate. And the aim of knowledge bases may be to enhance the individual or collective practices of a local group or to define and enhance the practice of the professional community at large.

Having a knowledge base for the professional community at large is not undisputed. As already indicated, Shulman (1987) stated:

> Discovering, explicating, and codifying general teaching principles simplify the otherwise outrageously complex activity of teaching. The great danger occurs, however, when a general teaching principle is distorted into prescription, when maxim becomes mandate. Those states that have taken working principles of teaching, based solely on empirical studies of generic teaching effectiveness, and have rendered them as hard, independent criteria for judging a teacher's worth, are engaged in a political process likely to injure the teaching profession rather than improve it.
>
> (p. 11)

In this warning, we see some important caveats while building knowledge bases for the professional community of teacher educators at large. Shulman and Shulman (2004) opted for a holistic approach and developed a model in which they combine the need for general professional knowledge with the recognition of the complexity of practice and of individual differences among professionals. According to the researchers, a knowledge base can be described as the shared knowledge of the community of professionals. They view such a knowledge base not as static, but as dynamic and growing in an ongoing interaction between the community and individual professionals. They define the different kinds of knowledge that should constitute a knowledge base using four clusters: vision, motivation, understanding and practice, which influence and enhance each other through reflective practice.

In sum, knowledge bases that aim to be relevant for the professional community at large have to include the complexity, the daily tensions and ambiguity of the work of teacher educators provided by practitioners and the results of (review) studies based on practitioner research provided by experts in the field and researchers.

Teacher educators

While there are several publications that discuss knowledge bases for teachers and knowledge bases for teacher education, studies on what a knowledge base for teacher educators can and should include are still scarce. Recent studies by Selmer et al. (2016) and Ping et al. (2018) offer a glimpse of what might be relevant for developing knowledge bases of teacher educators. Selmer et al. (2016) built on Shulman and Shulman's work and started building a knowledge base based on their own professional development as teacher educators. During a year, these three teacher educators mapped and analysed the knowledge they themselves needed.

They found three primary elements (general pedagogical knowledge, content specific knowledge and context knowledge), in which detailed subcategories could be distinguished. General pedagogical knowledge includes knowledge of learning, knowledge of teaching (cf. Loughran, 2014) and knowledge of curriculum. Content specific knowledge includes subject matter knowledge and pedagogical content knowledge. Context knowledge includes knowledge of local, state and national, and global contexts.

In 2018, Ping et al. published a review study on the professional learning of teacher educators, distinguishing professional learning content, professional learning activities and reasons for professional learning. Like the study of Selmer et al. (2016), this study focusses on what individual teacher educators learn during their work.

With regard to content knowledge, they found three main themes: pedagogy of teacher education, research and reflection, and professional identity. Pedagogy of teacher education refers to second-order pedagogy, to be distinguished from the first-order pedagogy that is a characteristic of teachers' work with students in schools (Murray & Male, 2005). It also refers to explicitly explaining the underlying reasons of teacher educators' teaching, and to mentoring and supervising students during their internship at schools. Research and reflection are important because research is conceived as an important requirement in higher education and, when research is focused on teacher educators' own practices, it supports and underpins reflection. Professional identity addresses the characteristics of teacher educators' profession – becoming a second order teacher, a mentor and a teacher educator-researcher – and can be seen as attempts to demarcate what really matters. Ping et al. emphasise that their findings are not a checklist necessary for all teacher educators to meet, but can be used as a framework to discuss teacher educators' work and professional learning and can be guiding for designing a professional program for teacher educators.

A comparison of Ping et al.'s (2018) study with the small-scale study of Selmer et al. (2016) shows that the theme 'pedagogy of teacher education' in this review study concurs with the general pedagogical knowledge element of Selmer et al. (2016), but that the other knowledge domains do not correspond with each other.

Designing a knowledge base

The literature discussed above teaches us that a knowledge base is intended to help professionals or the professional community in capturing the essential knowledge needed to underpin and improve their professional practices. Developing a knowledge base of teacher educators needs to take into account the broad variety of backgrounds, positions and professional interests of teacher educators. For example, the extensive survey InFo-TED carried out among institution-based teacher educators (see chapter 3) shows that in six European countries there are differences in teaching experience, in the level of the degrees teacher educators have and in their academic and educational interests. Moreover, the study of Lunenberg et al. (2014) emphasises the diversity of roles teacher educators have. Besides teacher of teacher and researcher, they can be coaches, assessors, curriculum developers and brokers between the world of schools and school-based teacher education and the world of university-based teacher education and research.

So, in addition to the caveats formulated in the first section, we may conclude that knowledge bases for the professional community as a whole should:

- include the diversity in the work of and among teacher educators and their learners;
- contain a basic structure reflecting the complexity and diversity of the work (or an aspect of the work) and also the integrative identity development of teacher educators;
- refer to different kinds of knowledge;
- be developed by the professional community of practitioners and researchers in the field;
- be communicative, open for discourse, revision, and expansion; and
- enhance reflection and development in identity and personal professional practice.

While respecting that student teachers often most value the practical experience of teacher educators (Murray et al., 2019), teacher educators also need to be informed about the research that can assist their complex work. Hence, building on the work of Loughran (2014), one could state that knowledge bases should offer the diversity of teacher educators 'landmarks and signposts' they need in their individual professional development journey, recognizing that there is not a single true or correct path for this journey.

Dutch knowledge base[1]

Context

Experiences with and research on Dutch professional development trajectories showed that teacher educators found it hard to find their way in the growing amount of available literature (Koster et al., 2008). This was a main reason to build the Dutch knowledge base of teacher educators.

The aim of the Dutch Knowledge Base project, which started in 2009, was to support teacher educators in studying and using the available research literature by developing a structured knowledge base of teacher educators. The idea was to offer an accessible and inspiring overview summarising the knowledge essential to the professional development of teacher educators.

Following Shulman and Shulman (2004), it was emphasised that this development should take place in interaction with individual teacher educators, take into account different kinds of knowledge and that the knowledge base should be open and dynamic.

Building the structure

The development of the knowledge base proceeded step by step. The first step was to identify possible domains of a knowledge base by conducting semi-structured interviews with stakeholders: the board and special interest groups of the VELON and some Dutch academics who had published extensively on the professional development of teacher educators and were also involved in the professional development of teacher educators; and by an extensive literature search. Next, to validate the format, an international expert meeting was organised with experts from the Netherlands, the United Kingdom, Australia, and the United States. In general, the participants recognised and acknowledged the identified domains.

The main discussion, at the international expert meeting, however, focused on the status of the various domains and the question of which domains represented the knowledge every individual teacher educator should have (i.e., what Shulman & Shulman (2004), call 'shared knowledge'), and which knowledge would be sufficient if available within a team or the professional community ('distributed knowledge'). The outcome of this process is represented in Figure 6.1.

The four core domains are basic and applicable to all teacher educators. The specific domains take into account the different contexts in which teacher educators work and their specialisation (e.g., a specific academic domain/subject or pedagogical content). The extended domains are in their most basic form relevant to all teacher educators, but in their full depth, they are intended for teacher educators specializing in such a domain[2]. This way, the knowledge base offers various entrances and meets the needs of individual teacher educators.

Building the content and creating ownership

The aim of the second stage was to fill the domains with content. A development group was installed, consisting of eight experts and members of various special interest groups of the VELON. Important criteria for inclusion were:

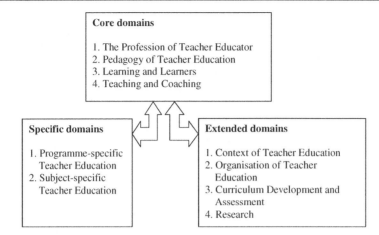

Figure 6.1 The ten domains of the Dutch knowledge base of teacher educators

people involved.

being active as a teacher educator, being involved in national networks of teacher educators, having a good overview of the research on teacher educators,
and, as a group, representing the diversity of institutions across the country in
order to assure a broad ownership.

The approach of this group was iterative and interactive. Leading questions,
covering the essence of the domains, were formulated as an inviting way of
structuring the domains for colleagues. It was also discussed that these leading
questions could be answered from several perspectives. The development group
decided to distinguish a theoretical, practical, reflective and a developmental
perspective. This way theoretical as well as practical knowledge would be
included, reflection would be stimulated and suggestions for further professional development would be offered. Hence, for each domain a matrix consisting of leading questions (rows) and perspectives (columns) was developed
(Table 6.1).

To stimulate ownership of the knowledge base by the professional community, the development group invited colleagues to contribute by filling the
matrix cells with content. The willingness to be part in the development proved
to be strong. Many teacher educator-researchers contributed to the theoretical
perspective of the knowledge base by writing encyclopaedic texts. This meant
that rich literature studies could be incorporated into the knowledge base. Even
more, teacher educator-practitioners wrote vignettes or sent video clips to fill the
cells from a practical perspective. In the end, almost 80 colleagues contributed to
the knowledge base. The reflection and the discussion cells (with questions for
reflection and discussion), and the development cells (with suggestions for further
reading) were filled by the development group. The filling of these cells also
offered the opportunity to build bridges between cells, point to additional or
competing visions and put contributions in contexts.

Teaching and coaching

Leading questions	Theoretical perspective	Practical perspective	Reflective perspective	Developmental perspective
What is teaching?				
How to take into account diversity of students' ages and experiences?				
How to support collaborative learning?				
When is teaching or coaching effective?				

Figure 6.2 Matrix for the domain Teaching and Coaching of the Dutch knowledge base

Use of the Dutch knowledge base

In the spring of 2011, the knowledge base was launched at the annual conference of the VELON. A survey carried out a year later, proved that the knowledge base was seen as relevant and useful (Attema-Noordewier et al., 2014). In the years that followed, the knowledge base became integrated in other national professional development initiatives. In 2012, the contents of the renewed Dutch professional standards of teacher educators were linked to aspects of the domains of the knowledge base of teacher educators. This way, the knowledge base offered teacher educators going through the registration procedure an accessible opportunity to theoretically underpin their work and their development plans.

The knowledge base also functioned as a theoretical frame of reference for a professional development programme for teacher educators that started in 2011 in the Netherlands and has been carried out annually since then. In this way, the knowledge base became embedded in a wider set of professional development activities in the Netherlands[3].

InFo-TED knowledge bases

Context

InFo-TED was established in 2013 by four experienced teacher educators from Belgium, England, the Netherlands, and Norway, who invited experienced teacher educators from Ireland and Scotland to join them. Colleagues from Israel, Australia, and the United States formed a supportive outer ring (for the history of InFo-TED, see chapter 1). At an early stage of InFo-TED, it became apparent that it was important to develop a shared understanding about teacher educators' professional development and a common language for further work. Hence, a conceptual model was developed to represent this shared language and understanding (Vanassche et al., 2015; see also chapter 2).

The aim of this model is to offer a 'practice-based' approach to the professional development of teacher educators and not a normative blueprint or fixed standards. In this model, the base of professional development is a teacher educator's professional stance, that is, being critical, inquiry-oriented, self-regulated, contextually responsive, and research-informed. The purpose of the conceptual model is primarily descriptive and communicative.

Figure 6.2 shows the conceptual model developed by InFo-TED. This model has as its focus the professional development of teacher educators,

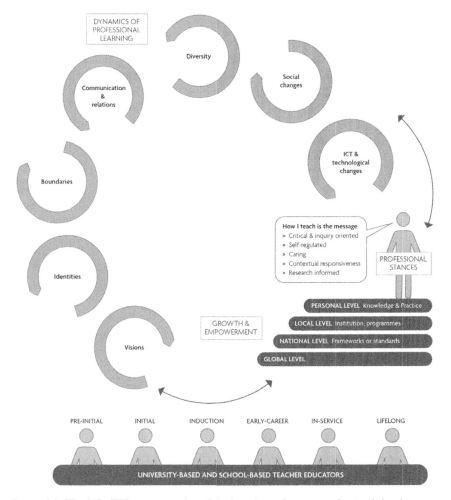

Figure 6.3 The InFo-TED conceptual model of teacher educator professional development

especially in their role as teachers of (prospective) teachers. The agreed starting point for this is their professional stance; that is, their practice rooted in the statement 'how I teach is the message' (Russell, 1997). But even in this aspect of the work of teacher educators, we see the diversity and complexity of the work: the professional learning of teacher educators takes place in the context of a university, other higher education institution or school, and is co-defined by (inter)national or regional policy contexts. The model also shows that teacher educators work in different workplaces and support teachers' learning at different stages of their career.

The 'dynamics of professional learning' in the diagram presents a non-exhaustive list of possible content domains for teacher educators' professional development.

Building the structure

In 2016, InFo-TED started to build a website, to share enacted practices of diverse teacher educators and to develop knowledge bases that should reflect and support as much as possible the whole range of the work of teacher educators in all its complexity and diversity. The knowledge bases were also meant to support the Summer Academy for experienced teacher educators, organised by InFo-TED (see chapter 8). The plural was used to stress that InFo-TED would not claim to build the ultimo generic knowledge base and to take seriously the stance of the conceptual model that the practice of teacher educators should be the starting point for professional development. It resulted in taking the different elements of the conceptual model as a basis for the building blocks. 'Research' and 'assessment', referring to other roles of teacher educators that were not represented in the conceptual model, were added as building blocks.

While acknowledging that in the future modifications to this set up could follow this decision meant that, to start with, 13 'building blocks' would be developed:

- ICT and technological change
- social change
- diversity
- communication and relations
- boundaries
- identities
- visions
- how I teach is the message
- personal, local, national, and global level
- stages of professional development
- university-based and school-based teacher educators
- research
- assessment.

Intertwined with the discussion about the structure was the discussion about the design of the knowledge bases; about how to optimise the open and communicative character, the accessibility and applicability for the broad variety of teacher educators' practices. First, it was decided to use a variety of presentation forms. For each of the 13 building blocks, an introductory text was written, an introductory video was made and a literature overview was added. Moreover, videos of good practices and overviews of web sources were added to the website, as well as blogs. Blogs offer the possibility to pose new research developments, share practices and challenge policies. Building blocks and blogs cross reference to each other.

The second decision was to offer teacher educators two main options to enter the knowledge bases-portal, namely directly via the building blocks based on the conceptual model (see Figure 6.3) or via a continuously expanding collection of blogs (see Figure 6.4).

Both, the discussion around the structure of the knowledge bases and the discussion about the entrances of the knowledge bases were very useful to sharpen our ideas.

Building the content and creating ownership

After the structure was decided on, and introduction texts and matching introduction videos for the 13 building blogs were completed, the circle of persons working on the knowledge bases was widened. Colleagues were invited to co-operate in videotaping good practices and in writing blogs. Moreover, the invitation to write blogs was published on the InFo-TED website. It was emphasised that the blogs could have a variety of focuses: research reports, literature summaries, examples of good practices, evaluations of pedagogical

Figure 6.4 Screenshot of the building block 'How I teach is the message'

Figure 6.5 Screenshot of the entrance page to the blogs

approaches, or policy responses. Already more than 50 colleagues with a wide variety in expertise and background have contributed to the blogs. Among others, blogs have covered the diversity of teacher educators, the roles of school-based and university-based teacher educators, an intelligently use of standards and the contribution of self-study research to the professional development of teacher educators.

Use of the InFo-TED knowledge bases

The InFo-TED knowledge bases serve as one of the pillars for the content of the international Summer Academy for experienced teacher educators (see chapter 8), that Info-TED organised in 2018 and will organise again in 2021. Another indication for the use of the knowledge bases is that more than 50,000 users from more than 150 countries visited the website between the launch of the website in October 2017 and the end of 2019. A solid qualitative evaluation of the relevance and use is still lacking, but the reactions on presentations of the knowledge bases at national and international conferences were generally positive.

Conclusion

Although literature on building knowledge bases of teacher educators is scarce (Selmer et al., 2016; Ping et al., 2018), it nevertheless offers us some points of attention for designing and building knowledge base(s). To start with, the literature offers a variety of ideas about what knowledge bases can be, generic or specific, starting from experiences of an individual teacher educator or developed by experts and so on.

With regard to the content, based on the literature, it seems obvious that knowledge of the work of teacher educators' as 'teachers of teachers' (Loughran, 2006; Murray & Male, 2005) should be a central issue. The work of teacher educators requests its own 'pedagogy of teacher education' (Loughran, 2006). As Russell (1997) states, teacher educators need to be conscious about 'the pedagogical turn' (p. 55) in teacher education, that is the power of being an explicit role model.

Broad empirical evidence for the choice of other contents, however, is scarce, but that knowledge bases should take into account the broad and complex work of teacher educators, and the variety of contexts they work in and the diversity of roles they fulfil, is generally agreed on.

More in general, in knowledge bases for teacher educators, there should be attention for scholarly and practical relevance and for reflection. Other themes that are mentioned in the literature about knowledge bases are space for competing explanations, perspectives and theories, and for context.

We will conclude this chapter by comparing and reflecting on the knowledge bases described above to formulate some recommendations. The four main questions to consider are as follows.

Question 1: what is the aim of the knowledge base?

The aim of the Dutch knowledge base project was to build an accessible and inspiring overview summarising the national and international knowledge essential for the daily work and professional development of the Dutch community of teacher educators. Following Shulman and Shulman (2004), the idea was that the building would be done in interaction with the professional community of teacher educators. Moreover, it was agreed that the knowledge base should be open and dynamic. The aim of the InFo-TED knowledge base project was based on the conceptual model for teacher educators. InFo-TED did not aim to build a generic knowledge base, but to develop building blocks that could support teacher educators to underpin and develop their practices. This practice-based approach was further stressed by adding blogs.

Recommendation 1

Be clear about the aim of your knowledge base(s). Make an underpinned choice for the kind of knowledge base that fits your aim. In case of a choice for a generic knowledge base, the work of Shulman (including the work of authors that build on his work) is a useful starting point.

Question 2: how to structure a knowledge base?

The structure of the Dutch knowledge base is based on a literature study and on interviews with Dutch experts and the special interest groups of the

VELON. The concept structure was discussed in an international expert meeting and established. The centre point of the structure is the core domains: the profession of teacher educators, the pedagogy of teacher education, learning and teaching. The structure of the InFo-TED knowledge bases is based on Info-TED's conceptual model, and has as its main theme the professional learning of teacher educators in their role as teachers of teachers. The centre point is 'how I teach is the message'. A few additions were added.

Hence, both structures are based on findings from the literature and a discussion among experts, and resulted in a model. In both structures, the variety of contexts teacher educators work in is taken into account, but more extensively in the InFo-TED knowledge bases than in the older Dutch knowledge base, where context is one of the extended domains. In the InFo-TED knowledge bases, the context gets attention by the emphasis on the different levels that influence the professional development of teacher educators as well as by the attention for university-based and school-based teacher educators.

Recommendation 2

Build the structure of knowledge bases for teacher educators around the central focus of the pedagogy of teacher education. The discussion and research on other contents is still ongoing and, as the two attempts described in this chapter show, developers of knowledge bases of teacher educators have their own rationale for their choices. Take into account the still increasing variety of contexts of teacher educators.

Question 3: how to develop content and form?

The literature emphasises that knowledge bases should include theoretical as well as practical knowledge, and space for different approaches. In the Dutch knowledge base, the content of each domain is approached from four perspectives: theoretical, practical, reflective and developmental. Typical for the InFo-TED knowledge bases is the non-exhaustive list of possible content domains. Each domain is briefly introduced, and the accompanying blogs and literature suggestions offer additional practical and theoretical perspectives. Both knowledge bases use a variety of forms, such as introduction texts, video clips, good practices, literature suggestions and web-based suggestions.

Recommendation 3

Give attention to theoretical as well as practical knowledge and use a variety of forms to serve the needs of the broad and diverse professional community of teacher educators.

Question 4: how to stimulate ownership?

In the development of both knowledge bases, a broad group of teacher educators has been involved. The basic structure of the Dutch knowledge base was built on interviews with Dutch special interest groups and experts, followed by a consultation of an international expert group. Then a development group took care of the further development, inviting experts as well as the broad community of Dutch teacher educators to contribute. After the structure of the InFo-TED knowledge bases was developed colleagues were invited to contribute examples of good practices and to write blogs. Moreover, an open invitation to write blogs was put on the InFo-TED website. Involving colleagues has enriched both knowledge bases.

In the next step to creating ownership, additional recent developments and conceptions were added and opened up for discussion. Also, explicitly linking the knowledge bases to professional development activities is essential for broadening the feeling of ownership and stimulating the use of the knowledge base. In the Dutch case, the link to VELON professional development activities and to courses for teacher educators, and in the InFo-TED case, the links to the Summer Academy are good examples.

Recommendation 4

To stimulate ownership and to assure that knowledge bases *for* teacher educators become knowledge bases *of* teacher educators, involving the professional community of teacher educators in the development is important, as is the linking of knowledge bases with professional development activities. Also, we would stress that constructing knowledge bases is an ongoing process and should be open to new developments and changing discourses regarding the teacher educator profession. Finally, we would recommend incorporating research about the perceived relevance and use of the knowledge bases in the development process.

Conclusion

In this chapter, we analysed the development of two knowledge bases. Acknowledging the limitation of this study, we feel that making an underpinned choice for the kind of knowledge base one wants to develop. Giving the pedagogy of teacher educators a central place and involving teacher educators from a variety of contexts in the development process are important issues to take into consideration. Moreover, knowledge bases for teacher educators should be open and flexible. Research on knowledge bases for teacher educators is still scarce, and more study is needed on both the development process and on the way knowledge bases are used by teacher educators in their practice.

Notes

1 More information can be found in Attema-Noordewier, S., Dengerink, J., Geursen, J., Korthagen, F., Koster, B., & Lunenberg, M. (2014). The Dutch case. In M. Lunenberg, J. Dengerink, & F. Korthagen (Eds.), *The professional teacher educator: Roles, behaviour, and professional development of teacher educators* (pp. 79–102). Sense Publishers.
2 Looking back at the structure of the Dutch knowledge base almost a decade later, one may conclude that nowadays research by teacher educators (including self-study research) and the co-operation with schools, that is, the role of broker, would ask for more attention.
3 Due to a renewal of the VELON-website, the original web-based knowledge base has been lost. Recently a pdf-reconstruction has been published (Dengerink & Lunenberg, 2020).

References

Achinstein, B., & Athansases, S. Z. (2005). Focusing new teachers on diversity and equity: Toward a knowledge base for mentors. *Teaching and Teacher Education*, 21(7), 843–862.

Achinstein, B., & Davis, E. (2014). The subject of mentoring: Towards a knowledge and practice base for content-focused mentoring of new teachers. *Mentoring & Tutoring: Partnership in Learning*, 22(2), 104–126.

Attema-Noordewier, S., Dengerink, J., Geursen, J., Korthagen, F., Koster, B., & Lunenberg, M. (2014). The Dutch case. In M. Lunenberg, J. Dengerink, & F. Korthagen, *The professional teacher educator: Roles, behaviour, and professional development of teacher educators* (pp. 79–102). Sense Publishers.

Berry, A. (2007). Tensions in teaching about teaching. Understanding practice as a teacher educator. *Self-study of teaching and teacher education practices* (Vol. 5). Springer.

Dengerink, J., & Lunenberg, M. (Eds.). (2020). *Reconstructie van de Kennisbasis Lerarenopleiders 2012* [*Reconstruction of the Knowledge Base of Teacher Educators 2012*]. Vrije Universiteit Amsterdam.

Dinkelman, T., Margolis, J., & Sikkenga, K. (2006). From teacher to teacher educator: Reframing knowledge in practice. *Studying Teacher Education*, 2(2), 119–136.

Goodwin, A. L., & Kosnik, C. (2013). Quality teacher educators = quality teachers? Conceptualizing essential domains of knowledge for those who teach teachers. *Teacher Development: An International Journal of Teachers' Professional Development*, 17(3), 334–346.

Hall, C., & Schulz, R. (2003). Tensions in teaching and teacher education: Professionalism and professionalisation in England and Canada, *Compare*, 33(3), 369–382.

Hiebert, J., Gallimore, R., & Stigler, J. W. (2002). A knowledge base for the teaching profession: What would it look like and how can we get one? *Educational Researcher*, 31(3), 3–15.

Koster, B., Dengerink, J., Korthagen, F., & Lunenberg, M. (2008). Teacher educators working on their own professional development: Goals, activities and outcomes of a project for the professional development of teacher educators. *Teachers and Teaching*, 14(5), 567–587.

Loughran, J. (2006). *Developing a pedagogy of teacher education: Understanding teaching and learning about teaching*. Routledge.

Loughran, J. (2014). Professionally developing as a teacher educator. *Journal of Teacher Education*, 65(4), 271–283.

Lunenberg, M., Dengerink, J., & Korthagen, F. (2014). *The professional teacher educator: Roles, behaviour, and professional development of teacher educators.* Sense Publishers.

Murray, J., Czerniawski, G., & Barber, P. (2019). Who is teaching me and what do they know? Student teachers' perceptions of their teacher educators and mentors. In J. Murray, A. Swennen, & C. Kosnik (Eds.), *International Research, Policy and Practice in Teacher Education* (pp 139–153). Springer.

Murray, J., & Male, T. (2005). Becoming a teacher educator: Evidence from the field. *Teaching and Teacher Education*, 21(2), 125–142.

Ping, C., Schellings, G., & Beijaard, D. (2018). Teacher educators' professional learning: A literature review. *Teaching and Teacher Education*, 75, 93–104.

Russell, T. (1997). Teaching teachers: How I teach IS the message. In J. Loughran, & T. Russell (Eds.), *Teaching about teaching: Purpose, passion and pedagogy in teacher education* (pp. 32–47). Falmer Press.

Selmer, S., Bernstein, M., & Bolyard, J. (2016). Multilayered knowledge: Understanding the structure and enactment of teacher educators' specialized knowledge base. *Teacher Development*, 20(4), 437–457.

Shulman, L. S. (1987). Knowledge and teaching: Foundations of the new reform. *Harvard Educational Review*, 57(1), 1–22.

Shulman, L. S., & Shulman, J. H. (2004). How and what teachers learn: A shifting paradigm. *Journal of Curriculum Studies*, 36(2), 257–271.

Vanassche, E., Rust, F., Conway, P. F., Smith, K., Tack, H., & Vanderlinde, R. (2015). InFo-TED: Bringing policy, research, and practice together around teacher educator development. In C. J. Craig, & L. Orland-Barak, *International Teacher Education: Promising Pedagogies(part C)* (Vol. 22, pp. 341–364). Emerald.

Verloop, N., Van Driel, J., & Meijer, P. (2001). Teacher knowledge and the knowledge base of teaching. *International Journal of Educational Research*, 35(5), 441–461.

: Teacher educators'
nal development

nd challenges

Kazuhiro Kusahara and Shotaro Iwata

Introduction

Research on teacher educators in Japan has gained momentum in the 2010s. In Oyanagi's (2018) review, a survey of the number of articles related to teacher educators published in 10-year intervals starting from the 1980s reveals negligible numbers in 1980–2000s and only two articles in the 2000s. According to an additional survey conducted by this chapter's authors, the number of publications reached 52 in the 2010s (Table 7.1). For Japan, the 'lost decade' in terms of economy was a 'high growth period' in terms of the professional development of teacher educators.

The above statistics pose a question of why interest in teacher educators in Japan has dramatically increased in the 2010s from the perspective of political and academic backgrounds inherent in this field. The purpose of this chapter is to answer this question.

The authors also describe a map of the recent trends in the research of teacher educators in Japan. Moreover, the academic conceptualisation and specific stories suggested by the InFo-TED studies in Europe are compared with those in Japan. In conclusion, the mutual implications from both research communities are presented in a complementary manner.

In the conclusion, in the context of politics, the establishment of professional schools for teacher education had essentially raised a controversy regarding Japanese teacher education. By contrast, in the context of academics, the

Table 7.1 Trends in research on teacher educators in Japan

	2010	2011	2012	2013	2014	2015	2016	2017	2018	2019
Number of articles (total 52)	2	5	9	3	2	7	2	4	5	12

Note. The search strings 'teacher educator', 'teacher education' and 'professional development' were searched in CiNii (Citation Information by National institute of Informatics), a database service for searching the academic information of articles, books, journals and dissertations published in Japan.

European research concepts had an enlightening impact on them. The European research trends are of significance to Japanese teacher educators because they have helped them recognise the implicit-explicit system embedded in teacher education in Japan. Some new research has emerged based on this recognition.

Political discussion background: why and how have teacher educators become a concern in Japan?

In Japan, an 'approval system' was introduced in 1949 after WWII to ensure the quality assurance of teacher educators (Katsuno, 2006; Yokosuka, 2013). According to the national law, 'In principle, the required credits are mastered in the university program that the Ministry of Education, Culture, Sports, Science and Technology (MEXT) deems appropriate to obtain the necessary qualifications in order to receive the school teacher's license' (MEXT, 2019).

The ostensible significance of this system is that the organisation and facilities for teacher education, the curriculum and the number of credits in each discipline area provide the external quality assurance of teachers, thereby facilitating standardisation of teacher performance in the real sense. However, greater essential significance of this system is that the performance of the teacher educators is assessed to ensure quality of teacher education, therefore ensuring quality of student learning as well as that of the teacher education program conducted by teacher educators. To receive accreditation by the approval system, the university with their faculty teaching in the teacher education program must pass a review by submitting to 'the approval system committee' in MEXT the relevant documents that list the classes specified by the law, the teacher educator of each class and their curriculum vitae, which includes information on book publications, academic papers, clinical records of practice that certify their competence, as well as proof that their classes are in accordance with the objectives of the teacher education program (MEXT, 2018).

Consequently, while this system has led to the centralisation of teacher education, in return for this system, the teacher educators in Japan have been given a double aegis, namely the political certification of their status and provision of an organisational base within the academic system; both these aspects are integrated consistently. Therefore, this Japanese context could be different from the context experienced by European teacher educators.

A new turning point in this system is the establishment of professional schools for teacher education in Japan in 2008. Japanese teacher education was based on bachelor's and master's degrees, but the induction of a professional degree program for the teaching profession caused controversy in the 2000s. The foundation of the professional graduate school for teacher education is an epoch-making reform; it is considered a shift into a professional program for enhancing teachers' competence through their practice and reflection in school sites from an academic-oriented master's program on school education. The new professional graduate school system has inevitably led to the emergence of teacher educators who can meet the demands of the institutional reform movement. The following three MEXT Council reports submitted to the minister of MEXT mark the origin and its change in the institutional reform.

First, in 2006, the report *The future of the pre-service education and teacher license system* was presented by the Central Council for Education (CCE, 2006). In this report, given the purpose and characteristics of teacher education, it was decided to categorise university teachers as 'clinical professors', as a new formal position. A clinical professor is required to be in charge of 30 percent of the faculty members teaching in the professional degree programs. Clinical professors are required to 'have a certain amount of work experience as a teacher, including as a supervisor or principal, and have excellent teaching experience' (p. 8). Moreover, they should be 'recognised as having advanced educational leadership in their field of specialization based on the practical report and empirical research at seminars/workshops as well as on their publications, etc.' (p. 8). However, they need not necessarily have the same aims and orientation as the traditional research faculty do.

Second, the report *Measures to comprehensive improvement of teachers' qualifications and skills throughout their professional career* appeared in 2012 (CCE, 2012). This report is substantially the first policy document in Japan that refers to the needs for the systematic professional development of teacher educators. The document states, 'in order to improve the quality of education and research in teacher education university and faculties, it is necessary to develop a system for training the faculty members to take responsibility for teacher education" (p. 19). Furthermore, it was argued that the doctoral programs in universities for teacher education should establish EdD programs for practitioners and provide a 'place of study for aspiring practicing teachers'. However, the document exhorted that PhD degree holders who graduate from research universities and who are currently teaching in the pre-service teacher education program should be given 'practical educational research experience, such as fieldwork in the school site' (p. 19).

Third, in 2015, the report *Improving the qualifications and skills of teachers who will play a role in school education in the future* was released (CCE, 2015). A noteworthy point in this report is that it propounds a recruitment system from teachers to teacher educators. The report proposes the development of teachers who have the foundation of practical skills related to the teaching profession and the ability to respond to new educational issues. Moreover, the report adds that teacher educators need to have problem-solving skills for adapting to recent practices and issues in order to meet the demand on teachers. Consequently, it was advocated that some in-service teachers should be trained as future teacher educator candidates, that the teacher education university should systematically train teachers who have the expertise in both theory and practice of their teaching subject in cooperation with the Board of Education, and that a pathway should be established for teachers who wish to advance their teaching career at the university teacher education program. In summary, the new recruiting scheme aims to train teacher educators in an educational site with a long-term perspective and select from within a pool of excellent teachers.

Focusing on the political context, potential teacher educators have shifted from research-oriented teacher educators to practice-oriented teacher educators with the trigger of the historical event called the 'professional school controversy'. Initially, the professional development of teacher educators was based on the requirements that practitioners should have a doctoral degree and researchers should attain experience in the field of education, according to their backgrounds and specialties. However, the focus of policymakers gradually shifted to methods of preparing teacher educator candidates in school sites. This policy shift in which the professional development as a researcher is neglected has led to the question of what it means to be a teacher educator in Japan.

As discussed in the introduction, the increase in the number of articles related to teacher education is also closely related to this policy shift. Himeno et al. (2019) have proposed the division of the educational culture in Japan, which classifies Japanese teacher educators into 'research professors' and 'clinical professors'. Under such a context, teacher educators' identities and careers have been carefully investigated, and the possible collaboration between 'research professors' and 'clinical professors' is suggested in the wake of the policy movement of the 2000s. These themes became the foundation for new research in the field of teacher education, eventually resulting in the publication of several academic research papers.

Academic literature review: why and how have teacher educators become a concern in Japan?

This section describes the previous research on the professional development of teacher educators in Japan. As the research trend shown in Table 7.1 confirms the rapid increase in the number of publications in the last ten years, the author focuses on the articles and books published since 2010.

According to the author's previous survey, the subject of the recent studies can be classified into Categories A, B and C: (A) the professionalism and identity of teacher educators, (B) the transition from researchers to teacher educators, and (C) the transition from teachers to teacher educators. The methodologies of educational science in Japan are customarily divided into three categories: (1) normative and theoretical research, (2) design and clinical research, and (3) experimental and empirical research (Japan Science Committee, 2019; Kusahara et al., 2015). Table 7.2 shows a matrix of the research subjects and methods, including the bibliographic information. The following description provides an overview of the academic research trends along this matrix.

Research on teacher educators in Category A has been dominated by studies based on normative and theoretical approaches. Okamura et al. (2015) and

Table 7.2 Review of previous research on teacher educators in Japan

	(A) Existence of Teacher Educator	*(B) Transition from Researcher to Teacher Educator*	*(C) Transition from Teacher to Teacher Educator*
(1) Normative, theoretical approach	Okamura et al. (2015) Kusahara (2018) Okamura (2018) Nagamura (2018) Oyanagi (2018, 2019)		Hamamoto et al. (2019) Kusahara (2019)
(2) Design, clinical approach		Maruyama et al. (2019)	
(3) Experimental, empirical approach	Himeno et al. (2019)	Iwata et al. (2018) Yamada et al. (2019) Yoshida et al. (2019)	Osaka et al. (2020)

Okamura (2018) presented an outline of concepts related to the professionalism and competence of teacher educators and discussed the role of clinical professors. Naganuma (2018) examined the strategy of professional development for university faculty members by reviewing J. Loughran's theories on the development of pedagogy in teacher education. Oyanagi (2019) argued the relationship between the identity and professionalism of teacher educators, quoting research frameworks such as self-study, professional capital and resident teachers presented by Western researchers. In addition, Oyanagi (2019) expanded on the earlier discussion and suggested the effectiveness of self-study as this method helps teacher educators present their practices and concerns based on data in order to contribute to the construction of the organisational common culture and, therefore, allow professional teacher education schools to fulfil their accountability. Kusahara (2018) critically read the European Commission's report and reconstructed the meanings of responsibility and challenges of teacher educators from the Japanese education context. He suggested an action plan to improve the profession of teacher educators in subject pedagogy.

An example of one of the few comprehensive empirical studies in Category A is Himeno et al. (2019). They conducted a questionnaire survey for research professors and clinical professors involved in the teacher education program at the national universities, and then clarified their perceptions on their job, their views of teacher development and their social relation construction within and outside the program. As described above, Category A articles share a common interest in identifying the issues in Japanese teacher education and suggesting reforms by drawing theoretical maps on the identity and professional characteristics in teacher educators.

The studies in Category B transitioned to empirical and experimental approaches. For instance, Iwata et al. (2018) determined the qualitative differences in the process of identity transformation and the reasons of differentiation by investigating the experiences of doctoral students who teach the subject pedagogy 'teaching methods of history-geography' as teaching assistants. Yamada et al. (2019) interviewed teacher educators who had transitioned from being subject discipline researchers into subject pedagogists. They examined the process of profession forming and the professional philosophy to integrate teaching, research, social service and administration to fulfil the academic responsibility. Yoshida et al. (2019) showed that the significance of team-based educational experiences for individual professional growth with continuous reflection on the educators' teaching as a graduate teaching assistant is a unique methodological case that integrates the techniques of self-study and lesson study.

Various approaches have emerged in Category C studies. Hamamoto et al. (2019) prepared the theoretical frameworks of professional development for teacher educators on the basis of a comparison of Anja Swennen and Kari Smith's research and practice. Kusahara (2019) described the curriculum of the higher education institutions in the Netherlands, Norway and the United States and argued that the differences in their educational strategies depending on the expected competencies of teacher educators, in conclusion, implicate the education system for teacher educators in Japan. Osaka et al. (2020) presented the reason why two former teachers of university-affiliated high schools could achieve a soft landing from teachers to teacher educators without causing stress. They discussed the peculiar function of university-affiliated schools in the development of teacher educators under the schooling context in Japan.

Thus, evidently, the studies in Categories B and C have indirectly responded to the professional school shock by describing the identity and professional growth as well as the development of teacher educators while applying the theories and concepts accumulated from the Category A research. It is noteworthy that the traditional method of professional development in Japan for in-service teachers, known as the lesson study (National Association for the Study on Educational methods, 2011), has been transferred to the development of teacher educators in order to build a relationship among colleagues and gain metacognition of their teaching practice.

While probing the background of the surge in the publications related to teacher educators in the 2010s, one cannot neglect the significance of the translation of some Western literature into Japanese in this decade. The following are a series of representative literature translated by Takeda and her colleagues (Takeda, 2012; Lunenberg et al., 2017; Loughran & Takeda, 2019, respectively): (a) *Linking practice and theory - the pedagogy of realistic teacher education* written by Fred A. J. Korthagen, (b) *Professional teacher educator: Roles, behaviors, and professional development of teacher educators* edited by Mieke Lunenberg et al., and (c) the major paper selections of John Loughran. It is interesting to note that the impact of Western research in an academic context has created not only a new research trend leading to Categories A, B and C studies in Japan but also a sustainable motivation for translating other work.

Implication of InFo-TED on the professional development of teacher educators in Japan

In accordance with the aforementioned research trends of teacher educators in Japan, the authors would like to discuss three points that the chapters on InFo-TED suggest for attaining deep understanding of the characteristics and challenges of teacher educators in Japan.

First, the status of a teacher educator in Europe and Japan differ, possibly due to the historical context in teacher education. The authors in chapter 1 define the typology of teacher educators as 'traditional teacher educators', 'mentors' and 'school-based teacher educators'. Although the 'traditional teacher educators' in Europe and those in Japan are similar to some extent in the diversity of their background, there are some notable differences in the social and academic stability. By contrast, it is possible to identify the difference in the 'mentors'. The mentors in Japan, known as 'supervisors' or 'consultants' of school education, have the institutional stability in the schooling system. They are appointed and dispatched by the board of education in every prefecture and municipality as educational civil servants as well as recognised as established professionals to support teachers' development at school and institutional sites (Shimada, et al., 2017).

On the other hand, 'school-based teacher educators' do not attract much attention in Japan compared with that in Europe. This can possibly be attributed to the main agents and places of teacher preparation in Japan. The period of teaching practicum for the pre-service teachers is as short as three weeks for elementary and junior high school teachers and two weeks for high school teachers (CCE, 2012). This results in a relatively small role and negligible responsibility of 'school-based teacher educators' in the development of pre-service teachers. In comparison with the European system, it can be concluded that university-based teacher educators lead an initiative in teacher preparation to a larger extent in Japan. However, the lack of teaching practicum is compensated by the lesson study conference as autonomous professional development conducted by 'school-based teacher educators' and by administrative guidance supervised by 'institution-based teacher educators' after beginning teaching as a career. By contrast, as discussed below, the relatively few opportunities to enhance the knowledge and experience of teacher educators are highlighted.

Second, the similarities between Europe and Japan in the career paths of teacher educators are revealed. In particular, in the academic circumstance, university-based teacher educators around the world may face some common expectations and tensions in promoting their research. The stories of teacher educators in Iceland, Israel, the Netherlands and Norway described in chapter 9, obviously represent the microcosms of teacher educators in Japan after the advent of the professional school controversy. This indicates the divergence of the backgrounds, passes and identities of Japanese teacher educators.

The authors must confess that any university-based teacher educators in Japan could face a conflict between teaching and research, practice and theory, collaboration with teachers, and promotion of large projects. This could also be applied to teacher educators in Japan: the conflict is between the three careers mentioned in chapter 3, namely 'cognitive career', 'community career' and 'organisational career'. The seeking of these career paths is promoted by the accreditation system as a driving force.

Nevertheless, in the case of Japan, a 'social career' must be added to the list of required careers, because the engagement in the lesson study conference conducted by in-service teachers in school and institution sites as an external advisor is essentially perceived as an academic responsibility undertaken by teacher educators. The lesson study conference for the collective reflection and problem solving under the collaboration of the universities, schools and institution-based teacher educators functions as the main crossroad of teacher educators in Japan (Kim, et al., in press). Thus, the blueprints presented for the profession of teacher educators in chapter 3 and chapter 9 provide Japanese teacher educators with a useful 'mirror' for a future perspective, encouraging a metacognition of their identity distribution.

Third, it is implicated that the institutional framework for the professional development of teacher educators has not been established in Japan, and it is indispensable to stimulate discussion on this issue. The national organisation called the Japan Association of the University of Education (JAUE) consists of 56 national universities managing the teacher education program. It also holds an annual conference and publishes in research journals (JAUE, 2020). The organisation requires teacher educators to deliver research presentations on their teaching and management as a team; therefore, it functions as an exceptional space for professional development in Japan. In fact, we need to consider the diversification and promotion of teacher educators (Iwata, 2016) after the professional school shock; however, that argument is addressed only in terms of political and academic contexts to start with. In that sense, the 12 principles of learning and design for teacher educators presented in chapter 5 could be a useful start-up kit for their consideration. In addition, a case of the Netherlands, where professional standards are set to reflect and qualify teacher educators in a knowledge base (chapter 6), and a case of international summer academics organised by InFo-TED to encourage research of teacher educators (chapter 8), would be of great significance to design a program to effectively meet the emerging double and triple tracks of teacher educators in Japan.

Conclusion

In closing this chapter, the authors emphasise again that the international comparative approach can be a useful method to activate more; it enables us to gain reflective insights as well as fruitful suggestions for both objects of comparison beyond their contexts.

References

Central Council for Education. (2006). *The future of the pre-service education and teacher license system (summary).* Ministry of Education, Culture, Sports, Science and Technology. [in Japanese]

Central Council for Education. (2012). *Measures to comprehensive improvement of teachers' qualifications and skills throughout their professional career (report).* Ministry of Education, Culture, Sports, Science and Technology. [in Japanese]

Central Council for Education. (2015). *Improving the qualifications and skills of teachers who will play a role in school education in the future.* Ministry of Education, Culture, Sports, Science and Technology. [in Japanese]

Hamamoto, A., Osaka, Y., Kusahara, K., & Iwata, S. (2019). A. Swennen and K. Smith's theory on teacher educator professional development. *Bulletin of the Graduate School of Education, Hiroshima University, Part II,* 68, 45–54. [in Japanese]

Himeno, K., Hasegawa, T., & Masuko, N. (2019). Roles of research professor and clinical professor in universities and their perspectives on teachers' development. *Journal of Teacher Studies,* 22(1), 25–35. [in Japanese]

Iwata, S. (2016). Recent policies on teacher education. In M. Oketani, M. Kobayashi, K. Hashimoto, & K. Nishii (Eds.), *What you need to know at the period of teaching practicum, adoption, and novice teaching: Becoming a resilient teacher* (pp. 3–6), Kyoiku Publishing. [in Japanese]

Iwata, S., Kusahara, K., & Kawaguchi, H. (2018). A qualitative study of the process of development for initial teacher educators: The influence of experiences as TA on identity development. *The Bulletin of Japanese Curriculum Research and Development,* 41 (1), 35–46. [in Japanese]

Japan Association of Universities of Education. (2020, July 15). Research activity, http://www.jaue.jp/ [in Japanese]

Japan Science Committee. (2019). The benchmarks for the curriculum design of psychology and educational science to qualify the disciplinary learning in higher education (tentative second report). [in Japanese]

Katsuno, M. (2006). Recent policies on accreditation and evaluation of teaching programs. *Annual Report of the Japan Society for Teacher Education,* 15, 26–32. [in Japanese]

Kim, J., Yoshida, N., Iwata, S., & Kawaguchi, H. (Eds.). (2021). *Lesson study-based teacher education: From Japan to the world.* Routledge.

Kusahara, K. (2018). Professional development of teacher educators who teach the social studies teachers: A reference to report of the European Commission. In T. Harada, H. Seki, & H. Nii (Eds.), *Possibilities of research of subject pedagogy* (pp. 281–290). Kazama Shobo [in Japanese]

Kusahara, K. (2019). Philosophy and methods of teacher educators' professional development: Case study on improving the quality of teacher education. In Education in the Social Studies Department Research Association (Ed.), *A Breakthrough of research on Social Studies: Theory into Practice* (pp. 308–318). Kazama Publishing. [in Japanese]

Loughran, L., & Takeda, N. (Eds.). (2019). *Teacher education and self-study advocated by J. Loughran: For those who educate teachers.* Gakubunsha. [in Japanese]

Lunenberg, M., Dengerink, J., & Korthagen, F. (2017). *The professional teacher educator: Roles, behaviour, and professional development of teacher educators* (N. Takeda, Trans.). Tamagawa University Press. (Original work published 2014) [in Japanese]

Ministry of Education, Culture, Sports, Science and Technology. (2018). Points to keep in mind regarding the application process for certification of teaching courses. General Education, Education and Human Resources Policy Division, Policy Bureau. https://www.mext.go.jp/component /a_menu/education/detail/__icsFiles/ afield file/2018/12/21/1411908_05.pdf [in Japanese]

Ministry of Education, Culture, Sports, Science and Technology. (2019). Approval system. https://www.mext.go.jp/b_menu/shingi/chukyo/chukyo3/siryo/06042105/012.htm [in Japanese]

Naganuma, M. (2018). A study on pedagogy of teacher education advocated by J. Loughran: For professional development of teacher educators in university. *Journal of Educational Studies*, 64(2), 607–612. [in Japanese]

National Association for the Study on Educational Methods. (2011). *Lesson study in Japan*. Keisuisya. [in Japanese]

Okamura, M. (2018). A study on concepts of professionalism and competency in teacher education. *Bulletin of the Graduate School of Education, Hiroshima University, Part III*, 67, 47–55. [in Japanese]

Okamura, M., Soma, M., Isemoto., D., & Masaki, H. (2015). How university-based teacher educators should be? Regarding 'practical-teaching-skills' and expectations for teacher educators with teaching experience at school. *Bulletin of the Graduate School of Education, Hiroshima University, Part III*, 64, 37–46. [in Japanese]

Osaka, Y., Kawaguchi, H., & Kusahara, K. (2020). How do Japanese teachers become teacher educators in higher education from in-service teacher? Focusing on three cases of continuous and stressless transition. *Journal of School Education Practice*, 26, 87–94. [in Japanese]

Oyanagi, K. (2018). A study on relationship between identity and professionalism of teacher educators: from the viewpoint of self-study, professional capital, and resilient teacher. *Journal of Graduate School of Teacher Education, Nara University of Education*, 10, 1–10. [in Japanese]

Oyanagi, K. (2019). A study on the concerns in carrying out purpose and role at school of professional development in education. *Bulletin of Teacher Education Centre for the Future Generation*, 5, 9–18. [in Japanese]

Shimada K., Kihara T., & Terashima K. (2017). Improvement of the rubric on the role of supervisor in board of education for the sustainable development of school-based practical researchers. *Research Report of JET Conferences*, 17(1), 535–542. [in Japanese]

Takeda, N. (2012). A proposal for educational practice in teacher education: To facilitate the professional development of teacher educators. *Annual Report of the Japanese Society for the Study on Teacher Education*, 21, 8–18. [in Japanese]

Yamada, H., Kusahara, K., Kawaguchi, H., & Osaka, Y. (2019). How do European researchers in education define their social responsibilities? A comparative study of three researchers in charge of subject pedagogy. *The Bulletin of Japanese Curriculum Research and Development*, 42(3), 41–54. [in Japanese]

Yokosuka, K. (2013). Current status and issues of approval system and its implementation. *Synapse*, 18, 62–63. [in Japanese]

Yoshida, N., Maruyama, Y., Matsuda, M., Kusahara, K., Iwata, S., Yodozawa, M., Miyamoto, Y., & Matsuura, A. (2019, September 3–6). *Lesson study-based training teacher educator: Case study on self-study and cooperative lesson study* [Conference presentation]. International Conference of World Association of Lesson Studies, Amsterdam, The Netherlands.

Chapter 8

Teacher educators' professional development during an international Summer Academy

Storylines as a powerful pedagogy

Helma Oolbekkink-Marchand, Paulien C. Meijer and Mieke Lunenberg

Introduction

Teacher education quality is seen as an important factor influencing the quality of teaching and students' achievements (European Commission, 2013). As a result, there is a growing interest in teacher educators: their identity, skills, roles and professional development (Loughran, 2014; Lunenberg et al., 2014). As mentioned in chapter 1, teacher educators enter their job coming from a variety of backgrounds, such as being an experienced teacher first but a novice in research, or by gaining a PhD degree first and entering teacher education without teaching experience. Davey (2013) described these pathways as the 'practitioner pathway' and the 'academic pathway'. One way or the other, teacher educators in most settings seem to be 'Janus-faced' (cf. Smith & Flores, 2019) due to the competing demands of excellence in both research and teaching.

Based on an extensive international study, the International Forum for Teacher Educator Development (InFo-TED, 2019) reported that these entry pathways partly relate to national policies or traditions (see also chapter 3). Also, professional development initiatives vary from country to country. In several European regions, for example, the Netherlands, United Kingdom, Norway and Flanders, there has been attention for the professional development of teacher educators for more than a decade. However, these initiatives vary, and embedding these initiatives in a systematic, national policy is still missing. Moreover, pan-national initiatives for the professional development of teacher educators are scarce. As Cochran-Smith et al. (2019) state:

> In no country is there a clear mapping out of these professional groups nor a comprehensive plan for their preparation and ongoing education. This suggests that across nations we need a framework for sorting out who is considered a teacher educator.
>
> (p. 15)

Recent studies have provided insights in professional development needs of teacher educators and in the preferences teacher educators have for professional development. In an international comparative study, Czerniawski et al. (2017) found that teacher educators have a strong desire for further professional learning but feel only moderately satisfied with their current opportunities. Although teacher educators work in different contexts and engage with different policies, MacPhail et al. (2018) identified common themes related to their professional development, for example, that teacher educators often indicate that professional development is 'self-initiated', and that they value professional development through collaboration with peers. Most teacher educators *needs.* appeared to feel the need to continuously develop their teaching, specifically because in teacher education, teaching on teaching is the focus, but they lack access to opportunities to develop their teacher education practices. Finally, teacher educators felt the need to link teaching and research, and therefore indicated the desire to seek opportunities to upskill in research.

Due to the limited sources for formal development, the way most teacher educators develop in their job is through (reflection on) experience and by connecting teaching and research. About three decades ago, teacher educators started to study their own practices, a movement that is now known as the self-study-movement (see e.g., Kitchen et al., 2020). As discussed in chapter 1, results from these studies have provided important insights into how teacher educators developed in their profession (Berry, 2007; Cochran-Smith, 2003; Kastner et al., 2019).

In this chapter, we aim to give insight in the (growing) complexity of teacher educators' professional development and explore a pan-national approach to contribute to teacher educators' professional development in-depth. The variety of backgrounds and nature of development of teacher educators formed a point of departure for a one-week international Summer Academy for teacher educators. In this chapter, we will describe the theoretical framework, context and set-up of the Summer Academy, and pay specific attention to the use of storylines as a way to encourage teacher educator development during that week. Storylines are used in research and teacher education to encourage teachers to make sense of their personal and professional story of becoming and developing as a teacher by drawing a line that indicates the highs and lows in their development. This approach was used in the context of the Summer Academy for teacher educators and will be illustrated and evaluated using participant reflections.

Context of the Summer Academy

An international group of experienced teacher educators (InFo-TED) initiated the Summer Academy with the aim to contribute to the professional development of teacher educators, to build networks among teacher educators and to support teacher educators to contribute to the professional development of (fellow) teacher educators. InFo-TED has been working on these goals through other activities also, such as creating an online knowledge base, blogs and policy events. The Summer Academy was the first face-to-face initiative for teacher educators from different European countries.

InFo-TED takes teacher educators' practice as a starting point for the professional development of teacher educators, assuming that teacher educators have good reasons for doing their job the way they are doing it. Taking this as a starting point, InFo-TED developed a conceptual model (see chapter 2).

The individual practice was also taken as a starting point in the Summer Academy and specific attention was paid to individual teacher educators' professional growth but also to collaborative professional growth. This was one central element of the Summer Academy. The other central element was to encourage experienced teacher educators to contribute to the professional development of other teacher educators by working on a professional product (e.g., supporting teacher education induction or integration of information and communications technology [ICT] in teacher education). The programme of the Summer Academy offered participants the opportunity for individual professional learning, for example, through individual reflection (see also Table 8.1), and for collaborative growth, for example, in the group work that was set up to encourage collaborative reflection. Also, teacher educators collaborated on a product during the collaborative group work that encouraged professional development of the teacher educator. In the setup of the Summer Academy, the following research-informed conceptual ideas were leading (see chapter 5):

- How I teach is the message: indicating the importance of congruent teaching and modelling (Russell, 1997). Becoming a teacher educator means a transformation from first-order teaching to second-order teacher and to have the 'intentionality about making the thinking behind my teaching visible' (Kosnik, 2007, p. 18).
- Critical and inquiry-oriented: encouraging critical discussions and inquiry in each other's practice as a teacher educator. Looking systematically into one's practice, using theory and supported by peers (Hadar & Brody, 2016).
- Research-informed: ensuring the use of research knowledge. For teacher educators, research has two goals: improving one's practice (see the previous point) and contributing to the broader knowledge base for teacher education and teacher educators (Cochran-Smith & Lytle, 2009; Smith & Flores, 2019).
- Self-regulated: ensuring that teacher educators have (and use) space to pursue their own learning goals. This design principle recognises the variety of backgrounds and working contexts of teacher educators and the need for a tailored professional development journey (MacPhail et al., 2018).

Table 8.1 Learning opportunities in the Summer Academy

Learning opportunities	How included in the Summer Academy	Relation to design principles
Thematic kickoffs	Diverse experts shared their insights in the dynamics of teacher educators as brought together in the conceptual model and the knowledge base for teacher educators developed by members of InFo-TED (See chapter 2 and chapter 6 of this book).	'How I teach is the message'; research-informed; critical and inquiry oriented
Storyline method	Participants shared their professional story, had dialogues about their stories and theorised their story based on insights from the thematic kickoffs	All design principles were taken into account in the instruction and facilitation of the dialogues around the storylines created by the teacher educators
Collaborative groupwork	Participants worked on shared products, related to professional learning for (other) teacher educators. Participating teacher educators were encouraged to develop a 'product' of their choice, which could be the design of professional learning activities or a research proposal regarding teacher educators' professional learning	In the facilitation of the group work, all design principles were taken into account.
Individual reflection	After each day, teacher educators made an individual private 'video-selfie' with their reflection on their learning throughout the day. On the last day, they made a public video-selfie that could be shared and discussed with their fellow participants (Kelchtermans & DeKetelaere, 2019).	Critical and inquiry oriented; self-regulated; caring; contextual responsive.

- Caring: ensuring a climate of care in which it is possible for every teacher educator to share their stories and practices, and to encourage each participant to care for each other. Including a focus on participants' professional identity development, which is personal and often emotional (Lunenberg et al., 2011), and makes a safe and supporting environment crucial.
- Contextual responsive: being responsive to what teacher educators need in the moment and also being responsive to the context each teacher educator brings in (Vanassche et al., 2015).

These conceptual ideas were the starting point for creating professional learning opportunities in the Summer Academy. Taking into account the design principles for professional development that InFo-TED developed (see chapter 5), a combination of thematic kick-offs, storylines, collaborative group work and individual reflection became the backbone of the Summer Academy. In the five-day programme, these professional learning activities were offered on a daily basis (see also Table 8.1). The thematic kick-offs were meant to share expertise and insights with teacher educators on, for example, school-based teacher educators and teacher educator professionalism. The storyline method was a threat during the week, which helped participants to articulate their personal and professional story and to collaboratively reflect on this story using theoretical concepts introduced during the thematic kick-offs. The collaborative group work was meant to encourage collaborative reflection and the development of a product related to teacher educators' professional development. Finally, individual reflection was encouraged by video selfies that participants created every day about their daily learning experiences.

In the next section, we will illustrate some of the learning that the participating teacher educators experienced. We interviewed two teacher educators on the basis of the storylines they created and further developed during the Summer Academy. Their learning was in line with what we know from literature: complex and dynamic. We found that the storylines, although completely unique and idiosyncratic, offered an opportunity for exploring some of the most powerful learning during the week, including what contributed to this learning. Below, we will first delve into the storyline technique and how we employed this during the Summer Academy. After that, we will illustrate teacher educators' experiences with the use of the storylines and the influence on their professional learning.

Capturing teacher educators' professional development: storylines

Storyline methodology fits in a narrative research tradition in which the importance of teachers' personal stories is emphasised. In other words, it is the way in which teachers make sense of the experiences and the events they encounter in their everyday teaching practice (Beijaard et al., 1999). As recommended by Beijaard et al. (1999), storylines are often accompanied by either a written or an oral explanation of the 'drawing' made by teachers. Storyline methodology was used in a range of studies that examined how people experience their development. In the area of teaching and teacher education, it has been used to examine beginning teachers' pathways into teaching (e.g., Meijer et al., 2011; Orland, 2000), experienced teachers' professional agency (Oolbekkink-Marchand et al., 2017) and teacher educators' professional development in a professional learning community (Brody & Hadar, 2018).

In the Summer Academy for experienced teacher educators, we chose to use storylines as a means for teacher educators to make sense of their story of becoming and developing as a teacher educator. More specifically, we used the storylines with a two-fold focus. The first focus is on the way teacher educators perceive their own development in the profession. We used storyline methodology to have teacher educators visualise their trajectory, to reflect on the moments of growth as well as downfalls, to analyse where they are now and to envision what they would develop next. We label this as 'storification'.

The second focus is on how teacher educators come to theorise their stories during the Summer Academy. This process of what we label as 're-storification' is particularly interesting, since it provides insight into how teacher educators give words and meaning to their own development and interpret their own development from a variety of perspectives in order to grow and expand their understanding of their development accordingly. Understanding one's own journey, revisiting it in terms of theories, we assumed, helps in working with educating teacher educators.

The creation of storylines can follow a number of procedures and relates to the reason(s) one wants to draw on (cf. Orland, 2000). In the context of the Summer Academy, a four-step procedure was followed, which is outlined in Table 8.2. In introducing the procedure, example storylines were provided and particular attention was paid to the idea that many pathways into and during a profession are best characterised as 'rocky roads' (Wood & Borg, 2010), which include both highs and lows. Highs may be periods of development as experienced by a teacher educator, for example, due to collaboration with colleagues, while lows are periods in which teacher educators may experience 'isolation' or feel left on their own. Understanding these and accepting the value of both highs and lows can help both [*why of storylines*] in valuing these experiences and positioning oneself as a teacher educator and help in making further decisions in one's profession. The instructor, a very experienced teacher educator herself, illustrated this with mentioning some of her own struggles and triumphs as a way of modelling the value, fun and vulnerability that accompany such 'storification'.

After the first session of storyline creation, participants from different countries exchanged and discussed their storylines in pairs. This appeared to be a very intense way of getting to know each other and each other's national contexts. Participants not only shared their stories, but also were surprised by other stories. Since all were experienced teacher educators, the impact of the various highs and lows was easy to understand. [*creates partnerships*]

After the second session, in which teacher educators linked the theories they had encountered during other parts of the Summer Academy to their own story, a second dialogue followed, first in pairs, then in small groups of four. In these dialogues participants were encouraged to 'zip practice and theory', which means they connected their practice to theoretical concepts and insights (see also chapter 2). Participants were free to further elaborate their storylines on a transparent overlay, which allowed for free associations that could easily be removed, rewritten, etc.

During the entire Summer Academy, the storylines were visible as they hung on the walls and provided input for dialogue during the week. As such, working on the storylines became intertwined with the other threads presented, in particular the collaborative group work and the thematic kick-offs. For example, the

Table 8.2 Procedure for storyline creation

Sessions	Steps and basic instruction	Questions to consider:
First session	(1) Creating storyline. Draw your professional storyline of how you became and developed as a teacher educator. Draw a line that captures the highs and lows in how you developed. (2) Dialogue about storyline. Share your storyline with a colleague and elaborate on the key moments	• Where do you start? Decide on your starting point. Why here? • What were key moments (highs and lows)? What happened? What did you do? Why were these important? Where does the InFo-TED conceptual model (or: do its elements) fit in? • Where are you now? What are your needs at this moment? You might use the model here If time allows: where do you want to go? • Can you elaborate on your storyline? What were the key moments for you? • What are similarities and differences between our storylines?

Second session	(3) Theorizing storyline. Reconsider your storyline using theoretical concepts: by 'zipping' practice and theory (Kelchtermans, 2018)
	(4) Dialogue about revisited storyline. Share your storyline and elaborate on the theoretical concepts you connected to your storyline
		• *Looking back:* How can you label elements / phases in your story using these (or other) theoretical concepts?
		• *Looking now:* What theoretical concepts reflect your situation
		  • At this moment in the Summer Academy?
		  • At your work at this moment?
		• *Looking forward:* What theoretical concepts reflect how you envision yourself / your work in the future
		  • When you come home (short term)
		• "Spot on the horizon"? (long term)
		• What theoretical concepts did you choose to add to your storyline (past, present, future)? Why did you choose these?
		• In what way do these concepts help you understand your story?

thematic kick-offs gave insights participants could add to their storylines or the storylines were revisited during collaborative group discussions.

Experiencing the storyline procedure: two cases

After the Summer Academy, we held interviews with two teacher educators about the storylines and their reflections. These teachers were chosen because they were experienced teacher educators and came from different national contexts. We were particularly interested in their (learning) experiences in the Summer Academy and in particular in relation to the storylines. Based on these interviews and the storylines of these teacher educators, Arthur and Brent (pseudonyms), we made case descriptions. In each case description, teacher educators reflect on creating the storylines, theorizing the storylines and dialogues about the storylines and their professional learning.

Case: Arthur

Arthur is one of the participants in the Summer Academy and is an experienced teacher educator (> 10 years) in a subject matter, a course coordinator and a researcher within his teacher education programme. He started to work in teacher education in one country and worked on his PhD. After four years, he moved to another country where he started to work as a teacher educator and a researcher.

Arthur indicates that the creation of the storyline for him was an 'astounding, amazing experience' and he remembered the moment of creating the storyline quite well because it was the first time he thought about his professional trajectory and what had brought him to teacher education. He thinks it was a really good 'exercise for reflection, just to think about our identity'. It was the first time after ten years of experience in teacher education that he was invited to reflect on what brought him to teacher education and to think about the highs and lows and the turning points in his professional trajectory.

Arthur's storyline is shown in Figure 8.1 and depicts the line he drew of his journey as a teacher educator. He drew a timeline in the middle of the figure indicating important years and important moments and feelings along the way. For example, an important moment in 2016 is his move to another country, which is an important turning point for him that led him to feel 'productive and useful'.

Arthur remembers quite well that he was talking to a group member and sharing the story about his professional life after drawing the storyline. He was enthusiastic about telling his story to another person and felt proud of his career at that point and about what he had achieved. He felt he had the chance to talk to someone in a safe space. According to Arthur, this dialogue about the storyline helps to further articulate the participant's story, it invites him to not only draw and write some things on a piece of paper but also to talk about his story to someone else, which helps to further explore his story. The Summer Academy also provided theoretical input on teacher educators' professionalisation, for example, by the thematic kick-offs on teacher educator professional development, which brought Arthur (during the second session) to a deeper level of reflection on the storyline and expanded his way of thinking about his own professional trajectory. 'It is like the combination of just yourself, another person and a theoretical perspective, it's like a lovely progression'.

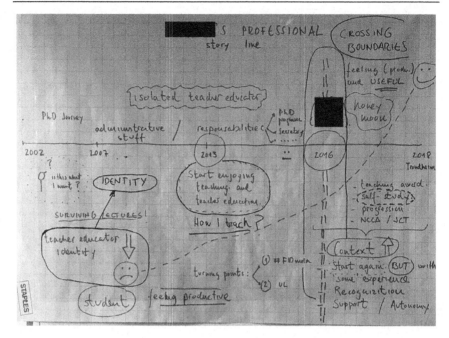

Figure 8.1 Arthur's storyline

Up until the moment Arthur drew his storyline, he did not consider himself a teacher educator. After so many years of working, he considered himself to be a teacher or an academic but not so much a teacher educator. In that sense, the drawing and reflection of the storyline was a way of professional learning and a turning point for him and a powerful moment that 'opened the door to his teacher educator identity'. It helped him to understand his profile and his professional career up until that point.

Arthur indicates that it was not just the storyline but the different learning opportunities and the informal conversations during the Summer Academy that helped him to identify as a teacher educator. Also, the Summer Academy contributed to his understanding of his own professional context in teacher education. After the Summer Academy, he used the storyline method with his own student teachers, using the same 'step–wise' approach, and letting students draw, share and revisit their storyline using theory.

Case: Brent

Brent is one of the participants in the Summer Academy and an experienced teacher educator (> 17 years) in a subject matter. He has multiple roles (e.g., mentor, researcher) within his teacher education programme in a higher education institute. He is also an educator of teacher educators and teaches a module around pedagogy of teacher education in another higher education institute.

Brent indicates that for him, creating the storyline was a process of going back to events and changes in his career as a teacher educator. He describes this:

> I remember that I went back to the periods I went through as a teacher educator and to connect these with my emotions, and that is what I remember: that I made a connection between my personal summary of events and what it did with my feeling of professional development.

Brent's storyline is shown in Figure 8.2 and depicts the line he drew of his development as a teacher educator. He draws a line with 'highs' and 'lows' in his development, indicating one clear period in which he is not satisfied with his development. After this period, he started a PhD, which increased his satisfaction with his development.

For Brent, not only drawing the storyline but the collaborative dialogue about the storyline was an essential element of working with the storyline. Drawing helps to 'order' your story, and talking about it gives you another perspective on your story. Brent remarked:

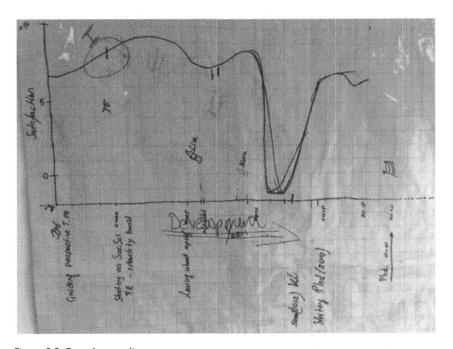

Figure 8.2 Brent's storyline

The world 'in my head' is not the same as the world I talk about … but as I start talking, I can bring these two together, it helps me to 'order' my story and to find words for my emotions and I also found that the conversation helps to get another perspective on your experiences.

Brent found that the relevant and sophisticated knowledge of other teacher educators was a help in getting another perspective on his experience. In addition, he highly valued collaboratively giving meaning to each person's development trajectory. The dialogue helps to give meaning to both positive and negative periods in the sense that he can see whether they had their value or he really knew that he did not want to go back there. Finally, Brent indicates that making a drawing is helpful in creating openness in the conversation in the sense that the storyline shows both successful and vulnerable moments in people's lives.

The storyline and the dialogue about the storyline contribute to Brent's professional learning because it provides a different perspective on his past and shows the potential he has for the future. 'Look at where I am now. If I look at the line upward, it also gives you at that moment a feeling of satisfaction and reassurance.' Brent also indicates that he broadened his perspective on the professional contexts in which teacher educators work.

There is also the insight that it is normal to 'search' your way… I went to the Summer Academy with the idea that I would be among high quality professionals, and it is good to see that they are also still searching and trying, … that connects.

Brent emphasised the value of the storyline method for professional learning, but indicated that the whole Summer Academy provided a meaningful context for professional learning. He indicated that both the learning opportunities provided, such as the thematic kick-offs and the group work, but also the informal conversation with colleagues during breaks, contributed to his professional development as a teacher educator.

Conclusion

This chapter reports on an opportunity for teacher educator professional learning across national contexts. In a collaborative effort and based on design principles grounded in theory, a Summer Academy was organised providing experienced teacher educators with diverse opportunities for learning. A storyline method was an important threat activity throughout the programme, providing teacher educators with the opportunity for 'storification' and 're-storification'. Experiences from the participants indicated the value of drawing a storyline, particularly in combination with dialogue with other teacher educators in a safe environment. This dialogue contributed to their understanding of themselves as teacher educators, provided new perspectives on their development and helped them gain insight in their future learning.

Adding theoretical perspectives contributed particularly to participant Arthur's understanding of his professional trajectory as a teacher educator. Both Arthur and Brent emphasised the importance of the entire context of the Summer Academy as a rich array of formal and informal professional learning activities that as a whole contributed to their professional development articulating their professional identity and understanding their professional context.

The storyline method seemed to be a powerful contributor to teacher educator professional development. Up until now, storylines were mainly applied in research and education of teachers, but this example shows that it is also a way to gain insight in teacher educators' professional development, especially as most teacher educators come from different pathways and tend to find their own way in teacher education.

Storylines may be valuable in future studies focusing on teacher educator's [*sees place for storyline elsewhere*] professional development, not only for higher education-based teacher educators but also for school-based and community-based teacher educators (cf. White, 2019). Comparative studies may give us more insight in the development of teacher educators' development in different contexts and over time.

This chapter showed the importance of a supporting context for teacher educators in which a storyline method may contribute to professional development. In future research it may be important to take a broad focus on the study of teacher educator development and to take into account both the personal trajectory of the teacher educator but also the environment in which he or she is working. The interaction between these elements may provide important insights that can be useful both for policies and practices in teacher education.

Finally, the Summer Academy as a whole proved to be a powerful learning experience for teacher educators. The design of the programme based on carefully underpinned design principles contributed to a learning environment which was supportive for teacher educator learning, for example, becoming aware of their identity as a teacher educator. Based on this experience, future Summer Academies are designed by InFo-TED making use of the insights gained. The conceptual ideas, including the pedagogies bases, may inform educators of teacher educators in other parts of the world to design learning environments for teacher educators and to contribute to the collaborative learning of teacher educators. This may contribute to building a strong profession responsible for the quality of education.

References

Beijaard, D., Van Driel, J., & Verloop, N. (1999). Evaluation of story-line methodology in research on teachers' practical knowledge. *Studies in Educational Evaluation*, 25(1), 47–62.

Berry, A. (2007). *Tensions in teaching about teaching: Understanding practice as a teacher educator* (Vol. 5). Springer.

Brody, D. L., & Hadar, L. L. (2018). Critical moments in the process of educational change: Understanding the dynamics of change among teacher educators. *European Journal of Teacher Education*, 41(1), 50–65.

Cochran-Smith, M. (2003). Learning and unlearning: The education of teacher educators. *Teaching and Teacher Education*, 19(1), 5–28.

Cochran-Smith, M., Grudnoff, L., Orland-Barak, L., & Smith, K. (2019). Educating teacher educators: International perspectives. *The New Educator*, 16(1), 5–24.

Cochran-Smith, M., & Lytle, S. (2009). *Inquiry as stance: Practitioner research for the next generation*. Teachers College Press.

Czerniawski, G., Guberman, A., & MacPhail, A. (2017). The professional developmental needs of higher education-based teacher educators: An international comparative needs analysis. *European Journal of Teacher Education*, 40(1), 127–140.

Davey, R. (2013). *The professional identity of teacher educators: Career on the cusp?* Routledge.

European Commission. (2012). Supporting the teaching professions for better learning. https://eur-lex.europa.eu/LexUriServ/LexUriServ.do?uri=SWD:2012:0374:FIN:EN:PDF.

Hadar, L. L., & Brody, D. L. (2016). Talk about student learning: Promoting professional growth among teacher educators. *Teaching and Teacher Education*, 59, 101–114.

The International Forum for Teacher Educator Development. (2019). The importance of teacher educators: professional development imperatives [White paper]. https://info-ted.eu/wp-content/uploads/2019/10/InFo-TED-White-Paper.pdf.

Kastner, J. D., Reese, J., Pellegrino, K., & Russell, H. A. (2019). The roller coaster ride: Our music teacher educator identity development. *Research Studies in Music Education*, 41(2), 154–170.

Kelchtermans, G., & Deketelaere, A. (2019, August 5). Show yourself! Video-selfies for feedback. InFo-TED website. https://info-ted.eu/show-yourself-video-selfies-for-feedback/.

Kitchen, J., Berry, A., Bullock, S. M., Crowe, A. R., Taylor, M., Guðjónsdóttir, H., & Thomas, L. (2020). *2nd International Handbook of Self-Study of Teaching and Teacher Education*. Springer.

Kosnik, C. (2007). Still the same yet different. In T. Russell, & J. Loughran (Eds.), *Enacting a pedagogy of teacher education: Values, relationships and practices*. Routledge.

Loughran, J. (2014). Professionally developing as a teacher educator. *Journal of Teacher Education*, 65(4), 271–283.

Lunenberg, M., Korthagen, F., & Zwart, R. C. (2011). Self-study research and the development of a teacher educator's identity. *European Educational Research Journal*, 10(3), 407–420.

Lunenberg, M., Dengerink, J., & Korthagen, F. (2014). *The professional teacher educator: Roles, behaviour, and professional development of teacher educators*. Springer.

Lunenberg, M., Murray, J., Smith, K., & Vanderlinde, R. (2017). Collaborative teacher educator professional development in Europe: Different voices, one goal. *Professional Development in Education*, 43(4), 556–572.

MacPhail, A., Ulvik, M., Guberman, A., Czerniawski, G., Oolbekkink-Marchand, H., & Bain, Y. (2018). The professional development of higher education-based teacher educators: Needs and realities. *Professional Development in Education*, 45(5), 848–861.

Meijer, P. C., De Graaf, G., & Meirink, J. (2011). Key experiences in student teachers' development. *Teachers and Teaching: Theory and Practice*, 17(1), 115–129.

Oolbekkink-Marchand, H. W., Hadar, L. L., Smith, K., Helleve, I., & Ulvik, M. (2017). Teachers' perceived professional space and their agency. *Teaching and Teacher Education*, 62, 37–46.

Orland, L. (2000). What's in a line? Exploration of a research and reflection tool. *Teachers and Teaching*, 6(2), 197–213.

Russell, T. (1997). Teaching teachers: How I teach IS the message. In J. Loughran, & T. Russell (Eds.), *Teaching about teaching: Purpose, passion and pedagogy in teacher education* (pp. 32–47). Falmer Press.

Smith, K., & Flores, M. A. (2019). The Janus faced teacher educator. *European Journal of Teacher Education*, 42(4), 433–446.

Vanassche, E., Rust, F., Conway, P., Smith, K., Tack, H., & Vanderlinde, R. (2015). InFo-TED: Bringing policy, research, and practice together around teacher educator development. In J. C. Craig, & L. Orland-Barak (Eds.), *International teacher education: Promising pedagogies (part C)* (Vol. 22, pp. 341–364). Emerald.

White, S. (2019). Teacher educators for new times? Redefining an important occupational group. *Journal for Education and Training*, 45(2), 200–213.

Wood, D., & Borg, T. (2010). The rocky road: The journey from classroom teacher to teacher educator. *Studying Teacher Education*, 6(1), 17–28.

Chapter 9

Teacher educators' professional life stories across four countries

Intertwining personal and contextual effects

Ainat Guberman, Ann MacPhail, Marit Ulvik and Helma Oolbekkink-Marchand

Introduction

'Teacher educators' as a term captures all those who are formally involved in the preparation and professional development of teachers (European Commission, 2013). This study deals with the first of the three types of teacher educators mentioned in chapter 1: the 'traditional group' of teacher educators who work in higher education institutes. This is an ill-defined professional group, with no abiding preparatory process or entry requirements, and multiple complex roles (Goodwin et al., 2014; Lunenberg et al., 2014). Many teacher educators enter teacher education with limited knowledge and skills required for their work, but acquire knowledge and skills through formal and informal learning opportunities while working (Lunenberg et al., 2014; Murray & Male, 2005). In view of teacher educators' significant influence in determining the quality of teachers in schools, teacher educators' qualifications, roles and professional development attract a growing interest among researchers. Many of these studies are either cross-sectional, looking into relatively large samples of teacher educators (cf. Czerniawski et al., 2017; Griffiths et al., 2014; Meeus et al., 2018; Van der Klink et al., 2017), or deal with individual teacher educators' professional experiences (cf. Loughran, 2014; Murray & Male, 2005; Smith, 2017). It is evident across such studies that teacher educators' work contexts influence to a great extent their professional trajectories (Kelchtermans et al., 2018; Vanassche et al., 2015). Nonetheless, insufficient studies have explored the interactions between teacher educators' personal characteristics and work contexts in a systematic manner. Such studies are needed in order to devise effective professional learning opportunities for teacher educators.

The current study explores the professional trajectories of four higher education-based teacher educators from four different countries: Ireland, Israel, the Netherlands and Norway. These trajectories exemplify how personal characteristics, institute contexts and national contexts interact to shape teacher educators' professional development.

Teacher educators' professional development

Teacher educators perform multiple roles. For example, they teach disciplinary content; engage in pedagogical theory and practice; develop curricula; serve as role models, coaches and gatekeepers; and conduct research (Lunenberg et al., 2014). Of these, teaching about teaching (also referred to as second order teaching) and research appear to be the more prominent roles. Studies that examined teacher educators' professional development needs found that both areas (teaching about teaching and research) were highly valued (Czerniawski et al., 2017; Griffiths et al., 2014; Murray & Male, 2005; Smith & Flores, 2019).

In order to teach about teaching, teacher educators need to present their practical knowledge and professional reasoning explicitly, and ground them in theory, exposing themselves to their students' critical scrutiny. They must adapt their teaching and assessment methods to adult learners in higher education and support their students as they attempt to develop their own ways of teaching (Griffiths et al., 2014; Lunenberg et al., 2014; Meeus et al., 2018; Murray & Male, 2005).

Teacher educators carry out different types of research to improve their teaching and contribute to the knowledge base in teacher education (Cochran-Smith, 2005; Loughran, 2014; Lunenberg et al., 2014). In reality, however, there are many tensions between, and within, the two complementary domains of teaching and research. For example, within academia, large scale theory-oriented studies are often preferred over practice-oriented research and specifically, practitioners' self-studies. This is regardless of the fact that many teacher educators believe that the latter types of research are crucial for their own, as well as for the teacher education profession's development (Cochran-Smith, 2005; Loughran, 2014). Research and teaching compete for teacher educators' limited resources of time (Czerniawski et al., 2017; Griffiths et al., 2014; Smith & Flores, 2019) and, while students greatly appreciate effective teaching, leaders of teacher education academic institutions often value research productivity (Smith & Flores, 2019).

Teacher educators' work contexts

Global context

Teacher educators' work is grounded in global historical, national, institutional and personal contexts (Kelchtermans et al., 2018; Vanassche et al., 2015). From a global perspective, we live in an era of performativity (Ball, 2003), with student achievement quantitatively measured and compared across countries. Teachers' evaluations rely upon their teaching practices and students' achievements. Academic institutions and staff members may receive financial benefits based on their research productivity. Under these circumstances, teacher educators who do not publish research in international peer-refereed academic venues feel undervalued (Griffiths et al., 2014).

National and institute contexts

Global tendencies can be amplified or moderated by national and Institutional work contexts. The types of support they provide can affect teacher educators' professional development, opportunities and choices.

During the last decades, three countries were subjected to the 'university turn', mentioned in chapter 1. Teacher educators in Ireland, Israel and Norway had to acquire research skills, accomplish doctorates and produce research publications as prerequisites for academic appointments and subsequent promotions (Gleeson et al., 2012; Guberman & Mcdossi, 2019). These demands are not as strong in the Netherlands, where teacher educators are eligible for promotion even without a PhD.

As for support, in Israel the Ministry of Education established the MOFET Institute that provides teacher educators' with opportunities for professional development in research, pedagogy and educational leadership. In the Netherlands, the Dutch Association for Teacher Educators (VELON) provides a voluntary registration trajectory that encourages teacher educators to reflect on the quality of their work and improve it (Timmermans, 2019). VELON has also initiated a research oriented programme (Kelchtermans et al., 2018). In Norway, the Norwegian National Research School in Teacher Education (NAFOL) supports teacher educators who are doctoral students (Cochran-Smith et al., 2020). There are no national professional development programmes for teacher educators in Ireland.

Within the national context, the level of institutional support for professional development varies greatly. Some institutes view professional development as an individual endeavour, whereas others encourage their staff to participate in their professional development, and provide technical as well as financial support.

Personal context

As chapter 1 explains, 'traditional teacher educators' are mainly recruited from schools and universities (Ping et al., 2018). The 'teacher' identity of teacher educators recruited from schools continues to be a central part of their professional identity and strengthens their interest in developing their pedagogy (Griffiths et al., 2014). In contrast, teacher educators recruited from universities have a stronger interest in research and academic writing professional development (Czerniawski et al., 2017).

Teacher educators' life stories

Teacher educators' identities develop over time through their work and interpretations of their professional experiences within social and cultural contexts (Swennen & Volman, 2019). It is possible to learn about these experiences and conceptualisations, as well as the social and cultural contexts in which these experiences occurred through teacher educators' narratives describing their professional life stories (Carter, 1993). Comparative studies across historical periods or national contexts can illuminate how ideologies, policies and infrastructure interact with personal characteristics and shape teacher educators' identities, practices and professional development. Such information is important for planning role definitions, work conditions and professional development opportunities for teacher educators that support high quality teacher education (Smith, 2017; Swennen & Volman, 2019).

Method

The context of the study

The study was conducted by members of the International Forum for Teacher Educator Development (InFo-TED; Kelchtermans et al., 2018; Vanassche et al., 2015). Previously, the group has conducted a survey on professional development needs of teacher educators (Czerniawski et al., 2017). The current study is based on semi-structured interviews with teacher educators who completed the survey and expressed their interest in being involved in a follow up study by supplying contact information for that purpose.

Participants

Four higher education-based teacher educators participated: three females (aged between late 40s and 60) and one male (early 40s) from Ireland, Israel, the Netherlands and Norway. Two entered teacher education after teaching in schools, while the other two had worked as researchers and lecturers in a university before entering teacher education. All four are currently active teacher educators. Together, they delineate the breadth of experiences and professional trajectories of higher education-based teacher educators, and the ways in which personal characteristics and background interact with institutional and national contexts to produce this variety of experiences.

Interviews

Semi-structured interviews were conducted. The interview guide followed the sections of the previously completed survey, exploring more deeply: (a) background and demographics, including recruitment into teacher education; (b) professional learning opportunities, activities and needs; and (c) teacher educators' attitudes towards and experiences with research. The face-to-face interviews lasted between 45 and 90 minutes and were conducted in each participant's native language (MacPhail et al., 2019).

Data analysis

Participants' descriptions of their professional trajectories were organised according to a timeline. Based on previous studies (Griffiths et al., 2014; Meeus et al., 2018), they were categorised into three main periods: (a) pre-induction and recruitment, that covers studies and work prior to joining teacher education, motivations for the transition and the recruitment process; (b) the induction period, that lasts up to two years from the transition into teacher education; and (c) later professional development.

Once the trajectories were organised according to a timeline, the challenge was to present each life story in English, ensuring each life story fitted into the three identified main periods. As a collective, we presented the themes in a case-by-phase matrix that gave an overview of the data from the time before the teacher educators were recruited into teacher education until the present, including professional learning opportunities and the relations between teacher education and research (Braun & Clarke, 2006).

The next phase was narrative analysis (Polkinghorne, 1995). We transformed the elements we extracted from the interviews into life stories and sought each participant's confirmation that the life story accurately represented their professional life. Each participant agreed to their respective narrative being published, and pseudonyms were used to provide anonymity. The final step was to explore the different stories with regards to recruitment, induction and career-long professional learning in relation to personal and contextual similarities and differences. The authors discussed their respective interpretations with the intent of arriving at a shared meaning of the data (Guest et al., 2012).

Findings

We present the four trajectories individually before presenting a collective analysis that aims to elucidate the interactions between personal, institutional and national factors that appear to have influenced our participants' professional trajectories.

Case: Carlos (Ireland)

Carlos studied in an undergraduate programme in a subject discipline, and was required to undertake an additional year of study at the master's level to obtain a teaching licensure. Carlos availed himself of the opportunity through a scholarship to undertake a PhD on completion of his master's. The four-year PhD scholarship afforded Carlos the opportunity to experience the role of teacher in the university, with opportunities to teach in the second, third and fourth year of his PhD. He became a lecturer in a university setting on completion of his PhD.

At that time, he identified as a teacher rather than a teacher educator, with the main concern at the time to survive as a teacher in the university context. It was not clear to Carlos if he was a teacher or a teacher educator, given the diverse career options of the student groups he was working with, acknowledging that working only with pre-service teachers would have more clearly led to an identity as a teacher educator. It was not until ten years after completion of his PhD, coinciding with a move to a university abroad, that Carlos began to identify as a teacher educator. This was not only due to the strong teacher education focus at the university he moved to, but also to admitting to himself that the ten years he had spent at his previous university had been a necessary time period for him to define the role of being a teacher educator as being confident and successful in teaching and research. He maintained that the opportunity to undertake a position at the university abroad was 'timely' with respect to having plateaued in his previous post.

Carlos identifies the move to another university as one of the most significant events in his career, acknowledging the cultural shift in moving from one country to another. On arrival, Carlos was able to access a formal mentor-mentee scheme, with an appointed mentor who provided a safe environment in which to share work-related experiences. Carlos also acknowledges the importance of the informal induction that took place at the same time with casual (but meaningful) conversations with colleagues in the corridor, as well as having access to activities that department members had already established, for example, a reading club. More recent significant events for Carlos have been his involvement in the InFo-TED 2018 Summer Academy, his involvement in specific projects with department colleagues, undertaking a programme leader position and seeking promotion.

Carlos identifies firstly as a teacher educator and secondly as a teacher educator of a specific subject discipline. In discussing areas of a teacher educator's work that require more upskilling, Carlos believes that upskilling opportunities have focused on research activities related to funded research projects and peer-review publications. In his own words, 'it is not enough to just teach'. There is a need to revisit our teaching to question the effectiveness of our teaching practices, share practices with colleagues and learn about different pedagogies. In sharing what upskilling opportunities were attractive, Carlos mentioned communities of learning, safe environments and informal conversations.

Even though Carlos is an experienced teacher educator, he admits that the roles of teaching and publishing research remain challenges, not only as individual endeavours, but also in attempting to ensure that the collective expectations across both are achieved. He fully understood the investment necessary to be competitive and warned against this taking over one's life.

Case: Shirley (Israel)

Shirley was a PhD student at a university's Department of Social Sciences. One of Shirley's former colleagues invited Shirley to join her college's research authority. Shirley liked the work and the people, and when one of her colleagues left the college, she accepted a permanent position at the college as a researcher and lecturer.

Shirley likes to mentor Master of Education students' research projects. The students are experienced teachers, and she likes to interact with them and learn about the realities in schools, given she has never taught in them.

Shirley participated in one of the MOFET institute's biannual (non-compulsory) study programmes (UK) that awards a teaching certificate for teacher education colleges. She chose to participate in an educational leadership program instead of a pedagogy-oriented program. After working as a teacher educator for several years, she was conscious that she was repeating similar tasks and, by association, her professional development had ceased. She aspired to attain leadership roles within her college. She was told that although her professional abilities were held in high regard, she was considered too young and that other, more experienced people were ahead of her in terms of promotion.

The turning point for Shirley came when she was asked to lead a large-scale research project for the Ministry of Education. The research resulted in her becoming a locally recognised name in her field and subsequently she was appointed head of the research authority at her college. In her current position, she is interested in research that impacts educational policies. Some of this research deals with general issues, such as mentoring and induction, in teacher education. Other research projects focus on her college's policies and, while conducted by other researchers, are supported by her.

Shirley's mission is to encourage other teacher educators to do research, and she hopes more teacher educators will be interested in large-scale research projects. She regrets that many teacher educators appear to lack ambition, opportunities and a skill-set to undertake research that is beyond the scope of the courses they teach. She would also wish to see more teacher educators avail themselves of assistance that would allow them to become more competent researchers. Shirley regrets that teacher educators are not sufficiently influential in determining policies within their areas of expertise, and she believes that this situation can be changed through teacher educators' research.

Case: Myriam (the Netherlands)

Myriam is an experienced teacher educator who has worked in two different higher education-based teacher education programmes in the Netherlands over the past 17 years. Her initial degree was granted after completion of a primary education teacher programme, followed by a Master's in Pedagogy (specialisation in child and family studies), which she combined with teaching in special education. After her studies, she met a teacher educator from her primary education teacher programme who, acknowledging the experience Myriam had amassed, invited her to work as a teacher educator. In becoming a teacher educator, Myriam became part of a group of early career teacher educators who collectively discussed their concerns. She also had support from an experienced teacher educator whom she could talk with and who provided her with feedback when preparing for classes.

Myriam became a coordinator of a new academic programme for primary teacher education. This was an opportunity for her to set up collaboration between a non-university-based and a university-based teacher education programme. After an intensive five years, she quit this part of her job due to the heavy workload associated with it. Myriam decided to 'go back' to teaching on the programme and to focus on her role as a pedagogue. She sought and found new (national) networks (i.e., a national network focused on pedagogy in teacher education) that encouraged her to develop as a pedagogue. As she developed more in this role, she discussed her pedagogical insights with her national network. In turn, the network asked her to work also as a teacher educator in a university-based programme to develop the role of the pedagogue.

Throughout her trajectory as a teacher educator, she struggled with the way teacher education is managed. Often there are opposing forces from outside and inside the organisation that hinder teacher educators' work. Management (inside) is searching to find a 'good enough' way to keep the ship on course, always going back and forth between different (outside) concerns. Over time, there were plenty of opportunities to develop as a teacher educator (such as reading literature with colleagues, professional development courses), although Myriam was keen to identify her own fields of professional interest related to teacher education pedagogy (e.g., combining relevant theory, teacher education practice and reflection). In the future, Myriam wishes to learn more about creating powerful learning environments for students looking beyond disciplinary borders, using positive psychology in teacher education and the role of art as a means to engage with students' experiences.

Myriam is involved in practice-based research on students' well-being and involvement in teacher education programmes. She is also interested in conducting self-study research as a teacher educator. She believes she has an important role in helping students value research. Nonetheless, she regrets that students often practice 'one type of research' (e.g., intervention studies) and strives to consider how best to extend students' exposure to other types of research methodology and methods.

Case: Mona (Norway)

Mona teaches secondary school math didactics in a one-year postgraduate programme for students with a master's degree and in a five-year integrated programme that leads to a master's degree at the university.

Mona started her career as a math teacher in upper secondary school. After nearly 20 years, she sought an additional job opportunity and contacted a teacher education institute. She joined the institute because she wanted new challenges, to improve teacher education and to contribute to good math teaching in schools. Mona believes math is the most important and interesting subject. In teacher education, it was not only about math. She had to fit into an environment she saw as more like the humanities. Furthermore, Mona shares that it was a shock to move from being an esteemed teacher of a prestigious subject in an upper secondary school to a teacher education institute environment where she struggled to feel like she belonged, given the prevailing interest and discourse that surrounded research activities. To enhance her sense of belonging, Mona, at the same time as being a staff member, secured a full-time PhD position in math didactics.

On completion of her PhD, Mona secured a permanent position at her current university and experienced what she describes as 'a good start'. During the first term, she did not have any teaching responsibilities. Furthermore, in securing university funding, she established a research and development project in cooperation with schools that was a basis for further teaching and research. While her colleagues are supportive, she feels that having contact with schools is important since there are only a few researchers in her math department who work with didactics.

When she started working in teacher education, Mona had come directly from teaching in school with rich experiences she could use in teacher education. However, on reflection, she believes that what and how she was teaching was not overly effective, initially not knowing much about the theory of math didactics. She believes that PhD studies contribute immensely to the quality of teacher educators' delivery as well as to having an overview of diverse perspectives. She found that her own PhD experience allowed her to refer to her own and others' research projects and associated work during her lectures, and was especially helpful when mentoring master's theses students. Being a teacher educator is, for Mona, to be able to create an interconnection between theory and practice.

Mona enjoys teaching as well as conducting research and development projects that contribute to math didactics. The support she experiences in her department is exceptional, allowing her to pursue whatever she believes will enhance her career. Mona admits that it is difficult to find time to write and that she needs to be more effective in protecting her time for such activity.

Interactions between personal, institute and national factors

We analyse the interactions between personal and contextual factors in each of the three career phases introduced earlier in the chapter: recruiting, induction and further professional development.

Recruiting

The participants confirm that teacher educators come mainly from schools and universities (Ping et al., 2018). Myriam and Mona have worked as schoolteachers, while Shirley and Carlos were university researchers. They each entered teacher education due to a combination of self-initiation and serendipity (Guberman et al., 2020). Shirley and Myriam were asked/head hunted by others to become teacher educators. Mona applied for a job in teacher education to extend her own learning, and Carlos secured a teacher education position in a university when he decided to move from a lecturing position.

Being a teacher educator is described as a multifaceted role (Smith, 2011). The different backgrounds, consequently, do not provide teacher educators with all the skills that are acquired on the job (Lunenberg et al., 2014). While Shirley lacked knowledge about schools, Mona and Myriam discovered that being a teacher educator was different from teaching, and not an easy task to fulfil (Loughran, 2006; Murray, 2014; Murray & Male, 2005). In the beginning of his work with students (some of whom were training to be teachers), Carlos did not view himself as a teacher educator at all. However, all four felt they had something to offer to teacher education. Shirley and Carlos had their discipline knowledge and research competence, while Myriam and Mona had experiences from school as well as disciplinary and pedagogical knowledge.

Induction

Upon entering teacher education, institutes offered support in different ways. Myriam participated in a group of early career teacher educators. She and Carlos had an experienced teacher educator as a mentor. Mona was released from teaching responsibilities and received funds for her projects. Shirley participated in a course that provided her with a teaching license for teacher education institutes. Interestingly, both Carlos and Mona were supported by the second (and not by their first) institute they worked in. These findings suggest that teacher educators' need for induction has slowly gained recognition by teacher education institutes. However, the specific forms of support are determined by institutional as well as national contexts (Kelchtermans et al., 2018). There is no comprehensive nor widely accepted conceptualisation concerning the desired form of induction for beginning teacher educators (Goodwin et al., 2014; Guberman et al., 2020). Harrison and McKeon (2008) found that the induction of teacher educators was often patchy and inappropriate, with generally poor mentoring and inadequate structured support. Peer support was valued but often arose by chance, so learning opportunities were missed. Our findings corroborate their conclusion.

Career-long professional learning

Professional learning activities are mainly self-initiated, and research has a significant role in the developmental trajectories of all four participants. Carlos and Mona use research to develop their pedagogy, whereas Shirley views research as a means to support evidence-informed policies. Myriam is mainly involved in practice-based research, reads research publications and is interested in conducting self-studies. Therefore, all four acknowledge that research productivity is highly regarded and rewarded, though there are some disagreements about what specific types of research are most beneficial (Czerniawski et al., 2017; Griffiths et al., 2014; Lunenberg et al., 2014; Smith, 2017).

Interactions between self-initiation (MacPhail et al., 2019) and local contexts have significantly affected our participants' professional trajectories. Moving from one institute to another changed Carlos's professional identity. Mona felt deskilled until she acquired a PhD and moved from a teacher education college to a research university. Shirley initially felt disadvantaged when college management implied that other colleagues would be supported in opportunities to develop their career before her. However, on being asked to lead a large-scale research project by an external body, college management acknowledged the achievement by appointing Shirley to a management and leadership role.

Unlike Carlos, Mona and Shirley, Myriam finds herself in a noticeably different space. She resents her institute's tendency towards uniformity, efficiency and performativity (Ball, 2003) which, in turn, does not support her pedagogical aspirations and research interests. This has resulted in her not yet fully actualising her plans related to her pedagogical role as a teacher educator.

National affordances have contributed to some participants' professional development. Myriam participated in a national network focused on pedagogy in teacher education. Shirley participated in a study programme for beginning teacher educators provided by an inter-collegiate institute. However, it seems that these national affordances are not coordinated with individual institutions. Myriam's institution does not provide her with opportunities to share what she learned with her colleagues and improve current programmes. Shirley's institute did not insist on her participation in pedagogy-oriented studies to compensate for her lack of school experience. It seems there is a need for coordinated policies of local institutes and national as well as international stakeholders.

Conclusion

Following four teacher educators from four different countries, we found that teacher educators' professional development is shaped by individual interests and skills as well as institutional, national and global contexts. Across the four countries, teacher education is still an 'incidental career' (White, 2019). The diversity of beginning teacher educators' knowledge and skills, as well as the multiplicity of their roles, justify the need for carefully planned induction and professional learning opportunities. However, although guidelines for effective induction and professional learning are available in the literature (c.f. Boyd et al., 2007; Griffiths et al., 2010; Livingston, 2014), and some support is offered in many countries, it is not tailored to address individual teacher educators' needs. Neither are national and institute resources pooled in a coordinated manner.

The main aim of our study was to gain in-depth insight into the interaction between teacher educators' personal characteristics and work contexts, since insufficient studies have explored these interactions in a systematic manner. While a limitation of this study is its small scale, we believe that the findings are suggestive of general trends and hope that they capture the attention of teacher education administrators and policy makers who wish to provide future teachers with well prepared and effective teacher educators.

References

Ball, S. (2003). The teacher's soul and the terrors of performativity. *Journal of Education Policy*, 18(2), 215–228.

Boyd, P., Harris, K., & Murray, J. (2007). *Becoming a teacher educator: Guidelines for the induction of newly appointed lecturers in initial teacher education*. Higher Education Academy Education Subject Centre.

Braun, V., & Clarke, V. (2006). Using thematic analysis in psychology. *Qualitative Research in Psychology*, 3(2), 77–101.

Carter, K. (1993). The place of story in the study of teaching Teacher Education. *Educational Researcher*, 22(1), 5–12.

Cochran-Smith, M. (2005). Teacher educators as researchers: Multiple perspectives. *Teaching and Teacher Education*, 21(2), 219–225.

Cochran-Smith, M. Grudnoff, L., Orland-Barak, L., & Smith, K. (2020). Educating teacher educators: International perspectives. *The New Educator*, 16(1), 5–24.

Czerniawski, G., Guberman, A., & MacPhail, A. (2017). The professional developmental needs of higher education-based teacher educators: An international comparative needs analysis. *European Journal of Teacher Education*, 40(1), 127–140.

European Commission. (2013). Supporting teacher educators for better learning outcomes. https://ec.europa.eu/assets/eac/education/policy/school/doc/support-teacher-educators_en.pdf.

Gleeson, J., Leitch, R., Sugrue, C., & O'Flaherty, J. (2012). *Understanding the role and potential for research capacity-building in initial teacher education (ITE) programmes North-South Ireland: A baseline and comparative study*. Centre for Cross Border Studies. http://hdl.handle.net/10197/4954.

Goodwin, L., Smith, L., Souto-Manning, M., Cheruvu, R., Tan, M. Y., Reed, R., & Taveras, L. (2014). What should teacher educators know and be able to do? Perspectives from practicing teacher educators. *Journal of Teacher Education*, 65(4), 284–302.

Griffiths, V., Thompson, S., & Hryniewicz, L. (2010). Developing a research profile: Mentoring and support for teacher educators. *Professional Development in Education*, 36 (1–2), 245–262.

Griffiths, V., Thompson, S., & Hryniewicz, L. (2014). Landmarks in the professional and academic development of mid-career teacher educators. *European Journal of Teacher Education*, 37(1), 74–90.

Guberman, A., & Mcdossi, O. (2019). Israeli teacher educators' perceptions of their professional development paths in teaching, research and institutional leadership. *European Journal of Teacher Education*, 42(4), 507–522.

Guberman, A., Ulvik, M., Oolbekkink-Marcand, H., & MacPhail, M. (2020). Teacher educators' professional trajectories: Evidence from Ireland, Israel, Norway and the Netherlands. *European Journal of Teacher Education.* DOI: doi:10.1080/02619768. 2020.1793948

Guest, G., Macqueen, K. M., & Namey, E. E. (2012). *Applied thematic analysis.* SAGE.

Harrison, J., & McKeon, F. (2008). The formal and situated learning of beginning teacher educators in England: Identifying characteristics for successful induction in the transition from workplace in schools to workplace in higher education. *European Journal of Teacher Education, 31*(2), 151–168.

Kelchtermans, G., Smith, K., & Vanderlinde, R. (2018). Towards an 'International Forum for Teacher Educator Development': An agenda for research and action. *European Journal of Teacher Education, 41*(1), 120–134.

Livingston, K. (2014). Teacher educators: Hidden professionals? *European Journal of Education, 49*(2), 218–232.

Loughran, J. (2006). *Developing a pedagogy of teacher education.* Routledge.

Loughran, J. (2014). Professionally developing as a teacher educator. *Journal of Teacher Education, 65*(4), 271–283.

Lunenberg, M., Dengerink, J., & Korthagen, F. (2014). *The professional teacher educator: Roles, behaviour, and professional development of teacher educators.* Sense Publishers.

MacPhail, A., Ulvik, M., Guberman, A., Czerniawski, G., Oolbekkink-Marchand, H., & Bain, Y. (2019). The professional development of higher education-based teacher educators: Needs and realities. *Professional Development in Education, 45*(5), 848–861.

Meeus, W., Cools, M., & Placklé, I. (2018). Teacher educators developing professional roles: Frictions between current and optimal practices. *European Journal of Teacher Education, 41*(1), 15–31.

Murray, J. (2014). Teacher educators' constructions of professionalism: A case study. *Asia-Pacific Journal of Teacher Education, 42*(1), 7–21.

Murray, J., & Male, T. (2005). Becoming a teacher educator: Evidence from the field. *Teaching and Teacher Education, 21*(2), 125–142.

Ping, C., Schellings, G., & D. Beijaard, D. (2018). Teacher educators' professional learning: A literature review. *Teaching and Teacher Education, 75*, 93–104.

Polkinghorne, D. E. (1995). Narrative configuration in qualitative analysis. *International Journal of Qualitative Studies in Education, 8*(1), 5–23.

Smith, K. (2011). The multi-faceted teacher educator: A Norwegian perspective. *Journal of Education for Teaching, 37*(3), 337–349.

Smith, K. (2017). Learning from the past to shape the future. *European Journal of Teacher Education, 40*(5), 630–646.

Smith, K., & Flores, M. A. (2019). The Janus faced teacher educator. *European Journal of Teacher Education, 42*(4), 433–446.

Swennen, A., & Volman, M. (2019). The development of the identity of teacher educators in the changing context of teacher education in the Netherlands. In J. Murray, A. Swennen, & C. Kosnik (Eds.), *International research, policy and practice in teacher education: Insider perspectives* (pp. 107–121). Springer.

Timmermans, M. (2019, November 17). Registration deepens and connects. *International Forum for Teacher Educator Development.* https://info-ted.eu/registration-deep ens-and-connects/.

Van der Klink, M., Kools, Q, Avissar, G., White, S., & Sakata, T. (2017). Professional development of teacher educators: What do they do? Findings from an explorative international study. *Professional Development in Education, 43*(2), 163–178.

Vanassche, E., Rust, F., Conway, P. F., Smith, K., Tack, H., & Vanderlinde, R. (2015). InFo-TED: Bringing policy, research, and practice together around teacher educator development. In J. C. Craig, & L. Orland-Barak (Eds.), *International teacher education: promising pedagogies (part C)* (Vol. 22, pp. 341–364). Emerald.

White, S. (2019). Teacher educators for new times? Redefining an important occupational group. *Journal of Education for Teaching*, 45(2), 200–213.

Chapter 10

Interlude: Teacher educators' professional development in the United States

Context and challenges

Frances Rust

Introduction

Teacher education is increasingly recognised worldwide as the linchpin of educational reform. As the initiators of the International Forum of Teacher Educator Development (InFo-TED) write in chapter 1 of this book, 'Pre-service teacher education has become a policy driver for bringing about changes in schooling through new and often fast changing policy requirements and the often systematic politicisation of teacher education' (INSERT REFERENCE PAGE). Absent until very recently has been attention to and support of those who prepare teachers. It is the remarkable work of InFo-TED described in this book and on the InFo-TED website (https://info-ted.eu), as well as in the numerous publications by members of the InFo-TED council and participants in the summer institute in Trondheim, that has brought serious scholarly and political attention to teacher educators as significant players in initiating and carrying out educational reforms.

InFo-TED has given visibility to the professional work of teacher educators, to the complexity of that work and to its importance. Critical to the influence of InFo-TED has been its stand against prescription about the work of teacher education. As a result, the InFo-TED initiative has engendered a conversation that steers clear of a 'blueprint' for action (see Vanassche et al., 2015). InFo-TED activities have enabled opportunities for expansive learning (Engeström & Sannino, 2010) that, as the authors in this volume suggest, can lead to thoughtful, high-level and board-based shifts in the practice of teacher educators. The various chapters of this volume make it clear that it is this openness to the complexity that history, culture and norms of practice present that have enabled participants in InFo-TED to embrace a pan-European conversation that is gradually being taken up beyond Europe where it was initiated.

In the United States, there is increasing interest in reshaping the narrative around teacher education by focusing on the professional learning of teacher educators as 'architects of the teaching profession' (Hollins & Warner, in press) and catalysts for educational change. For this, InFo-TED provides inspiration. However, to simply 'copy' the various activities of InFo-TED is to miss the essential qualities that have made it resonate well with teacher educators across Europe.

To develop a United States-appropriate InFo-TED will require attention to those historical and cultural factors that have shaped the highly contentious educational landscape that characterises education in the United States today. This chapter begins with a discussion of that history as it relates to teacher education and moves from there to describe the ways in which professional learning among university-based teacher educators has evolved and been supported. The chapter concludes with reflections on the implications of the work of the participants in InFo-TED for the professional development of university-based teacher educators in this country.

Background

The story of teacher educators in the United States is intricately woven into the fabric of teacher education itself: how teacher educators are perceived, known and understood has everything to do with the relative importance accorded at any moment in time to the preparation of teachers and that, too often, has related to how schools and schooling are perceived. As Fraser (2007) has written:

> For most of the history of the United States, from the American Revolution until well into the 1950s and 1960s, teacher preparation was a haphazard affair. The majority of teachers had no formal preparation, whether it was John Adams going from college to a teaching position in Worcester, Massachusetts in the 1750s or a thirteen-year-old Lucia Downing taking the teaching exam as a lark in the 1880s, passing, and soon being hired to teach; it was often the case that teachers were simply hired by school boards seeking the best person willing to work for the low pay offered.
>
> (p. 3)

There was no preparation of most of these teachers. At best, theirs was the 'apprenticeship of observation' of which Lortie (1975) writes.

As educational historians (Clifford & Guthrie, 1988; Cremin, 1961; Cuban, 1993; Fraser, 2007; Furman & Lazerson, 2005; Spring, 1986; Tyack, 1974) describe it, in the years after the American Civil War, as the nation's population grew and its boundaries expanded westward through Native American territories, policy makers at all levels gradually embraced the idea of free, public education. With this acceptance came the task of preparing teachers to teach in the nation's schools. Over this span of time, teacher education, as the formal preparation of teachers, grew gradually from small, local initiatives to state-wide and regional programs situated initially in normal schools and later in land grant universities.

Attention to who prepares teachers, who determines what they should know and be able to do, and who supports their professional learning over time – questions that point toward awareness of 'teacher education' as a professional endeavour and so of 'teacher educators' as professionals – only gradually began to surface as 'problems' with the nation's schools, were identified and ways to 'fix' those problems were needed (Fraser, 2007). As Cochran-Smith (2020) suggests, attention to these questions have only recently become part of the discourse around teacher education and teachers' professional learning.

In part, this 'fogginess' around who teacher educators are and what they do relates to a general lack of awareness of teacher education itself, but the story is bigger than teacher education. The work of preparing and supporting teachers in the United States is intimately tied to the country's conflicted history of schooling for democratic citizenship with the core question being focused on beliefs about who should be educated and how. As Tyack (1974) described it, the sheer complexity of that democratic task has confounded many attempts to develop a 'one best system' – a best way of conceiving of schools, curriculum and instruction, and so by inference, the preparation of teachers irrespective of where they might practice and whom they might teach. Instead, the history of schooling in the United States and of teacher education for those schools is a fragmented mosaic in which local, state and national interests sometimes coalesce and other times collide.

Schools (and teacher education) come into focus

Since the late 1950s, when the USSR's launch of Sputnik raised alarms about whether US public schools were adequately educating our children, the public's attention has increasingly been drawn by policy makers and the press to problems with public education. Concerns about education (meaning schools) reached a fever pitch with the publication of *A Nation at Risk* in 1983 under the aegis of Ronald Regan's secretary of education, William Bennett. In that document, the National Commission on Excellence in Education framed education in bellicose terms:

> Our Nation is at risk. Our once unchallenged pre-eminence in commerce, industry, science, and technological innovation is being overtaken by competitors throughout the world... the educational foundations of our society are presently being eroded by a rising tide of mediocrity that threatens our very future as a Nation and a people. What was unimaginable a generation ago has begun to occur – others are matching and surpassing our educational attainments.
>
> If an unfriendly foreign power had attempted to impose on America the mediocre educational performance that exists today, we might well have viewed it as an act of war. As it stands, we have allowed this to happen to ourselves. We have even squandered the gains in student achievement made in the wake of the Sputnik challenge. Moreover, we have dismantled essential support systems which helped to make those gains possible. We have, in effect, been committing an act of unthinking, unilateral educational disarmament.
>
> (p. 5)

The tenor of the debate about pre-K–12 education has rarely become less strident since then and, increasingly, teacher education has become the focus, initially, in this country and now globally.

The lens not applied, the perspective resisted as school performance is scrutinised, has been the lens of racial equity: in the same decade but preceding Sputnik were the US Supreme Court's *Brown v. Board of Education* decisions (1954, 1955) that declared the doctrine of 'separate but equal' education for Black children to be unconstitutional (Supreme Court of the United States, 1954) and tasked local federal judges with making sure that school authorities integrated the races in schools 'with all deliberate speed' (Supreme Court of the United States, 1955). These momentous decisions were immediately resisted by the White majority, and guided by the courts, a long slow movement toward integration of schools ensued. That public schools, despite massive legal efforts to integrate them throughout the country during the 1970s, '80s, and '90s, are now as segregated as they were in the late '50s demonstrates the power of the belief among policy makers at all levels that equity and social justice are unrelated to student achievement (Orfield & Ashkinaze, 1991; Orfield & Lee, 2005). It is a belief that is only now starting to crumble.

At the time of the initial efforts at school desegregation, children of colour, particularly in the southern part of the country, were taught in segregated schools by teachers of colour who lived in their communities (Foster, 1997). Within a few short years of the various court orders that mandated integrated schools, these teachers were removed from their schools and their teaching communities – spheres in which their knowledge and expertise were valued (Foster, 1997; Ladson-Billings, 2009; Walker, 2013) – and ordered into schools and classrooms where it was assumed that their presence would somehow enable integration.

For teacher education, the impact of this bifurcated approach to education and schooling in this country reflects the complexity of the politics at local, state and national levels that left many urban and rural public schools underfunded and attended largely by students of colour, and suburban public schools attended by White and middle-class students (Anyon, 1997; Fruchter, 2007, Orfield & Easton, 1996). Schools and colleges of education were not in the forefront in the shaping of curriculum and instructional practices that would support successful implementation of these policies. They were not focused on desegregation and preparing teachers to work collaboratively across racial and economic boundaries.

Thirty years after *Brown v. Board of Education* and Sputnik, Clifford and Guthrie (1988) wrote, 'generally, schools, colleges, and departments of education are politically impotent' (p. 40). Teacher education as a professional field, especially in the Research I universities that lead the field (Clifford & Guthrie, 1988), was coping with the feminisation of the profession and the low status accorded to professional preparation of almost any kind in liberal arts settings.

Clifford and Guthrie (1998) suggest that the framing of teaching as a feminine occupation has had 'consequences' for the status of teacher education 'among professions and among professional schools in universities' (p. 18). Fraser (2007) describes that status:

> In a hierarchy that places theory above practice and content knowledge above pedagogical knowledge, and, indeed, that adopts a condescending attitude toward students preparing for practical fields and the specialised faculty who attend them, education departments – whether in research universities or in recently renamed normal schools – are almost universally considered the bottom of the university pecking order.
>
> (p. 4)

Yet, schools and colleges of education were and are by far the major sites for the preparation of teachers in the United States and, like the majority of teachers in this country, their faculties of teacher educators are White (Ducharme & Agnes, 1982; Ladson-Billings, 2017) and are generally neither prepared nor supported as teacher educators (Bransford et al., 2005; Clifford & Guthrie, 1988). To maintain stature in the university, they are often divorced from the field. Ladson-Billings (2014, 2017) describes this schism of race and experience as identical to the 'demographic mismatch' between teachers and their students that exists in the pre-K–12 settings – the largely urban and rural schools that most need the expertise and support of teacher educators. She writes powerfully for a repositioning of teacher education that invites new roles, new coalitions and a deep and sustained commitment to studying teaching and teacher education with an eye to developing a 'culturally sustaining pedagogy' that can transform not only pre-K–12 classrooms but also those higher education classrooms where we prepare our teachers.

The possibility for such work comes as teacher education is being redefined, radically transformed, bending toward the democratic potential of public education. A Nation at Risk was a wake-up call and, though there is as Ladson-Billings (2017) suggests 'more uniformity than one might expect among teacher education programs' (p. 153), the arc of teacher education is extending toward what Zeichner (2020) describes as 'democratic professionalism' that

> centers students, families and communities in teachers' work and in teacher education programs, and is an alternative to both occupational and organizational professionalism that offers the potential to help productively manage the tensions and contradictions that have long existed between professional educators and the non-dominant communities that they are supposed to serve.
>
> (p. 41)

Beginning with the effort to define a 'knowledge base' for teacher education in the 1980s (see Reynolds, 1989) through multiple handbooks of research on teaching (e.g., Wittrock, 1986) and teacher education (e.g., Houston, 1990), and powerful calls from the Carnegie Endowment (Carnegie Task Force on Teaching as a Profession, 1986) and the Holmes Group (1986, 1990, 1995), the field has slowly moved toward professional norms and research-based practices. As Cochran-Smith (2020) describes it, 'the late 1990s and early 2000s were a turning point for teacher education' (p. 52). She writes:

> During this time, enormous pressure was exerted to make teacher education more standards- and evidence-based and more assessment driven (Education Commission of the States, 2000). However, concern was also growing among some teacher education scholars and practitioners that issues related to diversity, equity, and justice in teacher education were being marginalized and that the presumed consensus image of 'the professional teacher' (Sykes, 1999; Yinger, 1999) did not necessarily serve minoritized students or acknowledge the complex economic, social, and racialized contexts within which those practices had been verified.
>
> (p. 52)

As a result, there has been increasing pressure from within and outside of the university-based teacher education community towards genuine collaboration with schools in the form of clinical practice (Hollins, 2015; Yendol-Hoppey et al., 2019). As Yendol-Hoppey et al. (2019) make clear, 'the work of embedding clinical practice across teacher preparation programs began decades ago' (p. xi) with the calls from Goodlad (1988, 1990), the Holmes Group (1986, 1990, 1995) and more recently from teacher education organisations such as the American Association of Colleges of Teacher Education (AACTE, 2010, 2018a, 2018b) and accrediting organisations such as the National Council on Accreditation of Teacher Education (NCATE, 2010) and its successor, the Council for the Accreditation of Educator Preparation (CAEP, 2015). What seems newly possible is the 'remix' that Ladson-Billings (2014) envisions:

> The notion of a remix means that there was an original version and that there may be more versions to come, taking previously developed ideas and synthesizing them to create new and exciting forms… Such revisions do not imply that the original was deficient; rather, they speak to the changing and evolving needs of dynamic systems. Remixing is vital to innovation in art, science, and pedagogy, and it is crucial that we are willing to remix what we created and/or inherited.
>
> (pp. 75–76)

This reinvention requires that the role of teacher educator expands to become genuinely boundary-crossing.

Developing change

In the highly regulated and politicised environment of teacher education in the United States, 'the key levers for change are complex and difficult to manage' (Bransford et al., 2005, p. 451). What is needed are multiple and varied opportunities for invention, that is, the creation of 'third spaces' (Zeichner, 2009) or 'edge environments' (Gorodetsky & Barak, 2008), where there is room for experimentation, research and learning from the meeting of theory and practice.

Descriptions and discussions of such environments are increasingly the focus of scholarship in teacher education. See, for example, Darling-Hammond's (2006) presentation of powerful teacher education programs; Del Prete's (2010) description of university school partnerships; Ladson-Billing's (2014) description of her work with the hip-hop and spoken word program 'First Wave'; Hollins' (2019) deep analysis of a teacher education program; and Yendol-Hoppey et al.'s (2019) and Rust's (2020) studies of collaborations between universities and schools. Each of these pulls teacher educators out of the comfort zone of habitual practice and into the area of thoughtful collaboration. None alone will change the structure of teacher education. However, taken together and enabled by the type of collaboration modelled by participants in InFo-TED, the shift toward new understandings of teacher education as a dynamic, inclusive and culturally centred professional practice can take shape.

To accomplish such a shift, the redefining of the work of teacher educators that Darling-Hammond et al. (2005), Hollins (2015, 2019), Ladson-Billings (2014, 2017), Yendol-Hoppey et al. (2019) and the authors of this book point toward must go beyond picking school sites and placing student teachers. We've done that. The shift requires both an embrace of the broad definition of who a teacher educator is (see chapter 2) and the deep collaborative study of practice by these teacher educators to effect the development and implementation of dynamic spaces for learning. In essence, teacher educators must increasingly embrace their role as 'architects of the teaching profession' (Hollins & Warner, in press). To arrive at this new place will require re-thinking how teacher educators are identified, prepared and sustained.

Though it has been called for in the United States for some time (see Goodlad, 1990; Patterson et al., 1999), doctoral preparation of teacher educators is relatively new here and, for all the reasons cited throughout this chapter, it is neither invested in nor supported broadly as has been the case in Norway (see Smith, 2020). Teachers College, Columbia University, Alverno College and the University of Colorado-Boulder are among the rare doctoral programs in education where one can focus explicitly on the preparation of teacher educators for positions in higher education or as professional educators in schools. Like new teachers, the graduates of these programs cannot be expected in their first years to change the culture of higher education nor the programs that prepare and support teachers. As Goodwin and Kosnik (2013) remind us, 'one becomes a teacher educator as soon as one does teacher education, but one's professional identity as a teacher educator is constructed over time' (p. 334).

What we must look towards in the United States is a genuine embrace by university-based teacher educators of their school-based colleagues such that we can develop together what Cochran-Smith and Lytle (1999) describe as 'knowledge-*for*-practice', 'knowledge-*in*-practice' and 'knowledge-*of*-practice'. Such professional learning for university-based teacher educators is currently accomplished ad hoc through professional organisations: American Association of Colleges of Teacher Education (AACTE), Association of Teacher Educators (ATE), American Education Research Association (AERA-Division K) and through various specialty organisations serving early childhood educators: NAECTE and Associate Degree Early Childhood Teacher Educators (ACCESS), math educators (NCTM), language teachers (MLA), social studies (NCSS), special education (CEC) and numerous others.

Attendance at and participation in these groups can bring university-based teacher educators in contact with one another as well as with specialists and with school-based professionals. However, while the focus of these organisations is essentially on improving the professional practice of teacher educators in the discipline or content area, they do not offer the field an explicit, sustainable collaboration around teacher educators' professional learning that would enable radical changes in the preparation and support of teachers and the ensuing upgrading of practice in schools that such changes would signify. InFo-TED offers such an important opportunity to new and experienced teacher educators to engage as professionals in 'remixing' the field.

Conclusion

At this time in the United States when the need to lean into the challenge of democracy is proclaimed by a multiplicity of voices within and beyond the university, teacher educators are bid to come together to advance the field to benefit the lives of all of our children. The conceptual 'elasticity' of the InFo-TED model makes it an appropriate vehicle for consideration and emulation. How to pick up on the initiative that is InFo-TED in ways that can galvanise teacher educators in this country is an issue on which a number of teacher educators representing the diversity of the field are currently focused. Following the example of InFo-TED, our intent is to engage broadly with policy makers at all levels – in government, in our professional organisations, in the field – to enable the sorely needed vitalization of the field. Like the daring initiators of InFo-TED, we understand that teacher educators are essential to realising the purposes of education for democracy.

References

American Association of Colleges for Teacher Education. (2010). The clinical preparation of teachers: A policy brief.

American Association of Colleges for Teacher Education. (2018a). A pivot toward clinical practice, its lexicon, and the renewal of educator preparation: A report of the AACTE Clinical Practice Commission.

American Association of Colleges for Teacher Education. (2018b). A pivot toward clinical practice, its lexicon, and the renewal of educator preparation: Summary brief.

Anyon, J. (1997). *Ghetto schooling. A political economy of urban educational reform.* Teachers College Press.

Bransford, J., Darling-Hammond L., and LePage, P. (2005). Introduction. In L. Darling-Hammond, & J. Bransford (Eds.), *Preparing teachers for a changing world: What teachers should learn and be able to do* (pp. 1–39). Jossey-Bass.

Carnegie Task Force on Teaching as a Profession. (1986). *A nation prepared: Teachers for the twenty-first century.*

Clifford, G. J., & Guthrie, J. W. (1988). *Ed school: A brief for professional education.* University of Chicago.

Cochran-Smith, M. (2020). Teacher education for justice and equity: 40 years of advocacy. *Action in Teacher Education, 42*(1), 49–59.

Cochran-Smith, M., & Lytle, S. (1999). Relationships of knowledge and practice: Teacher learning in communities. *Review of Research in Education, 24,* 249–305.

Council for the Accreditation of Educator Preparation. (2015). *Accreditation standards.*

Cremin, L. (1961). *The transformation of the school: Progressivism in American Education, 1876–1957.* Knopf.

Cuban, L. (1993). *How teachers taught: Constancy and change in American classrooms, 1890–1990* (2nd ed.). Teachers College Press.

Darling-Hammond, L. (2006). Powerful teacher education. Lessons from exemplary programs. In L. Darling-Hammond, & J. Bransford (Eds.), *Preparing teachers for a changing world: What teachers should learn and be able to do.* Jossey-Bass.

Darling-Hammond, L., Pacheco, A., Michelli, N., Lepage, P., Hammerness, K., & Youngs, P. (2005). Implementing curriculum renewal in teacher education: Managing organizational and policy change. In L. Darling Hammond, & J. Bransford (Eds.), *Preparing teachers for a changing world: What teachers should learn and be able to do* (pp. 442–479). Jossey-Bass.

Del Prete, T. (2010). *Improving the odds: Developing powerful teaching practice and culture of learning in urban high schools.* Teachers College Press.

Ducharme, E. R., & Agnes, R. M. (1982). The education professoriate: A research based perspective. *Journal of Teacher Education, 33*(6), 30–36.

Education Commission of the States. (2000). In pursuit of quality teaching: Five key strategies for policy-makers.

Engeström, Y., & A. Sannino. (2010). Studies of expansive learning: Foundations, findings and future challenges. *Educational Research Review, 5*(1), 1–24.

Foster, M. (1997). *Black teachers on teaching.* The New Press.

Fraser, J. W. (2007). *Preparing America's teachers. A history.* Teachers College Press.

Fruchter, N. (2007). *Urban schools. Public will. Making education work for all our children.* Teachers College Press.

Fuhrman, S., & Lazerson, M. (2005). *The public schools.* Oxford University Press.

Goodlad, J. I. (1988). *The national network for educational renewal. Past, present, future.* Center for Educational Renewal.

Goodlad, J. I. (1990). *Teachers for our nation's schools.* Jossey-Bass.

Goodwin, A. L., & Kosnik, C. (2013). Quality teacher educators=quality teachers? Conceptualizing essential domains of knowledge for those who teach teachers. *Teacher Development*, 17(3), 334–346.

Gorodetsky, M., & Barak, J. (2008). The educational-cultural edge: A participative learning environment for co-emergence of personal and institutional growth. *Teaching and Teacher Education*, 24(7), 1907–1918.

Hollins, E. R. (Ed.). (2015). *Rethinking field experiences in teacher preparation*. Routledge.

Hollins. E. R. (2019). *Teaching to transform urban schools and communities: Powerful pedagogy in practice*. Routledge.

Hollins, E. R., & Warner, C. K. (in press). *Rethinking teacher preparation program design*. Routledge.

Holmes Group. (1986). *Tomorrow's teachers: A report of the Holmes Group*. Holmes Group

Holmes Group. (1990). *Tomorrow's schools: Principles for the design of professional development schools*. Holmes Group.

Holmes Group. (1995). *Tomorrow's schools of education*. Holmes Group

Houston, W. R. (Ed.). (1990). *Handbook of research on teacher education*. Macmillan.

Ladson-Billings, G. (2009). *The dreamkeepers: Successful teachers of African American children* (2nd ed.). Jossey-Bass.

Ladson-Billings, G. (2014). Culturally relevant pedagogy 2.0: a.k.a. the remix. *Harvard Educational Review*, 84(1), 74–84.

Ladson-Billings, G. (2017). The (R)Evolution will not be standardized. Teacher education, hip hop pedagogy, and culturally relevant pedagogy 2.0. In D. Paris, & H. S. Alim (Eds.), *Culturally sustaining pedagogies: Teaching and learning for justice in a changing world* (pp. 141–156). Teachers College Press.

Lortie, D. (1975). *Schoolteacher: A sociological study*. University of Chicago Press.

National Commission on Excellence in Education. (1983). A nation at risk. U. S. Department of Education.

National Council for Accreditation of Teacher Education. (2010, November). *Transforming teacher education through clinical practice: A national strategy to prepare effective teachers*. Blue Ribbon Panel on Clinical Preparation and Partnerships for Improved Student Learning.

Orfield, G., & Ashkinaze, C. (1991). *The closing door: Conservative Policy and Black opportunity*. University of Chicago Press.

Orfield, G., & Easton, S. (1996). *Dismantling desegregation: The quiet reversal of Brown v. Board of Education*. The New Press.

Orfield, G., & Lee, C. (2005). *Why segregation matters: Poverty and educational inequality*. Harvard University.

Patterson, R. S., Michelli, N. M., & Pacheco, A. (1999). *Centers of pedagogy: New structures for educational renewal*. Jossey-Bass.

Reynolds, M. C. (1989). *Knowledge base for the beginning teacher*. Pergamon Press.

Rust, F. (2020). Expansive learning within a teachers community of ongoing learners (TCOOL). *Frontiers in Education*, 5.

Smith, K. (2020). Expansive learning for teacher educators: The story of Norwegian National Research School in teacher education (NAFOL). *Frontiers in Education*, 5.

Spring, J. (1986). *The American school, 1642–1985*. Longman.

Supreme Court of the United States. (1954). Brown v. Board of Education of Topeka. 347 U.S. 483.

Supreme Court of the United States. (1955). Brown v. Board of Education of Topeka II. 349 U.S. 294.

Sykes, G. (1999). Teacher and student learning: strengthening the connection. In G. Sykes, & L. Darling Hammond (Eds.), *Teaching as the learning profession: Handbook of policy and practice* (1st ed., pp. 151–180). John Wiley & Son.

Tyack, D. B. (1974). *The one best system. A history of American urban education*. Harvard University Press.

Vanassche, E., Rust, F., Conway, P., Smith, K., Tack, H., & Vanderlinde, R. (2015). InFo-TED: Bringing policy, research, and practice together around teacher educator development. In J. C. Craig, & L. Orland-Barak (Eds.), *International teacher education: Promising pedagogies (part C)* (Vol. 22, pp. 341–364). Emerald.

Walker, V. S. (2013). Ninth annual Brown lecture in educational research: Black educators as educational advocates in the decades before Brown v. Board of Education. *Educational Researcher*, 42(4), 207–222.

Wittrock, M. C. (1986). *Handbook of research on teaching* (3rd ed.). Macmillan.

Yendol-Hoppey, D., Dana, N. F., & Hoppey, D. (2019). *Preparing the next generation of teacher educators for clinical practice*. Information Age Publishing.

Yinger, R. (1999). The role of standards in teaching and teacher education. In G. Griffin (Ed.), *The education of teachers: Ninety-eighth yearbook of the National Society for the Study of Education* (pp. 85–113). University of Chicago Press.

Zeichner, K. (2009). Rethinking the connections between campus courses and field experiences in college- and university-based teacher education. *Journal of Teacher Education*, 61(1–2),89–99.

Zeichner, K. (2020). Preparing teachers as democratic professionals. *Action in Teacher Education*, 42(1), 38–48.

Chapter 11

Designing professional development for teacher educators

Creating long-term learning for the workplace

Jean Murray, Warren Kidd, Bregje de Vries, Andrea McMahon and Sheeba Viswarajan

Introduction

issue 1

Many forms of professional development opportunities for teacher educators occur *away* from the workplace, and particularly away from the immediate arena of practice[1]. Yet, as chapter 1 of this book signals, research consistently shows how central learning *in* and *from* the arena of practice can be for authentic and meaningful professional development (Lunenberg et al., 2014, McNamara et al., 2014). In fact, for many teacher educators, some form of learning, close to, on or in the arena of practice, is their major form of learning (Cochran-Smith et al., 2019).

This chapter aims to develop new knowledge and understanding of how *goal* professional development activities might be planned and implemented in order to provide integrated, practice-relevant and enduring forms of learning with high relevance for the workplace. It achieves this by exploring the specific learning opportunities offered by the Summer Academy (henceforth referred to as the Academy) and the Virtual Learning Environment (VLE) within the International Forum for Teacher Educator Development (InFo-TED) project. Chapter 5 and chapter 8 of this book describe the event, the learning structures and the pedagogical principles and practices deployed for the Academy in more detail. But, in summary, this was a one-off, face-to-face, structured learning event, implemented in a setting far from the workplaces and the daily practices of most of the attending teacher educators

The research questions to be considered here are:

1 What learning occurred for the participating teacher educators *during* the Academy, and did that short-term learning contribute to longer-term and 'practice-relevant' learning back *in* the workplace and the immediate arenas for participants' practice?

2   If so, what structures within the Academy facilitated this learning, both short- and long-term?

3   What might be the wider implications of this study for designing professional learning opportunities?

These questions structure the chapter: the first section presents findings about the short- and long-term learning resulting from the Academy for individuals; the second analyses the structures that facilitated that learning; and the third considers the wider implications of these findings for those designing and implementing professional learning. It also offers further ideas for forging practice-relevant learning opportunities. The conclusion stresses that teacher educators themselves must be the drivers of their own professional development trajectories within and beyond their workplaces.

Contexts for the study

Chapter 1 outlined many aspects of what is already known about teacher educators' professional learning. Of particular relevance for this current chapter is the importance of both formal and informal learning in and on the arena of practice as the immediate and central part of the workplace (Lunenberg et al., 2014; McNamara et al., 2014; Murray & Male, 2005). Learning which occurs in such professionally and personally relevant contexts often involves experiential and informal learning[2]. Additionally, professional development in the workplace has the potential to generate 'expansive learning' (Engeström, 2001, 2015; Engeström & Sannino, 2010), an active, open and social form of learning that can create new knowledge and practices, often for a newly emerging activity. As stated in chapter 1, workplace learning in teacher education is generally not well theorised (McNamara et al., 2014).

Yet for teacher educators, some professional development opportunities may also beneficially occur away from the workplace. Certainly, teacher education institutes of all forms often arrange formal one-off learning events, such as short courses, workshops and meetings focused on contemporary issues relevant to the organisation. These activities are often viewed as important for institutional stability, consistency and growth, and attending them may also be important and beneficial for teacher educators as employees.

Other formal face-to-face events may be productive for addressing key areas of individual development. In their large-scale survey of teacher educators, for example, Czerniawski et al. (2017) found that well-targeted seminars, courses and workshops were popular options for developing research skills (see also chapter 3 of this book). Such face-to-face, formal events were also seen as effective ways of enhancing ICT (information and communications technology) skills and meeting specific teaching needs. But overall, attending formal events such as courses did not attract high levels of interest, and participants 'expressed a strong preference for professional learning events that are continuous and based around experiential learning' (Czerniawski et al., 2017, p. 11).

One-off formal provision alone then is often not a popular form of learning, *[issue]* and it may not exert a major, long-term impact on teacher educators' development. This will be particularly true if that provision is poorly planned and/or largely decontextualised from the immediate arena of practice.

For the purposes of this chapter, the key characteristic of the Academy was that it was a one-off, face-to-face professional development event, held in a location geographically distant from nearly all the participants' workplaces. Led by two Dutch teacher educators, it was designed to be an interactive event that celebrated contextually-rich professional learning through all its values, structures, content and pedagogies. Participants had to go through an application process and have permission for five full days of attendance away from their normal workplaces. A range of collaborative learning activities was planned during the week, as detailed in chapter 8. Participants worked every day in small groups. The aim was to achieve sustainability of the learning through group plans made during the week; all were asked to create future, communal activities, with plans for 'a clear path forward with a time line and deliverables' (Rust & Berry, 2019). Further details of the underpinning design principles can be found in chapter 5 of this book.

Preparations for the Academy involved the construction of a VLE (virtual learning environment) embedded in the wider InFo-TED website. This was intended to develop participant interaction pre- and post-event on a collaborative, interactive and asynchronous model (Murray & Kidd, 2016), using private fora there, participants could collaborate and interact across geographical and professional boundaries before the event itself.

Data for the study

[data based on participant feedback + report of InFo-TED]

This chapter draws upon two reports of the Academy: firstly, Kelchtermans and Deketelaere (2019), an internal evaluation document; and secondly, the full, public evaluation (Rust & Berry, 2019). The internal evaluation used data captured daily during the event by means of 'video selfies' in which all the participants recorded their experiences and significant learning points. The external evaluation also drew on this data supplemented by retrospective interviews and communications with a selected sample of participants (see Rust & Berry, 2019, for further details). The chapter also draws on the official report of the InFo-TED project prepared for the European Commission (Smith, 2019). For all these documents, data collection and analysis were rigorous and systematic.

These general evaluation data are supplemented by auto-ethnographical *[also this]* reflections in the form of vignettes and journal writing from three other Academy participants[3]. One participant came from the Netherlands (participant 1 below) and two from England (participant 2 and participant 3). This final tranche of data was collected retrospectively (up to 18 months after the event) and on an ad hoc basis when personal opportunities allowed.

In terms of conventional research, there are distinct limitations to this additional data set: the sample is very small; there was no formal or extensive sampling strategy; self-reported data collection methods were used; and researcher positionality is complex as all stages of the research were carried out by people involved in the InFo-TED project. Nevertheless, all aspects of the research aimed for authenticity, dependability and reciprocity, as valued alternative criteria for evaluating qualitative research.

The strength of these alternative criteria extended to the overall data analysis also. Here all the data sources found in the two evaluation reports, together with the individual data generated by the auto-ethnographies, were analysed using established techniques derived from grounded theory (see, e.g., Corbin & Strauss, 2015; Charmaz, 2014). Here the precise procedures used were that an initial content analysis generated 13 interconnected codes; these were then refined and grouped to create the recurring themes presented under research questions one and two below. The chapter now turns to discussion of the first of the three interlinked research questions that structure this chapter.

What learning occurred for the participating teacher educators during the Academy, and did that short-term learning contribute to longer-term and 'practice-relevant' learning back in the workplace for the participants' practice?

The formal report to the European Commission (Smith, 2019) records the Academy as an 'intensive learning experience' (p. 26) for the participants. It lists the learning outcomes as including: enhanced professional awareness, improved teaching skills and knowledge of professional literature, and increased awareness of their personal development trajectories. The thematic analysis across the two evaluations and the participant data show that the overall effect of the Academy was to offer those learning outcomes in three areas: 'identity forging'; personal practice, including the inter-relationships between teaching, research and scholarship; and recognising the importance of professional development. Some of this learning was initiated during the Academy itself, but it often generated new practice-relevant professional activity and growth back in the arena of practice, and the endurance of this learning is striking. There were certainly aspects of the Academy that were less positive, and these are also noted below.

Due to constraints of space in this chapter, only a summary of all these themes are presented below; for further details, readers are referred to the two evaluation reports (Kelchtermans & Deketelaere, 2019; Rust & Berry, 2019) on the InFo-TED website.

Identity forging

As Rust and Berry (2019) conclude in evaluating the Academy, 'the week enabled [the participants] to see and claim themselves as teacher educators' (p.

2). For some, this was a 'professional life changing' opportunity for identity development. For participant 3, it was 'inspiring, offering a rare chance [for] time to reflect on my own professional journey, which for me was the crossing over from being a teacher to a teacher educator in higher education'. Geert Kelchtermans's session on how teacher educators confront their own vision and identity was a key learning accelerator for her, leading to the reflection that we have multiple identities, which often overlap and can at times create a 'pedagogy of discomfort' (to explain, this term was used by Kelchtermans during the Academy, signalling that pedagogical change is not always easy or comfortable).

For this participant, a new teacher educator at the time, this work on identity development had both immediate and long-term effects. As she says, since participation in the Academy, 'I have developed more confidence in my new role and an understanding of its overlapping complexities. I am aware of the journey I am on to developing a new professional identity that reflects the nature of higher education'.

Developing personal practices in research-informed teaching

Identity development led to consideration of personal knowledge of teacher educators' work. In both the general evaluations, participants reported that knowledge and understanding of their practices and workplaces were challenged and reconceptualised. As participant 1 describes:

> First, my story[4] helped me to articulate what I knew of teacher education and of myself as a teacher educator. Next, it supported me in articulating what I did *not* yet know. Being in an environment that was full of expertise in relation to teacher education, my reflection seemed to sharpen and make clear what I did not [yet] know or possess as a teacher educator. This same environment, however, invited me instantly to recapture this and become aware of my own strengths.

For this participant, the Academy became a 'professional life changing opportunity' for 'an emergent transfer of new ideas… to be further explored and shared at the workplace back home'.

For participant 2, the diverse 'micro-communities of practice' formed during the Academy repeatedly allowed her to share interests, discuss concerns and reflect on the 'zipper' analogy for bringing together theory and practice (the 'zipper' or 'zipping' was used by Kelchtermans, as an analogy for teacher education practice in which theory and practice are 'zipped' together or brought together). She realised that:

> In order to merge the theory into practice, I would need to zip them together, so professional learning requires a conscious action to be taken, that is, enacting on what I took away from the sessions. If… conflict,

unease, problematisation… brings us to a pedagogical discomfort triggering a heightened self-awareness and close reflection I can learn so much during this discomfort. This part of the learning could… involve disconnecting from my previous learning and starting afresh. *un karning theme*

Following Engerström (2001), this may be seen as 'expansive learning': knowledge of practice is being remade and renewed; some previous knowledge is being questioned; this process is not simple or straightforward as it may bring discomfort. The end result is positive though, as it gives additional insights into pre-existing practice and knowledge. Thinking about her students' learning needs and comparing it to her own experiences, she asks:

> Isn't this the same for our student teachers too? What they take away from our professional sessions vary depending on their interpretive framework and as teacher educators, surely, we can support them explicitly in taking conscious action on it, that is, help them in zipping up.

Rust and Berry (2019) report that other teacher educators also 'wrote about (*future*) plans to integrate practices from the Academy into their teaching' (p. 3), again citing most frequently the storylines (in this activity, each teacher educator was encouraged to re-construct their professional history and to share it with others), voice over teaching, zipping (defined above), modelling and the idea of a pedagogy of discomfort (as defined above). The evaluators conclude then that it would seem that, after the event, 'how I teach is the message' is being carried over into practice; that is, they saw knowledge and practice moving from the Academy to the workplace, often in new and creative ways.

The importance of professional learning

Participation in the Academy also increased or enhanced commitments to professional learning in their own workplaces, both for themselves and for their colleagues. As participant 3 commented, 'There should always be a place in our busy work lives for our own personal and professional development. This is… key to our growth as individuals'. Participant 1 saw 'the experience of being in a multinational pool of teacher educators for days and getting to know each other's stories, showed me the importance of lifelong learning through drawing, reading, and discussing stories'. She described implementing changes in the way she worked with other teacher educators back in her workplace in order to ensure on-going professional cooperation and enhanced learning opportunities for them all. These changes included more team working and more regular sharing of practice.

Participant 3 said that learning provision was needed not least to alleviate 'some of the initial feelings of inadequacy that are common amongst teacher educators' and to improve teacher educators' own professional practice throughout their careers and hence will lead to better quality and experiences of their student teachers'.

Other participants were also convinced of the need for local and national learning programmes for teacher educators (Rust & Berry, 2019). In summary, participants' insights into the 'multi-layered phenomenon of professional development' were more conscious, concrete and complex, and their attitudes towards the importance of teacher educator learning were 'further grounded and strengthened' (Kelchtermans & Deketelaere, 2019, p. 6).

Differentiated experiences and outcomes

The findings here are largely positive but there were some less successful aspects of the Academy. Rust and Berry (2019) include one section on 'suggestions for improvement' in which some participants recommend 'spending less time on product oriented working in groups that may not have complete buy-in from all participants, particularly when the time allotted was too short to finish the product' (p. 12). Others note 'concerns about continuation of dialogue and support… that is, sustainability' (Rust & Berry, 2019, p. 12).

Sustainability was certainly one of the more difficult aims for the Academy to achieve. In effect, only one group achieved this through its long-term planning: its focus was on developing and researching practices to use new technologies in teaching; its members have since co-presented their emerging findings at an international conference; publication of a journal article is forthcoming; and plans for mutual visits are in place. Other groups have stayed in contact and engaged in some informal, shared activities, but it is fair to say that these groups are currently without clear plans for sustainability. *[handwritten: not a lot of sustainability]*

The VLE did not function as fully as intended. Rust and Berry (2019) noted participants' comments that the online engagement was 'helpful… for knowing who else was coming and giving them something of an idea of what to anticipate' (p. 15), but in general, use before and after the Academy was limited. This was disappointing, not least because the design principles tried to maximise ownership by participants.

Overall, the analysis of the Academy as a one-off event shows that, for many participants, it both generated short-term learning *and* had some legacy in contributing to further learning back in the workplace. New forms of learning, practice and identity clearly emerged during the 'immersion' in the learning environment provided by the event, and some of them evolved and grew back in the participants' workplaces. Here then, 'off-the job learning' had relevance for enhanced professional learning *in* the workplace; participants were active in co-creating and enacting new learning for themselves and colleagues during the event, but they then continued to develop that learning back in their own workplaces and immediate arenas of practice.

Having explored the first research question and indicated the forms of learning occurring at and after the Academy, the chapter now moves to consider learning structures.

What structures within the Academy facilitated learning, both short- and long-term?

In this analysis, the inter-linked structures within the Academy, which facilitated the integration of short-term formal and informal learning *away* from the workplace and some longer-term, largely informal, learning *in* the workplace, can be summarised as follows.

Firstly, all aspects of the event were informed by relevant research, both empirical and conceptual, on teacher educators' professional learning. They were also made as 'practice-relevant' as possible from the earliest stage of the design process. As Rust and Berry (2019) record, planned learning opportunities during the Academy provided focused 'curriculum content', incorporating cutting-edge teacher education research and deploying relevant and engaging pedagogies. These varied pedagogical methods aimed to provide models of the 'teach-as-you-preach' principle and to spark inspiration for personal practice back in the workplace. Participants were repeatedly asked to consider 'what does this mean for me in my practice?' and to reflect on how that practice, particularly their interrelated teaching and research roles, might change. Importantly, the programme was underpinned by clear values and conceptual principles for teacher educators' learning, as earlier chapters of this book indicate.

Secondly, the pan-European working groups were heterogeneous, deliberately set up to include participants from diverse professional backgrounds and contexts, and at different career points. The participants were then working amongst groups of teacher educators, identifying different experiences and varied learning needs in their storylines. Across this diversity of contexts, there were inevitably both similarities and differences. Key here was identification of tensions between what Kelchtermans and Deketelaere (2019) called 'different normative views on good (teacher) education' (p. 4) and professional beliefs and pedagogies. This led to rich discussions of differences and similarities in education policies and in forms of regulation and monitoring of teacher educators' practices. The working groups formed then diverse 'micro-communities of practice' (Murray, 2008). Overall, colleagues were mutually supportive, but at the same time ready to challenge, debate and critique. This happened through the swift generation of senses of community and trust within the groups, resulting in the building of 'a safe and yet constructively challenging learning environment' (Kelchtermans & Deketelaere, 2019, p. 3).

Thirdly, a degree of sustainability for individual learning was built into the Academy structures. Rust and Berry (2019) report that teacher educators 'wrote about [future] plans to integrate practices from the Summer Academy into their teaching' (p. 3), citing most frequently the storylines (see chapter 8 for further details). The evaluators conclude then that 'how I teach is the message' is being carried over into practice, with key ideas being transposed from the Academy to the workplace in new and creative ways.

All these structures together gave space for participants to stand back from their own arenas of practice in order to re-evaluate their existing identities and practices and to re-think their future personal and professional priorities. Many of these structures replicate those which Engestrom (2001) and Engestrom and Sannino (2010) see as characteristic of an expansive learning environment (as above, this is defined as an open and positive environment with the potential for expansive learning to take place). Using Engestrom's work, Fuller and Unwin (2004) identified the features of such environments. Using those features for analysis of the Academy's learning structures shows that it:

- gave experiences of immersion in a well-planned learning environment away from the workplace, giving time and 'mind space' for sustained reflection;
- adopted a multi-dimensional view of expertise;
- fostered breadth of learning through cross-national experiences and boundary crossings;
- used these experiences to enable the reanalysis and recreation of professional identities and practices;   '' υnleaɾn ˮ
- gave opportunities for engaging in heterogeneous micro-communities of practice which quickly formed high trust environments and in which collaboration was valued and knowledge and skills were developed; and
- focused on learning content and skills that had high relevance for the workplace and could generate further professional learning back in the arena of practice (p. 138).

Having explored the learning structures for the Academy that facilitated learning, the chapter now moves to consider the third and final research question. Here the move is far beyond the Academy itself to consider its wider implications. Right at the end of the chapter, there is, however, a 'loop back' to that powerful learning event.

What might the wider implications of this study be for designing professional learning opportunities?

The wider implications of this study about the InFo-TED Academy and the learning it produced are clearly limited by its small-scale and design. But it still raises important considerations for those designing and implementing professional development programmes using different forms of learning. A particular interest is in what facilitates the integration of short-term formal and informal learning *away* from the workplace in becoming an integrated and meaningful part of longer-term (and largely informal) learning *in* the arena of practice. And, how might different forms of professional development best be articulated to achieve learning with high relevance for teacher educators' practice. Following Vanassche and Kelchtermans (2014), this is not an attempt to identify 'best practices', but rather a preliminary sketch of ideas that may support research and practice into achieving the professional development of teacher educators.

Various issues stand out at this point: first and most importantly, the end purpose of any professional development for teacher educators should be to generate and sustain longer-term and 'practice-relevant' learning back in the participants' workplace. This learning needs to be authentic and meaningful if it is to be effective; it is about ensuring the quality of the teaching and research that teacher educators undertake alongside their pre-service students and serving teachers, mentors and teacher educator colleagues in both higher education institutions and schools. Fundamentally then, the quality of that professional learning has implications for the future in affecting how teacher educators teach and research. This in turn affects the quality of teaching and learning in schools; and that is, 'the ultimate horizon and justification' (Kelchtermans & Deketelaere, 2019, p. 5) for the design of all professional development for teacher educators.

Secondly, one conclusion from Czerniawski et al.'s (2017) large-scale survey of teacher educators' professional development needs, cited above, was that overall, participants expressed a strong preference for professional learning opportunities that are continuous and based around experiential learning' (p. 12). The Academy experience met these criteria in that it involved such learning and was continuous, albeit only across a limited time span of five days of highly concentrated learning. This inspired longer-term and relevant professional development plans back in participants' workplaces.

Another point is that the formation of micro-communities of practice was a key learning structure within the Academy. Working in communities of practice is, of course, an established form of professional learning for teacher educators (see, e.g., Brody & Hadar, 2018; Willemse et al., 2016). In the Academy, such groups were again successful, but these were small (not just communities but *micro-communities*), heterogeneous and high trust spaces in which participants were able to both support and challenge each other's ideas. Those communities built 'safe and yet constructively challenging learning environment(s)' (Kelchtermans & Deketelaere, 2019, p. 3). They were therefore able to form what Cochran-Smith et al. (2019), in the context of self-study research, call 'edgy critical communities', which found 'ways to get beneath the surface and interrogate their own and others' assumptions' (p. 17). Unless the design of future CoPs ensures these things, then the value of this form of learning may be limited to simply confirming current practice, and often not getting very far toward teacher educators' deep learning and unlearning (Cochran-Smith et al., 2019) and failing to contribute to shared knowledge about the professional development of teacher educators (Zeichner, 2007).

The learning structures within the Academy had a deliberately 'practice-relevant' design. This phrase is not used to imply a restricted focus on teacher educators' practices or the workplaces within which they take place, nor is it intended to imply a one-size-fits-all model for professional development. In a pan-European event attended by teacher educators from across Northern Europe and beyond, the heterogeneity of participants, their practices and working contexts were inevitable and welcome. As described above, this was also factored into the design for the Academy to create rich and well-structured opportunities for learning from differences and diversities, as well as from similarities and homogeneities. Here then the learning structures were, in important ways, both contextualised and decontextualised; within them, participants encountered both the known and the unknown, the familiar and the strange in terms of the multiple contexts for teacher educators' practices, the organisations and immediate arenas of practice and belief systems in which those practices occurred. These ideas of learning through both simultaneous contextualisation and decontextualisation are intriguing, not least because the easy assumption for making learning 'practice-relevant' is to situate it in familiar and therefore safe contexts, often 'boundaried' by national parameters. Further exploration of these ideas in the design of teacher educators' professional development would be timely.

As acknowledged above, the VLE designed to support the Academy did not function as fully as intended, despite its attempts to instantiate the principle of 'ownership' for its participants. Similar patterns of only partial engagement in online environments can be observed in other professional learning projects (see, e.g., Fowler et al., 2013). Nevertheless, it is impossible to imagine that professional development using multiple forms of technology will *not* be part of the future-scape of teacher educators' learning (Murray & Kidd, 2016). Learning using technological mediums can, of course, be a stand-alone mode, but here the interest is in the place technology can play in creating links between different modes of learning. Redesigned VLEs will play a part here, particularly in interlinking formal learning at face-to-face events and informal learning in the workplace.

Finally, as chapter 1 indicates, workplace learning for teacher educators is not well theorised compared to the strength found in other professional fields (McNamara et al., 2014). Developing this area of research is clearly important; that could well be achieved by drawing on the InFo-TED conceptual model of professional development (see chapter 2 of this book), alongside the ideas in this study.

Conclusion

Consideration of all the above issues could lead to the further development of effective forms of professional development for teacher educators, which is one of the long-term goals of InFo-TED. Overall, we believe that it is clearly important to listen to teacher educators' voices when designing authentic and high-quality professional development. Furthermore, teacher educators themselves, whether as individuals or as part of communities of practice, must be the drivers and owners of their professional learning trajectories and the key change agents (Cochran-Smith, 2005) within their own arenas of practice.

Seen as a tool for ripple effect

Finally, to complete the circle by returning to the starting points for this article, that is, the learning within the Academy itself and the issue of its long-evity, Rust and Berry's (2019) evaluation concludes that, 'the impact of the Summer Academy may, like a pebble thrown into a pond, have a ripple effect reaching and influencing the practice of teacher educators far beyond... [those] who participated in it' (p. 5). In terms of the success of the Academy and the long-term learning of the teacher educators involved in it, it is very much hoped that this will be so, but only time and longer-term evaluations will tell.

Notes

1 This term is used to signify the spaces and places where teacher educators work with their students, colleagues and mentors in higher education institutes and schools and where their practice occurs and is enacted.
2 This learning is defined here as being that which takes place alongside work, but is not the primary goal of that work.
3 For details of the data collection strategies for both evaluations, readers are referred to the original documents on the InFo-TED website (https://info-ted.eu/). Some of the supplementary data and the collection strategies for this chapter were originally reported in Kidd et al. (2019). Permission for the reproduction of the material has been obtained from the editor and publisher of this latter journal (*Research in Teacher Education*).
4 This is a reference to the 'storylines' activity reported in full in chapter 8. In this activity, each teacher educator was encouraged to reconstruct their professional history and to share it with others.

References

Brody, D., & Hadar, L. (2018). Critical moments in the process of educational change: understanding the dynamics of change among teacher educators. *European Journal of Teacher Education*. 41(1), 50–65.

Charmaz, K. (2014). *Constructing grounded theory*. SAGE.

Cochran-Smith, M. (2005) Teacher educators as researchers: Multiple perspectives. *Teaching and Teacher Education*, 21(2), 219–225.

Cochran-Smith, M. Grudnoff, L., Orland-Barak, L., & Smith, K. (2019). Educating teacher educators: international perspectives. *The New Educator*, 16(1), 5–24.

Corbin, J., & Strauss, A. (2015). *Basics of qualitative research: Grounded theory procedures and techniques*. SAGE.

Czerniawski, G., MacPhail, A., & Guberman, A. (2017). The professional development needs of higher education-based teacher educators: An international comparative needs analysis. *European Journal of Teacher Education*, 40(1), 127–140.

Engeström, Y. (2001). Expansive learning at work: Toward an activity theoretical reconceptualization. *Journal of Education and Work*, 14(1), 133–156.

Engeström, Y. (2015). *Learning by expanding: An activity-theoretical approach to developmental research* (2nd ed.). Cambridge University Press.

Engeström, Y., & Sannino, A. (2010). Studies of expansive learning: Foundations, findings and future challenges. *Educational Research Review*, 5(1), 1–24.

Fowler, Z., Stanley, G., Murray, J., Jones, M., & McNamara, O. (2013). Research capacity building with new technologies within new communities of practice: reflections on the first year of the Teacher Education Research Network. *International Journal of Professional Development*, 32(2), 182–203.

Fuller, A., & Unwin, L. (2004). Expansive learning environments: Integrating organisational and personal development. In H. Rainbird, A. Fuller, & A. Munro (Eds.), *Workplace learning in context* (pp. 126–144). Routledge.

Kelchtermans, G., & Deketelaere, A. (2019). *Output 7.1 evaluation report of the EPDP and the VLP*. International Forum for Teacher Educator Development.

Kidd, W., McMahon, A., & Viswarajan, S. (2019). Developing a pan-European approach to teacher educators' collaborative learning: Learning about, learning how and learning from. *Research in Teacher Education*, 9(2), 39–45.

Lunenberg, M., Dengerink, J., & Korthagen, F. (2014). *The professional teacher educator: Roles, behaviour, and professional development of teacher educators*. Sense Publishers.

McNamara, O., Murray, J., & M., Jones. (Eds.). (2014). *Workplace learning in teacher education*. Springer.

Murray, J. (2008). Teacher educators' induction into higher education: Work-based learning in the micro communities of teacher education. *European Journal of Teacher Education*, 31(2), 117–133.

Murray J., & Kidd, W. (Eds.). (2016). *Using emerging technologies to develop professional learning*. Routledge.

Murray, J., & Male, T. (2005). Becoming a teacher educator: Evidence from the field. *Teaching and Teacher Education*, 21(2), 107–115.

Rust, F., & Berry, A. (2019). *Output 7.2 evaluation report of the E-InFo-TED Project*. Norwegian University of Science and Technology.

Smith, K. (2019). *E-InFo-TED: Final report of the Erasmus+ Funded Project, produced for the European Commission*. International Forum for Teacher Educator Development.

Vanassche, E., & Kelchtermans, G. (2014). Teacher educators' professionalism in practice: Positioning theory and personal interpretative framework. *Teaching and Teacher Education*, 44, 117–127.

Willemse, M., Boeil, F., & Pillen, M. (2016). Fostering teacher educators' professional development on practice-based research through communities of inquiry. *Vocations and Learning*, 9, 85–110.

Zeichner, K. (2007). Accumulating Knowledge across self-studies in teacher education. *Journal of Teacher Education*, 58(1), 36–46.

Chapter 12

Influencing professional development at national levels

Learning from reciprocity and diversity

Jean Murray, Ann MacPhail, Paulien C. Meijer, Helma Oolbekkink-Marchand, Marit Ulvik and Ainat Guberman

Introduction

This chapter focuses on analysing the influence the International Forum for Teacher Educator Development (InFo-TED) project has had to date in four national contexts. Dissemination, impact and sustainability are key concepts in developing and implementing professional initiatives of any kind. This trio of interlinked concepts illustrates the required dimensions for all European Commission (EC) grants, including the Erasmus+ scheme, which funded InFo-TED. Current guidance on this scheme defines impact as the effect of Erasmus+ activity on individuals, organisations and society, and dissemination as 'essentially communicating the project outcome and successes to ensure that the results are conveyed as widely as possible' (EC, 2019, p. 37) and sustainability as 'the potential for the continuation of the project's activities, outcomes, and impacts after the Erasmus+ funding has finished' (EC, 2019, p. 35). Furthermore, this last term can also refer to 'the integration of results and innovation into the management or pedagogy of participating organisations and... new curricula' (EC, 2019, p. 37). The guidance states that 'impact and dissemination are key parts of any Erasmus+ project, and are contractual obligations' (EC, 2019, p. 8). These criteria are also central evaluation criteria when judging the quality of applications.

These requirements meant that means of achieving dissemination, impact and sustainability were built into the InFo-TED project from its inception. Dissemination, for example, was widespread and systematic, and repeated attempts were made to engage policy makers and stakeholders. For example, in addition to the regular presentation of research at academic conferences, the Info-TED project planned for a number of transnational events to achieve these things. Formal events included organising three transnational meetings – or multiplier events – for policy makers in Scandinavia, the Low Countries, and the British and Celtic Isles (InFo-TED, 2019; Rust & Berry, 2019). These seminars were attended by a total of 78 policy makers. There were also two meetings in Brussels attended by 41 pan-European policy makers. The group held an invited seminar for the European Educational Research Association in Bolzano, Italy, in September 2018. The event was attended by more than 45 stakeholders and policy makers in teacher education from 18 different countries, 11 in Europe (including European nations as diverse as Poland, Denmark and Spain) and seven, wider international nations, including Japan, Hong Kong, Australia and Canada.

But dissemination and engagement do not necessarily add up to impact and long-term sustainability; both of these things are much more difficult to achieve. This is not to say that the InFo-TED project did not have any impact or was not sustainable. Rather, as the final report to the European Commission (Smith, 2019) shows, the project did achieve some degrees of both measures. For example, by the end of the funded project on 31 August 2019, the website had received nearly 44,000 views from 170 countries, with the largest number of searches coming from India.

As Penfield et al. (2014) point out, however, the concept of impact is generally difficult to define, and there are distinct challenges around understanding and evaluating it. In particular, they point to issues around how to capture impact including its developmental nature and the associated time lags, its attribution, the concept of 'knowledge creep' and the multiple ways of capturing rigorous evidence. The sustainability of research-led initiatives has also gained attention from funders in recent years, with emphases on the longer-term endurance of project outcomes on the target educational areas or structures.

In a complex and multi-faceted project such as InFo-TED, we acknowledge how difficult it is to 'prove' more extensive impact, particularly given the general issues of time lag and the collection of relevant evidence. We would therefore stress that it is not our intention to provide 'hard indicators' or 'measurable outputs' of InFo-TED's impact and sustainability in the case study countries. Rather we deliberately use the word 'influence' here, but only in the sense of identifying the effects which these ideas have upon pre-existing national contexts and without any of the connotations of power or moral ascendancy which that word can imply (definitions from the Oxford English Dictionary; Oxford, n.d.).

A further point is that, as earlier chapters of this book have indicated, InFo-TED is not an institution but a forum where teacher educators meet, exchange ideas and work together on projects to inspire and support their own professional development and that of others. This is a reciprocal process; members share their experiences with and research on professional development initiatives in their countries with others. The relevance of the new ideas and knowledge generated in the forum may then be further developed to create new initiatives or enhance existing provision in ways relevant to their own national contexts. In a sense then, InFo-TED functions as a kind of seedbed in which ideas about authentic professional development can germinate and grow.

Finally, we acknowledge that there are limitations to this study: these are not case studies in the conventional sense, not least because they reflect the differential uptake of the InFo-TED project in the countries. Furthermore, because this chapter was co-researched by six people closely involved in the project, we need to acknowledge our positionality[1].

In this chapter, we refer to four European case studies within the project. First, Ireland has a new National Teacher Education and Teacher Educator Forum that gives collective support for teacher educators' learning. Then, the Netherlands has the Dutch Association for Teacher Educators (VELON), which has long engaged with stakeholders to develop professional development opportunities for teacher educators in schools, colleges, and universities. These activities are of particular significance since VELON's activities were founding influences for InFo-TED. Our next case studies are from Norway and Israel, where the work of InFo-TED aligns with, and at some points enhances, existing structures and policies for ensuring the diversity and high-quality of teacher educators' professional development activities.

In each case study country, these initiatives aimed to engage a range of stakeholders and policy to create national professional learning communities. Influence was, of course, achieved from differing starting points in each of these countries; nevertheless, our analysis points to some common factors in achieving this measure across the cases. Having acknowledged the limitations around the case studies, we start our analysis with the new structures emerging in Ireland.

goal is to get important people on board

Case study 1: the influence of InFo-TED in Ireland

There were no pan-national initiatives to support teacher educators' professional development in Ireland prior to the start of the InFo-TED project, but involvement in that project, led to the development of the National Teacher Education and Teacher Educator Forum (denoted as 'Forum'). Notable in this development was the use of professional connections made between Irish and Israeli InFo-TED Council members[2] (see below for further details).

Using Erasmus funding for reciprocal visits, two teacher educators on the InFo-TED Council and based at the University of Limerick arranged a visit to the MOFET Institute in Israel in May 2017. MOFET colleagues were then invited to present their work and institute infrastructure to teacher educators in Ireland in November 2017. That meeting then provided the impetus to hold the inaugural meeting of the Forum where the approximately 70 Irish teacher educators in attendance discussed common interests and requirements. These included: a clear interest in an inclusive networking space; the need for a collective voice and collective consideration of the teacher education continuum to inform teacher education; an acknowledgement of the necessity for resource pooling and institutional support; and the centrality of pre-service teachers and school placement. There was unanimous support from attendees for the notion that working as a collective and collaborative group could possibly establish a platform for teacher education that would inform both current and future teacher education policies. *work was started in Ireland*

Three teacher educators from different universities are currently responsible for the facilitation of the Forum, with one of them also being central to the work of the InFo-TED Council. Since its inception in November 2017, the Forum has held biannual seminars in October/November and March/April. ①
Each seminar lasts for one day; any member can offer to host it. The purpose of these events is firstly, to discuss issues and developments in Teacher Education and, resulting from those discussions, to formulate position/discussion papers that can contribute to teacher education in Ireland; and secondly, to engage in ② professional development activities for teacher educators across the career continuum. It has 140 teacher educators on a Forum mailing list, capturing the names of those who have attended at least one of the seminars to date.

The second development within the Forum was the establishment of special interest groups (SIGs) as small groups of teacher educators with an interest in a specific area of teacher education. Two of these SIGs – 'school placement in Initial Teacher Education (ITE)' and 'criteria for accreditation of ITE programmes' – led the discussions at the first two seminars. The third SIG, 'teacher education and teacher educator identity', was proposed at the October 2018 seminar and has had a presence at subsequent seminars.

The Forum has gained momentum in being approached to provide perspectives from teacher educators generally and, in particular, being proactive in submitting responses to teacher education related (policy) developments. In April 2018, a joint higher education institution position paper exploring school placement challenges was submitted to the national Teaching Council, which is the professional standards body in Ireland for the teaching profession that promotes and regulates professional standards in teaching. The position paper was prepared by teacher education colleagues across nine Irish teacher education institutes. *outcomes*

In November 2018, the Forum furnished a report in response to a request to attend the Teaching Council and provide a teacher education perspective on issues that were being considered for the future reconfiguration of teacher education programmes. These issues were: school placements, ITE programme structures and mandatory areas, and research and portfolios. In the same month, the Forum was invited by the Information and Communications Technology (ICT) Policy Unit of the Department of Education and Skills (DES) to propose three to four members who would meet with the Implementation Advisory Group subgroup with a view to setting up a working group to examine and progress the Digital Strategy for Schools. A key objective of the Digital Strategy for Schools (2015–2020) is to embed digital technologies across the continuum of teacher education, that is, ITE, induction and continuous professional development. A key action in this regard is to cooperate with ITE providers to ensure that pre-service teachers acquire the skills, knowledge and confidence to use digital technologies to support teaching and learning in their classroom practice.

In May 2019, the Forum was formally made aware that the Teacher Education Policy Unit is commencing work on the preparation of an overarching policy statement on ITE, which will help bring together, in one place, a picture of the many different issues that impact on ITE provision in Ireland. In response to the call for submissions from the DES to a policy statement for ITE, the co-facilitators of the Forum made a submission in September 2019 to comment on two of the 'overarching themes' identified in the call that have been a focus of attention in the Forum: student placements and connections to schools, and teacher educators. In December 2019, informed by its November 2019 meeting, the Forum made a submission in response to a consultation document from the Teaching Council that set out standards for ITE, including school placement. The report presented a summary of the related Forum discussion, with particular reference to school placements, staffing of ITE programmes and research.

In summary, it can be said that the impact of the InFo-TED project on development in and on teacher education in Ireland has been significant, notably through the development of the Forum. Since its establishment in 2017, the Forum has created a space for supporting the professional development of teacher educators through networking and policy influencing. Importantly, it has also contributed a new collective voice on shaping national teacher education and related research discourse (MacPhail & O'Sullivan, 2019). Overall, the Forum has enhanced consciousness that professional responsibility demands 'keeping open spaces and opportunities' (Solbrekke & Sugrue, 2014, p. 19) to articulate as a community the purposes and the values of the work of teacher educators and thereby shape the discourses of reform of research and teacher education nationally and internationally.

Case study 2: the influence of InFo-TED in the Netherlands

In the Netherlands, the Dutch Association for Teacher Educators (VELON) was established in 1975 with three-fold aims: being a meeting platform for teacher educators, stimulating the professionalization of both individual teacher educators and their professional community, and looking after the concerns of that community, in which quality is paramount. This association has also been responsible for the creation of a professional standard and for the certification of teacher educators; it has been the catalyst for the development of a knowledge base and several professional learning programmes for teacher educators. It could be said that in the Netherlands, after some decades of work, many features of an encompassing professional development system (Ingvarsson, 1998) are now in existence. This may be an important reason why, in the international survey of teacher educators' professional development needs (see chapter 3; Czerniawski et al., 2017), Dutch teacher educators recorded relatively high satisfaction rates with the learning opportunities available to them, compared to their international colleagues.

The strength and longevity of this national focus on teacher educators' professional development has meant that the reciprocity between the Dutch experiences and the InFo-TED initiatives has been inspiring. A notable influence on the early work of InFo-TED was the work of Lunenberg et al. (2014), which pointed to the diversity of roles teacher educators fulfil and the importance of professional development. This work also played a role in the professional development programme at VU University Amsterdam, which focuses on so-called second order pedagogy (Koster et al., 2008; Murray, 2002) as an approach to pedagogy in teacher education.

Dutch participants in the InFo-TED project could then build on existing structures and networks in which teacher educators' professional development, professionalism and work were already 'live' topics of discussion. The influence of InFo-TED in the Netherlands took place mainly through three key Dutch individuals involved in the Council and its activities.

The first individual, an InFo-TED council member, belongs to the Board of VELON. Hence, board meetings have discussed the policy implications of the InFo-TED White Paper (InFo-TED, 2019). This analysis was enriched by the additional reflections of another Dutch VELON member, originally given at one of the InFo-TED policy meetings with pan-European policy makers and stakeholders, mentioned above (Brussels, May 2019). An increasing awareness of the importance of teacher educator professionalism and professional development can also be found in policy discussions by key stakeholders in various other national fora. For example, another Dutch InFo-TED Council member sits on the Inter-university Council of University-based Teacher Education, where similar discussions have focused on these issues.

The second individual inspired a spin-off based on the experiences of Dutch teacher educators during the Summer Academy (see chapter 8). Dutch participants developed their practices as teacher educators and/or as educators of teacher educators. For example, one person, together with a group of international colleagues, developed a pedagogy for 'dealing with discomfort' as a teacher educator. The aim here was to encourage dialogue between teacher educators about their professional identities, starting from tensions they experienced in their daily practices. A participant developed a pedagogy called 'the diamond' that aims to look at the experience of 'being a teacher educator' from various angles. This pedagogy encourages early career teacher educators to discuss the goals of teacher education collaboratively, and thereby to raise awareness of the diversity of those goals and to encourage new educators to take a 'preliminary stance' (Aardema & Elvira, 2020). These pedagogies have since been shared and enacted during national and international meetings and conferences (Meijer et al., 2019).

For the third participant, the Summer Academy proved to be a valuable preparation for becoming the new coordinator of the revised VU professional development programme for teacher educators. The InFo-TED conceptual model has been introduced to participants there. Dutch participation in the InFo-TED Summer Academy also led to an increasing number of blogs and conference contributions on aspects of teacher educators' work in the

Netherlands. For example, the 18 Dutch blogs, posted on the Info-TED website (see chapter 6), cover a wide range of topics, including ICT (Walraven, 2018), voice-over teaching for teacher educators (Oldeboom, 2018) and the VELON registration trajectory (Timmermans, 2019).

A third spin-off from the InFo-TED project is the multiplier event for the Low Countries (see above), planned to connect people involved in the professional development of teacher educators. In addition to representatives from VELON and the Flemish Association for Teacher Educators (VELOV) in Flanders, responsible for professional development trajectories in both countries, this included representatives from the Ministries of Education and stakeholders involved in policy making in pan-European teacher education. The already strong national networks of teacher educator professionalism in the Netherlands and Flanders expanded further after this meeting.

In summary, in the Netherlands the InFo-TED project was able to contribute to and strengthen on-going work on teacher educators' professional development, as well as contribute to national agendas to strengthen professionalism. Looking to the future work of InFo-TED, we recognise the importance of connecting wider European and Dutch networks for teacher educators, not least through sharing pedagogies for professional development. Making these public, for example through blogs, contributes to the visibility of the work and pedagogies of teacher educators and shows policy makers and other stakeholders the complexities of our work.

Although work on the professional development of teacher educators in the Netherlands is relatively well developed, most initiatives are loosely coupled and their interrelationships are often based on personal connectivity, rather than sustained organisational networks. More time is needed to deploy these contributions into a stable knowledge infrastructure. It should also to be taken into account that the Dutch system of state governance and lump-sum funding gives a lot of autonomy to institutions and professional groups to set their own standards. Overall, a key point from the Netherlands then is that influencing policy takes time.

Case study 3: the influence of InFo-TED in Norway

In Norway, as in the Netherlands, the InFo-TED project has aligned with and in some ways strengthened an ongoing development in supporting teacher educators' professional development. Notably, Norway has had a National Research School in Teacher Education (NAFOL) since 2010. The government has also funded formal education for mentors as school-based educators for 20 years. InFo-TED has had influence on both of these areas of development, but here we focus on the former initiative.

To contextualise, Norway has had a range of reforms within teacher education in which the importance of both the academic and the practical components of teacher education have been emphasised. Mirroring the Europe-wide 'university turn' (Murray, 2015) identified in chapter 1, many university colleges have now become universities through mergers. University affiliation or aspirations have created pressures on individuals and institutions to adapt to the conventional academic expectations of the university sector. Moreover, all teacher education has now moved to master's level, and teacher educators are expected to supervise student teachers' research-based theses. Many teacher educators, especially at university colleges, were ill-equipped to undertake such supervision.

To prepare for the 2017 reform, NAFOL was established in 2010 as a partnership, with nearly all teacher education institutions in Norway working together to support teacher educators in gaining doctorates (Cochran-Smith et al., 2019). NAFOL recognises teacher educators' unique position in academia by offering specialised education for teacher educators who want to achieve a PhD.

The leader of InFo-TED between 2013 and 2019 was also the leader of NAFOL. This meant that the InFo-TED project could align with NAFOL as an ongoing professional development. This influence has been felt in a variety of ways. Firstly, teacher educators, leaders of teacher education institutions and policy makers have become more aware of teacher educators as a unique professional group through a range of InFo-TED activities. These included the multiplier event for the Scandinavian countries in 2018, regional seminars, the Summer Academy in Trondheim in 2018 and the website (https://info-ted. eu). There have also been many presentations of InFo-TED work at conferences and seminars in Norway and the other Nordic countries.

Secondly, InFo-TED research has contributed to Norwegian research about teacher educators in the form of articles that have put the topic more firmly on the agenda in Norway. Thirdly, Norwegian policy makers have participated in and learned from InFo-TED policy events, including the pan-Scandinavia meeting in Bergen in 2018 and two pan-European seminars in Brussels in 2017 and 2019.

Accelerated by NAFOL and InFo-TED then, there is a growing understanding in Norway of teacher educators' multiple responsibilities, but there are also challenges when it comes to meeting diverse and sometimes seemingly conflicted professional development imperatives. For example, to obtain a permanent position in teacher education in Norway today, a doctorate is normally required (Elstad, 2010), and research production is often what receives recognition and promotion. Unsurprisingly then, teacher educators themselves are often concerned about their professional development needs (Finne et al., 2014). The InFo-TED survey findings for Norway show that this development is needed to increase their research competence, even when a majority of the participants held a doctorate (Czerniawski et al., 2017).

Other contextual changes in Norway mean that teacher educators are also expected to maintain a proximity to the practice field. Notable here is the new national curricula for teacher education, which has created more homogeneity across programmes and led to more time spent in field placements. Many

Norwegian teacher educators also face increasing demands from student teachers, schools and policy makers for 'relevance' in their programmes (Elstad, 2010).

Recent reports show, for example, that Norwegian student teachers often criticise their teacher educators' teaching competence and the relevance of teacher education (Ulvik & Smith, 2019). This can be challenging for teacher educators, as many of those entering higher education in recent years have no experience as schoolteachers (Ulvik & Smith, 2019). This means that even whilst Norwegian teacher educators place high value on research, they also want to develop their teaching and their contacts with schools, recognising that their work is multifaceted.

A final issue for Norwegian teacher education to address is that there is no formal induction phase for new teacher educators, rather professional learning on entry to teacher education relies on ad hoc and self-initiated learning in the workplace (Cochran-Smith, et al, 2019). There is then work to be done in a number of ways in strengthening and interlinking professional development priorities for the multifaceted roles of teacher educators in Norway. InFo-TED, working alongside NAFOL and its participating universities, has strong potential to support this future work.

Case study 4: the influence of InFo-TED in Israel

Of our four case study countries, Israel has the most systematic support system for teacher educators and their professional development. Nevertheless, InFo-TED has still had considerable influence on the augmentation of existing provision. To provide a context here, the MOFET Institute was founded in 1983 by the Israeli Ministry of Education to contribute to the professionalization of teacher education and to support teacher educators' professional development. MOFET is thus positioned at the nexus between academia, the educational system and politicians. From there, it works with all teacher education institutes to develop programmes for teacher education, offer teacher educators diverse learning opportunities and implement relevant research policies. It also hosts over 30 Communities of Practice (CoP), deploying these as a chosen model for teacher educators' professional development (Brody & Hadar, 2018).

All these activities have multiple interactions with those of InFo-TED. Notably, involvement in InFo-TED has assisted MOFET to develop its pan-European professional networks, enabling Israeli teacher educators and policy makers to benefit from wide sources of international expertise. Here formal activities have included supporting Israeli teacher educators' participation in InFo-TED's Summer Academy and sponsoring a group of early career leaders in teacher education to visit Ireland and meet Irish InFo-TED members. During the latter visit, the MOFET group looked at how the Irish educators combined teaching and close-to-practice research, and analysed how multiple stakeholder perspectives play out in teacher education policymaking in Ireland.

As a spin-off from the Summer Academy, there were two presentations of InFo-TED research at a recent MOFET conference. Other InFo-TED Council members have also visited MOFET to share their knowledge and experience, and one of the project evaluators has been appointed to advise Israeli policy makers on devising coherent, residency-based and rigorous teacher preparation programmes.

A further area of InFo-TED influence has been in the area of professional development for school-based teacher educators. In Israel, these people perform diverse roles, including being: a cooperating teacher who supervises student tea- *close* chers' work; a mentor who coaches beginning teachers; a leader of teachers' CoPs; and a coordinator of disciplinary (subject) studies at their respective school. *proximity*

As chapter 3 of this book details, because of the paucity of research on school-based teacher educators' professional development, in 2019 InFo-TED initiated an international survey for this group. One InFo-TED member at MOFET has been centrally involved with planning and implementing this survey, and the initiative has been supported by policy makers who believe that the results will help Israel to improve current induction and on-the-job support programmes for school-based teacher educators. Here the work of InFo-TED has been supplemented by Israeli participation in another European Erasmus+ project (named *Promentors*) that aims to create a new model for mentors' education. Together, it is hoped that experience gained from participation in these two European projects will result in innovative mentor preparation and professional development programmes in Israel.

The Israeli Ministry of Education has now initiated study days for policy makers to analyse conceptualisations of mentoring in teacher education throughout teachers' careers, starting with recruiting student teacher candidates and culminating in mentoring educational leaders. The aim of this initiative is to consolidate role definitions, qualifications, preparation and professional development for mentors, and the integration of mentoring into the education system. This initiative is informed by InFo-TED's model, viewing teacher education as a career-long process.

Furthermore, insights from InFo-TED research and publications are assisting MOFET with the construction of both theoretical and practical conceptualisations beyond mentoring of all school-based teacher educators' work. Such conceptualisations are needed in Israeli teacher education to clarify the following: similarities and differences the varied roles within this group of teacher educators; the types of knowledge, skills and values that those different roles require; and whether there is a recommended 'chronological' order of those roles when working with pre-service teachers. Here part of MOFET's role has been to mediate InFo-TED's conceptualisations and accumulated knowledge for Israeli teacher educators and for policy makers in the Ministry of Education. In return, MOFET members on the InFo-TED Council have been able to discuss with international colleagues the lessons learned from these national initiatives, set within their established and longstanding infrastructures for Israeli teacher educators' professional development.

Conclusion

Our case studies show that the InFo-TED project has had positive influences in the four focus countries, sometimes aligning with on-going initiatives or strengthening existing provision, and sometimes generating new activities. In Ireland, where there was no pre-existing, nationwide group focusing on teacher educators' professional development, the project led to the creation of a new National Forum. This now gives collective support for Irish teacher educators' voices and learning. In the Netherlands, the InFo-TED project became integrated alongside national priorities and developments, in part within VELON, enhancing previous work. Here, there were also new initiatives with stakeholders to create and publicise innovative pedagogies and senses of agency for teacher educators' professional development.

Whilst Norway does not have the same kind of strong professional interest group as VELON in the Netherlands, it does have a unique national investment in teacher educators' professional development, notably NAFOL. Again, the work of InFo-TED has been able to align with this pre-existing structure and the associated policies. This same pattern can be seen in Israel; of our four case studies, this is the country with the most systematic and long-term infrastructure for supporting teacher educators' professional development. But here, the influences of InFo-TED included the further development of professional networks, enabling Israeli teacher educators and policy makers to benefit from wide sources of pan-European expertise. Research and policy development on conceptualising school-based teacher educators' roles were also informed and enriched by InFo-TED work, including its conceptual model and the forthcoming, international survey on this group's learning needs (see chapter 3).

There is still work to be done in each of these contexts, of course. In Ireland, the Forum needs a social media and online presence to alert teacher educators to its work and the opportunities for contributions. It also needs funding on a more systematic level. On-going conversations between the Forum and the heads of Schools of Education in Irish institutes will help to identify the professional challenges ahead, including how all stakeholders with an interest in teacher education could work collectively to address these. In the Netherlands, the lack of recognition for teacher educators' multi-faceted roles and the consequent devaluation of their expertise is still a live issue. In Norway, discussions are underway about the development of future plans to strengthen national support systems for teacher educators' research competence. Systematic and nationwide induction support for all new teacher educators is also an issue. And in Israel, important work is still on-going to develop professional learning provision for all types of school-based educators.

An analysis of specific factors involved in achieving the successes shown in the case studies indicates the following patterns. First, the work of InFo-TED was often aligned alongside any existing structures, policies and practices for teacher educators' development, creating a sense of congruence and integration with existing national priorities. Second, where there was innovation, as in the creation of the Irish Forum and the forging of new pedagogies in the Netherlands, there was also a strong sense of coherence with existing professional values and agendas. Third, some of this work was undertaken by key actors in each national teacher education context, whose knowledge ensured their abilities to align the InFo-TED work in relevant ways. Fourth, the key actors in each context were able to enrich their work and that of their national colleagues by drawing on strong international networks, forged within InFo-TED and beyond. Fifth, the positionality of those actors meant that they had good connections with key stakeholders and policy makers in their countries of origin. These enabled them to ensure high levels of communication between educational researchers and practitioners, as well as policy makers institutionally and nationally.

The chapter shows how an international project such as InFo-TED can align with and enhance provision within national systems. It is also apparent that connections can be built across congruent national activities and networks in order to facilitate the professional development of teacher educators internationally. We are therefore confident in our claim that the project, to date, has had definite influence in these four national contexts. We maintain that those influences, particularly when they are reciprocal and generative, are important and meaningful legacies for any project. We acknowledge, however, that achieving such influence on existing infra-structures, practices and policies for teacher educators' professional development takes time. This is true even with a strong and viable project, such as InFo-TED, propelled by the concerted efforts of key agents and stakeholders.

Notes

1 In conventional social science research traditions, this positionality would not be seen as a strength of the research. In other traditions for educational research, however, including self-study research, it could be reinterpreted as reinforcing the findings.
2 Conversations with Dutch colleagues were also important here.

References

Aardema, A., & Elvira, Q. (2020). Opvattingen van beginnende lerarenopleiders over het opleiden van toekomstige leraren: de diamant als werkvorm [Visions of beginning teacher educators on teaching student teachers: the diamond as a teaching format]. *Tijdschrift voor lerarenopleiders, 41*(2), 78–86.

Brody, D. L., & Hadar, L. L. (2018). Critical moments in the process of educational change: Understanding the dynamics of change among teacher educators. *European Journal of Teacher Education, 41*(1), 50–65.

Cochran-Smith, M. Grudnoff, L., Orland-Barak, L., & Smith, K. (2019). Educating teacher educators: International perspectives. *The New Educator, 16*(1), 5–24.

Czerniawski, G., Guberman, A., & MacPhail, A. (2017). The professional developmental needs of higher education-based teacher educators: An international comparative needs analysis. *European Journal of Teacher Education, 40*(1), 127–140.

Elstad, E. (2010). University-based teacher education in the field of tension between the academic world and practical experience in school: A Norwegian case. *European Journal of Teacher Education*, 33(4), 361–374.

European Commission. (2019). Key action 203 (KA203). Guide for applicants: Erasmus+ 2020 Call. Strategic Partnership Projects for Higher Education. https://www.erasmusplus.org.uk/file/28499/download.

Finne, H., Mordal, S., & Stene, T. M. (2014). *Oppfatninger av studiekvalitet i lærerutdanningene 2013* [Perceptions of study quality in teacher education 2013]. Stiftelsen for industriell og teknisk forskning. https://www.sintef.no/globalassets/upload/teknologi_og_samfunn/teknologiledelse/sintef_1127901_oppfatninger-av-studiekvalitet-i-larerutdanningene-2013.pdf.

Ingvarson, L. (1998). Professional development as the pursuit of professional standards: The standard-based professional development system. *Teachers and Teaching*, 14(1), 127–140.

The International Forum for Teacher Educator Development. (2019). The Importance of teacher educators: Professional development imperatives [White paper]. https://info-ted.eu/wp-content/uploads/2019/10/InFo-TED-White-Paper.pdf.

Koster, B., Dengerink, J., Korthagen, F., & Lunenberg, M. (2008). Teacher educators working on their own professional development: Goals, activities and outcomes of a project for the professional development of teacher educators. *Teachers and Teaching*, 14(5–6),567–587.

Lunenberg, M., Dengerink, J., & Korthagen, F. (2014). *The professional teacher educator: Roles, behaviour, and professional development of teacher educators*. Springer.

MacPhail, A., & O'Sullivan, M. (2019). Challenges for Irish teacher educators in being active users and producers of research. *European Journal of Teacher Education*, 42(4), 492–506.

Meijer, P. C., Oldeboom, B., McMahon, A., Rust, F., Oolbekkink, H., Calderon, A., Kleeman, S., Placklé, I., & Dufloo, F. (2019, July 1–5). *Reflection in collaboration as heuristic for teacher educator development: An international case study* [Conference presentation]. Biennial Conference of the International Study Association on Teachers and Teaching (ISATT), Sibiú, Romania.

Murray, J. (2002). Between the chalkface and the ivory towers? A study of the professionalism of teacher educators working on primary initial teacher education courses in the English education system. *Collected Original Resources in Education (CORE)*, 26, 1–550.

Murray, J. (2015). Teacher education and higher education. In G. Beauchamp, L. Clarke, M. Hulme, M. Jephcote, A. Kennedy, G. Magennis, I. Menter, J. Murray, T. Mutton, T. O'Doherty, & G. Peiser (Eds.), *Teacher education in times of change* (1st ed., pp. 179–200). Policy Press.

Oldenboom, B. (2018, November 5). 'Voice-over teaching' for teacher educators. *International Forum for Teacher Educator Development*. https://info-ted.eu/voice-over-teaching-for-teacher-educators/.

Oxford English Dictionary. https://www.oed.com/view/Entry/95520?rskey=aKLgPO&result=2&isAdvanced=false#eid.

Penfield, T., Baker, M., Scoble, R., & Wykes, M. (2014). Assessment, evaluations, and definitions of research impact: A review. *Research Evaluation*, 23(1), 21–32.

Rust, F., & Berry, A. (2019). *Output 7.2 evaluation report of the E-InFo-TED Project*. Norwegian University of Science and Technology.

Smith, K. (2019). *E-InFo-TED: Final report of the Erasmus+ Funded Project.* International Forum for Teacher Educator Development.

Solbrekke, T. D., & Sugrue, C. (2014). Professional accreditation of initial teacher education programmes: Teacher educators' strategies: Between 'accountability' and 'professional responsibility'? *Teaching and Teacher Education, 37,* 11–20.

Timmermans, M. (2019, November 17). Registration deepens and connects. *International Forum for Teacher Educator Development.* https://info-ted.eu/registration-deepens-and-connects/.

Ulvik, M., & Smith, K. (2019). Preparing for professionalism in teaching - a Norwegian perspective. In J. Murray, A. Swennen, & C. Kosnik (Eds.), *International research, policy and practice in teacher education: Insider perspective.* Springer.

Walraven, A. (2018, June 29). Professionally developing teacher educators with regard to ICT. *International Forum for Teacher Educator Development* /https://info-ted.eu/professionally-developing-teacher-educators-with-regard-to-ict/.

Chapter 13

Teacher educators' professional development

Looking to the future

Ruben Vanderlinde, Kari Smith, Jean Murray and Mieke Lunenberg

Introduction

With the publication of this book, the International Forum for Teacher Educator Development (InFo-TED) aims to share its seven years of learning with a broader public, that is, everybody involved in supporting teacher educators' professional development. The book offers an evidence-based way of looking at teacher educators' professional development that will guide policy makers, academics, practitioners and all other stakeholders involved in providing professional development for teacher educators or in researching this area.

The 12 previous chapters have drawn together research and professional initiatives in the field and used these strands to contribute new and valuable knowledge and understanding. Those chapters variously pay attention to issues including conceptual elaborations, empirical data results, insights from concrete professional development initiatives, the voices and trajectories of teacher educators, and the connections between national and international policies and initiatives.

The book is academically rigorous on the one hand, and practice and policy relevant on the other. It aims to inform and inspire researchers who want to explore the professional development of teacher educators; to inform and inspire practitioners involved in the design, implementation and evaluation of professional learning opportunities; and to inform and inspire policy makers with ingredients for developing systematic and structural plans for the professional development of teacher educators.

As teacher educators educate the next generation of teachers, they need ample and rigorous attention by those policy makers. This became very clear while writing this concluding chapter in a year when the educational system on a global level was confronted with unseen challenges. Although not the focus of this book, the effects of the Covid-19 crisis and the Black Lives Matter movement urge teacher educators to rethink their professional practices and to formulate responses to global problems. Society is clearly looking to teacher educators as people who are shaping the education of the future and as professionals who can formulate answers about a range of questions including implementing distance education on an institutional scale, providing anti-racist education to support social diversity and organising blended learning in class-rooms and/or homes. This book then can be seen as a public statement in which teacher educators and their professional learning and practices are finally placed at the heart of the debate about the future of education.

The book takes the stance that teacher educators are characterised by second order professionalism (Murray, 2002) with multiple identities and different roles (Lunenberg et al., 2014; see also chapters 1 and 2), which require their own specific conceptual language. This book embraces the recognition and positive appreciation of the complexity, messiness and unpredictability that characterises teaching and teacher education (see chapter 2). As such, this stance is a counterbalance to documents that describe teacher education (and teacher educators) as a problem, or define teacher educators in a technical-rational or instrumental way.

This final chapter presents some of the recurring themes and issues discussed in the previous chapters, clearly looking to the future and redirecting attention again to academics, policy makers and practitioners. In this context, it becomes clear that a real and international community (with special issues in journals and with conferences) has grown over the last ten years, with different stakeholders involved in the planning, design, implementation and evaluation of professional development initiatives for teacher educators. In this growth, InFo-TED may have acted as a catalyst. The foci, discussed below, that we have found impor-tant for the future are (a) school-based mentors, (b) innovative research meth-ods, (c) diversity and social justice and (d) informal technology supported learning activities.

Focus on school-based mentors

In chapter 1 and chapter 2, teacher educators are broadly defined as 'all those who actively facilitate the (formal) learning of student teachers and teachers' (European Commission, 2013, p. 8). This broad definition is also visible in the conceptual model presented in chapter 2. Although all authors of the book embrace this broad definition, it becomes clear throughout the different chap-ters that InFo-TED primarily has focused its work on higher education-based teacher educators.

For instance, the international comparative research data presented in chapter 3 is based on survey data from 1,158 higher education-based teacher educators, and the professional learning trajectories presented in chapter 9 are based on four similar teacher educators. The full recognition of mentors as school-based teacher[1] educators is then relatively new, even though this group has been working with student teachers for more than 30 years in schools in some countries (see chapter 1 for further details). This emphasis is relatively new in some of the research literature on teacher educators, but it is also new for mentors to explicitly identify themselves as teacher educators. Mentors, acting as school-based teacher educators, have then in some countries become recognised as a relatively new professional sub-group employed within schools, with their professional learning as not yet firmly part of the focus of those interested in teacher educators' professional learning.

Mentors are described as school-based teacher educators who work in schools and support student teachers' during their teaching practicum. This means that mentor teachers are mostly experienced teachers who support student teachers in learning how to teach (Crasborn & Hennissen, 2010; Tillema & Smith, 2009). In the last decade, in many countries, mentors have gained more responsibility for teaching student teachers and for supporting beginning teachers as a form of in-service teacher education.

In Norway, for instance, the practical component in teacher education has been expanded and the professional role of mentors has received increased attention. For the last decade, there has been governmental funding for mentor education offered by all universities; and in 2018 the government issued a national framework for mentoring of beginning teachers in pre-school and school, which includes the requirements of mentor education. Mentor teachers are considered a hidden professional group of educators in the research literature (e.g., Clarke et al., 2014). This is not because researchers, practitioners and policy makers are not interested in this group. On the contrary, this group of teacher educators is rather invisible as they do not always identify themselves as teacher educators. Alternatively, Czerniawski et al. (2019) describe them as having 'hybrid, poly-contextualised identities'.

During the last decades, information has been gathered about professional learning needs of teacher educators from an international perspective (Czerniawski et al., 2019; see also chapter 1), but also embedded in national contexts and policy discussions (see, e.g., Tack et al., 2019; who conducted a policy evaluation study on teacher educators' in the context of Flanders). The next step to be taken is to focus in more depth on the professional development needs of this emerging group, taking account of what Reynolds et al. (2013) describe as the potentially transformative challenge of those teacher educators working 'the interface between the academic world, the world of teacher education and the world of the practising teachers' (p. 309).

InFo-TED is currently undertaking an international survey of school-based teacher educators to explore their professional development needs and to provide recommendations for policy makers and other stakeholders, but more colleagues could join this journey in order to have more fine-grained information of this group of teacher educators. In doing so, the research community will be able, for instance, to expand the design and further empirically test the design principles for teacher educators professional learning presented in chapter 5. It will also be able to revise the current knowledge bases as presented in chapter 6, to present new professional development initiatives as presented in chapter 8 and to describe mentors' learning patterns and professional trajectories as was done in chapter 9 for higher education-based teacher educators.

Focus on innovative research methods

Since researchers began to study the professional learning of teacher educators, several topics and themes have emerged, such as pedagogies for teacher education (Loughran, 2014), professional roles (Lunenberg et al., 2014), teacher educators' identities (Murray & Male, 2005; Murray, 2014) and professional learning needs and activities (Tack, 2017). These topics have been explored in chapter 1. As that chapter states, Ping et al.'s (2018) literature review shows what, how and why teacher educators learn is a diverse topic, set within a growing research field. The chapters in this book also reflect these broad themes and this research growth. These chapters here further reflect that varied research methods are used to study teacher educators' professional learning. While most of the studies reported in this book use qualitative research methods (see, e.g., chapter 9, chapter 11), some studies (see, e.g., chapter 3) also use quantitative research methods. This aligns with the international research literature on teacher educators (Tack, 2017).

This emphasis may be partly due to the origins of research on teacher educators. Following the large-scale Research About Teacher Education (RATE) surveys published annually in the United States in the 1980s, interest in teacher educators began to grow as evidenced in the work of Ducharme and colleagues (Ducharme, 1986; Ducharme & Agne, 1989).

In the AERA-conference in 1992, four teacher educators presented a symposium entitled *Holding up the mirror: Teacher educators reflect on their own teaching,* sharing their research on their personal practices as beginning teacher educators. They explained that they felt the need to start these studies because they could not find any research to support them (Hamilton et al., 1992). A year later, Ducharme (1993) published his seminal book *The lives of teacher educators.* There he characterised the identity of teacher educators as 'Janus-like': 'school person, scholar, researcher, methodologist, and visitor to a strange planet' (p. 6), and showed how limited the available knowledge was on teacher educators then. That publication was rapidly followed by research by others including Russell and Korthagen (1995) and Loughran and Russell (1997). Nevertheless, as chapter 1 identifies, although research on teacher educators and their professional development is growing, the studies often remain small-scale, qualitative and practice-based, with a paucity of longitudinal and large-scale studies reducing the potential cumulative and developmental impact of the research (Zeichner, 1999).

But what is of particular interest here is that within the growing research field, innovative methods are used and developed. An example is the 'video selfies' method, described in chapter 11, in which teacher educators recorded their experiences and significant learning points; another is the storyline method, described in chapter 8, to encourage teacher educators to make sense of their personal and professional story of becoming and developing as a teacher educator by drawing a line indicating the highs and lows in their development.

Internationally, there is also an increasing use of art-based methods (see, e.g., Hiralaal et al., 2018). This illustrates that researchers studying teacher educators' professional development are also methodologically contributing to the research community.

In this context, it's worth repeating the interesting call for more design-based research reported in chapter 5. These authors argue that in order to increase the 'maturity' of research in the field, design-based research on teacher educators' professional development is needed to make a connection explicitly between the design principles of professional development initiatives on the one hand, and the resulting learning processes of teacher educators on the other. Design-based research might be one way to further increase the maturity of the research field, but the review study of Ping et al. (2018) also illustrated the fragmented focus of the field. A fragmented focus is probably typical for an emerging research field but it needs more coherence. To put this differently, studies need to build on each other and to use the same conceptual language; they should also formulate critiques of similar work. This means that the research community needs to create an integrated research agenda with topics to address in the coming years. International forums like InFo-TED have a major role to play in setting-up such a research agenda.

Such an integrated research agenda will also further support the theorisation of teacher educators' professional development. As chapter 11 has discussed, this is much needed because workplace learning for teacher educators, in particular, is not well theorised compared to that for other occupational groups and professional fields, including doctors, nurses and social workers (McNamara et al., 2014). Developing this area of research is clearly important and can be achieved by an integrated research agenda and by drawing on the InFo-TED conceptual model of professional development (see chapter 2).

In this context, we can also learn by developing knowledge bases. Although the concept of knowledge bases is contested and not always easy to understand correctly (Shulman, 1987; Selmer et al., 2016), insights from chapter 6 are interesting. Acknowledging the limitations of that study, we feel that making transparent and well rationalised choices for the kind of knowledge bases to be developed, giving the pedagogy of teacher educators a central place and involving teacher educators from a variety of contexts in the development process are important issues to take into consideration. Moreover, knowledge bases for teacher educators should be open and flexible. Research on knowledge bases for teacher educators is still scarce, and more study is needed on both the development process and on the way knowledge bases are used by teacher educators in their practices.

Focus on diversity, inclusion and social justice

One of the themes that needs to be placed on the research agenda for the next five years is how teacher educators should deal with growing social diversity, and how to embrace this theme in their professional development activities and initiatives. Nowadays, our societies are rapidly transforming, and inequality and social justice are becoming key challenges, as the recent increasing attention to the Black Lives Matter movement emphasises once more. This is particularly the case in those countries that have a history of migration, in the past and more recently. Such histories often mean that the student body in classrooms is steadily becoming more diverse due to demographic changes.

Educational systems implement initiatives to ensure that access to regular education is guaranteed for every student and that no one is left behind (Organisation for Economic Co-operation and Development [OECD], 2019; United Nations Educational, Scientific and Cultural Organization [UNESCO], 2017; European Commission, 2017). This encourages teachers to adapt their teaching to a variety of pupil characteristics such as ethnic, linguistic and socio-economic backgrounds; physical and mental abilities; interests; and motivations (Akyeampong, 2017). But teachers often report that they struggle to respond to the educational needs of a diverse range of pupils and that this causes them feelings of pressure, insecurity and stress (Vandervieren & Struyf, 2019). Research also shows that teacher education programmes have aimed to address diversity, sometimes with little success (McDonald, 2005; Yuan, 2018). In this respect, not only (student) teachers report feeling unprepared to work in diverse classrooms, but also teacher educators themselves often share these feelings of being unprepared (Florian et al., 2010).

Many teacher educators may not have had experience of 'teaching for diversity', nor may they agree with its associated approaches to teaching and learning (Cochran-Smith et al., 2016). For example, in Norway, a recent report on a national initiative called *Competence for Diversity* concludes that teachers did not find that the in-service training provided by higher education institutions met the professional development needs they had as practising teachers. The providers, teacher educators from higher education institutions, were found to be more enthusiastic about the initiative, especially because it brought them closer to the reality of school. Yet, they also experienced it as challenging and they questioned their own competence to prepare teachers for multi-cultural classrooms (Lødding et al., 2018). There seems to be an urgent need to address the issue of educating teachers for a diverse society starting with teacher educators (Florian et al., 2010).

Focusing on teacher educators' ability to deal with diversity is considered one of the main challenges in teacher education because 'if teacher educators are not competent to teach about diversity, they will not be able to prepare their students for work in a diverse and inclusive learning environment' (Vranjesevic, 2014, p. 473). A first attempt to organise the available literature on this theme can be found in the InFo-TED knowledge bases, where five perspectives to investigate diversity are listed: the perspectives of the teacher educators, curriculum, institutional context, local or national context, and theoretical underpinning (Lunenberg & Guberman, 2019).

One problem that has received limited attention is that many teacher educators themselves are not conscious of the influence of their own position in relation to the diversity of student teachers. Self-study research may offer insights. Pennington et al. (2012) emphasise that change is only possible as teacher educators, teachers and students gain critical insights into how their identities have been constructed by and in a specific culture, and how their cultural narratives of teaching have shaped their personal and professional subjectivities.

The study of Bair et al. (2010), who explored the role of emotions in teacher education classrooms, with particular attention to the connections between faculty, student and institutional cultures, confirms this. They found that black teacher educators often felt that they functioned in a space where blackness was discredited and devalued. Students stereotyped them, questioned their qualifications and challenged their intellectual authority. The study by Han et al. (2014) focused on becoming conscious of the challenge of teacher educators to empower diverse students by cultivating their cultural integrity, as well as their individual abilities and academic successes. Other issues are the often-limited experience of teacher educators in teaching for diversity, or the hidden messages in learning materials.

Studies on teacher education dealing with diversity agree that a central component of any successful pre-service programme is teacher educators modelling best practice in instructional strategies for working with a diverse student population (O'Hara & Pritchard, 2008; Vranjesevic, 2014). For this to occur, teacher educators need to engage in ongoing professional development and have access to appropriate resources and supports (Vavrus, 2002; Keppens, 2020). In this respect, then the research identifies that preparing student teachers for diversity should not be the responsibility of a few faculty members skilled in these areas. Rather all faculty members in teacher education institutes should share these responsibilities and must have (or develop) the requisite knowledge, skills and attitudes to address issues of diversity throughout the teacher education programme (O'Hara & Pritchard, 2008).

In this context, several insights presented in this book are helpful to put diversity on the agenda, including the design principles for professional learning (see chapter 5), or the key idea that teacher educators themselves must be the drivers of their own learning trajectories and the key change agents within their professional workplaces (see chapter 11). We suggest then that all stakeholders in education need to address two questions: what professional development provision is required to enable teacher educators to become confident in preparing teachers to teach in diverse contexts?; and how can teacher educators themselves engage in this area of professional learning, which for many is a new and challenging responsibility?

Focus on informal technology supported learning activities

The global crisis around Covid-19 has affected all teacher education systems, and thus also all teacher educators and all their professional learning. As schools and universities closed their premises, most teacher educators continued to work, fulfilling all their roles and responsibilities to their students and colleagues (see chapter 1), but in an almost entirely virtual environment and supported, initially a least, by what Murphy (2020) has characterised as 'emergency e-learning'. During the pandemic, using technology-based and online learning went from being something many teacher educators thought they *ought to* integrate into their teaching (Czerniawski et al., 2017), to something they *had to* make use of (Smith et al., 2020).

For many this was a steep learning curve, especially in the early stages, but accounts of creative and innovative online learning provision are now emerging. These include the work of Smith et al. (2020) with a multinational InFo-TED research group, Ferdig et al. (2020) in the United States, and Kidd and Murray (2020) in England. In these accounts, it is clear that as teacher educators' learning rapidly increased, so did their confidence, with many finding ways to align online technologies with their pedagogical visions and to incorporate teacher learning in critical and reflective ways. Some accounts also show the potential to model good practice online (see the examples of 'kitchen chemistry' and 'online home-schooling' given in Kidd & Murray, 2020). It seems that the strategies – described in past literature (see, e.g., Tondeur et al., 2012; Røkenes, & Krumsvik, 2014) – that teacher educators could use to foster technology integration are now actually implemented in systematic practices.

Much of this professional learning took place from necessity, occurring in micro-communities of practice with teacher educators working alongside their colleagues in universities and schools (Kidd & Murray, 2020), often assisted by 'third space workers' (Whitchurch, 2012), such as university 'learning technology advisers'. For other teacher educators though, learning was undertaken in professional isolation as they struggled to implement high quality teaching online (Smith et al., 2020).

Whether collaborative or solitary, this was workplace learning at its most rapid and immediate: informal and responsive, sometimes uneven, but constantly evolving and important. This then was *essential* professional development at a time of global crisis, but there is now clearly great potential for wider communal learning and for collective knowledge to be shared for the benefit of all. In our view, professional development using multiple forms of technology has now become an essential part of the future-scape of teacher educators' learning (see chapter 5), either using technology in a stand-alone mode or using it to create links between different modes of professional development.

This book has clearly illustrated the importance of informal, online professional development activities alongside formal provision. As chapter 6 describes, InFo-TED has developed a repository on its website, containing knowledge bases, blogs, talking heads videos and many other resources to develop teacher educators' professional learning. To date, this website has approximately 930 visitors and 1,700 page views per month from across the world (see Figure 13.1).

Figure 13.1 Geographical location of InFo-TED website visitors
Note: Data based on June 2020 statistics for the previous 30 days

But what we do not know, of course, is the influences that these various resources may have had on the learning of teacher educators individually or communally. This then is an example of technology providing resources for informal, self-initiated but ultimately unquantified learning benefits. Further research into this area would undoubtedly be beneficial.

Another interest in this book is in possible roles for the use of technology to create hybrid forms of learning (i.e., both on- and off-line, synchronous and asynchronous modes of professional development). Here we ask, what is the role of technology in interlinking informal learning either in the workplace or through personal enquiry, and formally planned professional development 'events' (whether in the 'real' world or in online spaces)? In particular, is there a role for technology in facilitating how short-term formal learning *away* from the workplace might become an integrated and meaningful part of longer-term, and largely informal, learning *in* the arena of practice?

As chapter 11 describes, InFo-TED experimented with a virtual learning environment (VLE) as a link for participants between personal practices and professional learning in their workplaces and their development through the Summer Academy as a face-to-face event (see chapter 8, chapter 11). But the technologies involved in such VLEs still have a long way to go to achieve meaningful integration between different modes of professional development.

Here we see redesigning those VLEs as one essential task for future creators of professional development for teacher educators.

Finally, as chapter 11 has also identified, this book highlights that teacher educators themselves, whether as individuals or as part of communities of practice, must be the drivers and owners of their professional learning trajectories and the key change agents (Cochran-Smith, 2005) within their own arenas of practice. This has clear implications for those designing and implementing professional development programmes using different forms of learning (see chapter 5), as does the observation that professional development works well as a bottom-up process and sometimes becomes shallower when it is enforced by a top-down decision or reform (Kelchtermans et al., 2018).

Conclusion

In this final chapter some key themes for the further professional development of teacher educators (school-based mentors, innovative research methods, diversity and inclusion, and informal technology supported learning activities) are presented, based on the reading of all chapters included in this book. These themes, together with the content of all chapters, reflect challenges for the future for researchers, policy makers and practitioners involved in supporting teacher educators' professional development.

The Interlude chapters in this book (chapter 4, chapter 7 and chapter 10) give an overview of the challenges for teacher educators' professional development in Australia, Japan and the United States next to the more European-oriented perspective of the other chapters. These chapters clearly illustrate the importance of creating professional development initiatives that align with and enhance provision within national systems. The book then aims to support initiatives, programmes and activities for teacher educators' professional development that are reciprocal and generative, which might have lasting influences, creating important and meaningful legacies.

Our experiences in the seven years of InFo-TED work have strengthened our conviction that teacher educators can and will have an important role to play in their own professional development. As such in this conclusion, we ask for both professional and institutional agency. This also implies that we ask for connections to be built across congruent national activities and networks in order to facilitate the professional development of teacher educators internationally.

Of course, such requests are strongly connected to a warning that one size does not fit all. This is of crucial importance for teachers' professional development (Merchie et al., 2016) and thus also for teacher educators' professional development. In other words: it is about accepting that teacher education and all education is contextual; or it is about adaptation and not imitation. In this way, achieving and influencing existing infrastructures, practices and policies for teacher educators' professional development takes time, even with a strong and viable project and the concerted efforts of key agents and stakeholders. This is contrary to the often short-term or ad hoc decisions made that are swayed by the issues of the day. Here, we also argue for the need for teacher educators to have stronger voices and to engage in the public and political debates on education and teacher education.

To conclude, InFo-TED aims to continue to work on teacher educators' professional development in general and on the themes outlined in this last chapter in particular. We already mentioned that the group recently launched a new international comparative survey to study the professional learning needs of school-based teacher educators, but InFo-TED is also preparing new project applications with a focus on diversity, inclusion and social justice. Together with these initiatives, this last chapter can be read as an invitation for collaboration across the globe to keep teacher educators at the centre of the public educational debate.

Note

1 The definition of the term 'school-based teacher educators' varies between national contexts. For example, in England it is used to denote a specific sub-group fully involved in *all* aspects of the organisation of school-led pre-service routes, including but extending beyond mentoring (see White et al., 2015). But in other countries, such as Norway, the term can also be used to denote only those mentoring, as stated in this chapter.

References

Akyeampong, K. (2017). Teacher educators' practice and vision of good teaching in teacher education reform context in Ghana. *Educational Researcher*, 46(4), 194–203.

Bair, M. A., Bair, D. E., Mader, C. E., Hipp, S., & Hakim, I. (2010). Faculty emotions: A self-study of teacher educators. *Studying Teacher Education*, 6 (1), 95–111.

Clarke, A., Triggs, V., & Nielsen, W. (2014). Cooperating teacher participation in teacher education: A review of the literature. *Review of Educational Research*, 84(2), 163–202.

Cochran-Smith, M. (2005). Teacher educators as researchers: Multiple perspectives. *Teaching and Teacher Education*, 21(2), 219–225.

Cochran-Smith, M., Ell, F., Grudnoff, L., Haigh, M., Hill, M., & Ludlow, L. (2016). Initial teacher education: What does it take to put equity at the center? *Teaching and Teacher Education*, 57, 67–78.

Crasborn, F. J. A. J., & Hennissen, P. P. M. (2010). The skilled mentor: Mentor teachers' use and acquisition of supervisory skills [Doctoral dissertation, Eindhoven School of Education]. https://www.researchgate.net/profile/Frank_Crasborn/publication/254879513_The_skilled_mentor_Mentor_teachers'_use_and_acquisition_of_supervisory_skills/links/5890b275aca272f9a556bcc4/The-skilled-mentor-Mentor-teachers-use-and-acquisition-of-supervisory-skills.pdf

Czerniawski, G., Guberman, A., & MacPhail, A. (2017). The professional developmental needs of higher education-based teacher educators: An international comparative needs analysis. *European Journal of Teacher Education*, 40(1), 127–140.

Czerniawski, G., Kidd, W., & Murray, J. (2019). We are all teacher educators now: Understanding school-based teacher educators in times of change in England. In A.

Swennen, C. Kosnik, and J. Murray (Eds.), *International research, policy and practice in teacher education* (pp. 171–185). Springer.

Ducharme, E. (1986). Teacher educators: Description and analysis. In J. Raths, & L. Katz (Eds.), *Advances in Teacher Education* (Vol. 2, pp. 39–60). Ablex.

Ducharme, E. (1993). *The lives of teacher educators.* Teachers College Press.

Ducharme, E., & Agne, R. (1989). Professors of education: Uneasy residents in academe. In R. Wisniewski, & E. Ducharme (Eds.), *The professors of teaching: An inquiry* (pp. 67–86). University of New York Press.

European Commission. (2013). Supporting teacher educators for better learning outcomes. https://ec.europa.eu/assets/eac/education/policy/school/doc/support-teacher-educators_en.pdf.

European Commission. (2017). Preparing teachers for diversity: The role of initial teacher education. Public Policy and Management Institute. https://op.europa.eu/en/publication-detail/-/publication/b347bf7d-1db1-11e7-aeb3-01aa75ed71a1.

Ferdig, R., Baumgartner, E., Hartshorne, R., Kaplan-Rakowski, R., & Mouza, C. (Eds). (2020). *Teaching, technology, and teacher education during the COVID-19 pandemic: Stories from the field.* Association for the Advancement of Computing in Education (AACE).

Florian, L., Young, K., & Rouse, M. (2010). Preparing teachers for inclusive and diverse educational environments: Studying curricular reform in an initial teacher education course. *International Journal of Inclusive Education, 14*(7), 709–722.

Hamilton, M-L., Pinnegar, S., Laboskey,V., & Guilfoyle, K. (1992, April 20–24). *Holding up the mirror: Teacher Educators reflect on their own teaching* [Conference presentation]. American Educational Research Association Symposium, San Francisco, CA, United States.

Han, H. S., Vomvoridi-Ivanović, E., Jacobs, J., Karanxha, Z., Lypka, A., Topdemir, C., & Feldman, A. (2014). Culturally responsive pedagogy in higher education: A collaborative self-study. *Studying Teacher Education, 10*(3), 290–312.

Hiralaal, A., Matebane, R., & Pithouse-Morgan, K. (2018). Learning through enacting arts-informed self-study research with critical friends. In J. Ritter, M. Lunenberg, K. Pithouse-Morgan, P. Samaras, & E. Vanassche (Eds.), *Teaching, learning and enacting self-study methodology: Unraveling a complex interplay* (pp. 295–312). Springer.

Kelchtermans, G., Smith, K., & Vanderlinde, R. (2018). Towards an 'international forum for teacher educator development': An agenda for research and action. *European Journal of Teacher Education, 41*(1), 120–134.

Keppens, K. (2020). Videography in teacher education: A study on inclusive teaching competences [Doctoral dissertation, Ghent University]. https://biblio.ugent.be/publication/8642985/file/8642986.pdf.

Kidd, W., & Murray, J. (2020). The Covid-19 pandemic and its effects on teacher education in England: How teacher educators moved practicum learning online. *European Journal of Teacher Education, 43*(4), 542–558.

Lødding, B., Rønsen, E., & Wollscheid, S. (2018). Utvikling av flerkulturell kompetanse i lærerutdanningene, grunnopplæringen og barnehagene: Sluttrapport fra evalueringen av Kompetanse for mangfold [Development of multicultural competence in teacher education, basic education and kindergartens: Final report from the evaluation of Competence for diversity]. Nordisk institutt for studier av innovasjon, forskning og utdanning (NIFU). https://nifu.brage.unit.no/nifu-xmlui/handle/11250/2493141.

Loughran, J. (2014). Professionally developing as a teacher educator. *Journal of Teacher Education*, 65(4), 271–283.

Loughran, J., & Russell, T. (1997). *Teaching about teaching*. Falmer Press.

Lunenberg, M., Dengerink, J., & Korthagen, F. (2014). *The professional teacher educator: Roles, behaviour, and professional development of teacher educators*. Sense Publishers.

Lunenberg, M., & Guberman, A. (2019, August 6). *Teacher educators and diversity*. International Forum for Teacher Educator Development. https://info-ted.eu/diversity.

McDonald, M. A. (2005). The integration of social justice in teacher education: Dimensions of prospective teachers' opportunities to learn. *Journal of Teacher Education*, 56(5), 418–435.

McNamara, O., Murray, J., & Jones, M. (Eds.). (2014). *Workplace learning in teacher education*. Springer.

Merchie, E., Tuytens, M., Devos, G., & Vanderlinde, R. (2016). Evaluating teachers' professional development initiatives: Towards an extended evaluative framework. *Research Papers in Education*, 33(2), 143–168.

Murphy, M. (2020). COVID-19 and emergency eLearning: Consequences of the securitization of higher education for post-pandemic pedagogy. *Contemporary Security Policy*, 41(3), 492–505.

Murray, J. (2002). Between the chalkface and the ivory towers? A study of the professionalism of teacher educators working on primary initial teacher education courses in the English education system. *Collected Original Resources in Education (CORE)*, 26(3), 1–550.

Murray, J. (2014). Teacher educators' constructions of professionalism: A case study. *Asia-Pacific Journal of Teacher Education*, 42(1), 7–21.

Murray, J., & Male, T. (2005). Becoming a teacher educator: Evidence from the field. *Teaching and Teacher Education*, 21(2), 107–115.

O'Hara, S., & Pritchard, R. H. (2008). Meeting the challenge of diversity: Professional development for teacher educators. *Teacher Education Quarterly*, 35(1), 43–61.

Organisation for Economic Co-operation and Development. (2019). The road to integration: Education and migration. http://www.oecd.org/education/the-road-to-integration-d8ceec5d-en.htm.

Pennington, J. L., Brock, C. H., Abernathy, T. V., Bingham, A., Major, E. M., Wiest, L. R., & Ndura, E. (2012). Teacher educators' dispositions: Footnoting the present with stories from our pasts. *Studying Teacher Education*, 8(1), 69–85.

Ping, C., Schellings, G., & Beijaard, D. (2018). Teacher educators' professional learning: A literature review. *Teaching and Teacher Education*, 75, 93–104.

Reynolds, R., Ferguson-Patrick, K., & McCormack, A. (2013). Dancing in the ditches: Reflecting on the capacity of a university/school partnership to clarify the role of a teacher educator. *European Journal of Teacher Education*, 36(3), 307–319.

Røkenes, F. M., & Krumsvi, R. J. (2014). Development of student teachers' digital competences in teacher education: A literature review. *Nordic Journal of Digital Literacy*, 9(4), 250–280.

Russell, T., & Korthagen, F. (1995) *Teachers who Teach Teachers*. Falmer Press.

Selmer, S., Bernstein, M., & Bolyard, J. (2016). Multilayered knowledge: Understanding the structure and enactment of teacher educators' specialized knowledge base. *Teacher Development*, 20(4), 437–457.

Shulman, L. (1987). Knowledge and teaching: Foundations of the new reform. *Harvard Educational Review*, 57(1), 1–22.

Smith, K., Ulvik, M., Curtis, E., Guberman, A., Lippeveld, L., Viswarajan, S., & Berglas, T. (2020). Meeting the black swan: Teacher educators' use of ICT- pre, during and eventually post Covid19. *Nordic Journal of Comparative and International Education*.

Tack, H. (2017). *Towards a better understanding of teacher educators' professional development. Theoretical and empirical insight into their researcherly disposition* [Doctoral dissertation, Ghent University]. https://biblio.ugent.be/publication/8532727/file/8533022.

Tack, H., Rots, I. Struyven, K., Valcke, M., & Vanderlinde, R. (2019). Uncovering a hidden professional agenda for teacher educators: A mixed method study on Flemish teacher educators and their professional development. *European Journal of Teacher Education*, 41(1), 84–104.

Tillema, H. H., & Smith, K. (2009). Assessment orientation in formative assessment of learning to teach. *Teachers and Teaching: Theory and Practice*, 15(3), 391–405.

Tondeur, J., van Braak, J., Sang, G., Voogt, J., Fisser, P., & Ottenbreit-Leftwich, A. (2012). Preparing pre-service teachers to integrate technology in education: A synthesis of qualitative evidence. *Computers & Education*, 59(1), 134–144.

United Nations Educational, Scientific and Cultural Organization. (2017). A guide for ensuring inclusion and equity in education. https://unesdoc.unesco.org/ark:/48223/pf0000248254.

Vandervieren, E., & Struyf, E. (2019). Facing social reality together: Investigating a pre-service teacher preparation programme on inclusive education. *International Journal of Inclusive Education*. DOI: doi:10.1080/13603116.2019.1625451

Vavrus, M. (2002). *Transforming the multicultural education of teachers*. Teachers College Press.

Vranjesevic, J. (2014). The main challenges in teacher education for diversity. *Zbornik Instituta za pedagoska istrazivanja*, 46(2), 473–185.

Whitchurch, C. (2012). *Reconstructing identities in higher education: The rise of 'third space' professionals*. Routledge.

White, E., Dickerson, C., & Weston, K. (2015). Developing an appreciation of what it means to be a school-based teacher educator. *European Journal of Teacher Education*, 38(4), 445–459.

Yuan, H. (2018). Preparing teachers for diversity: Literature review and implications for community-based teacher education. *Higher Education Studies*, 8(1), 1–17.

Zeichner, K. (1999). The new scholarship in teacher education, *Educational Researcher*, 28(9), 4–15.

Index

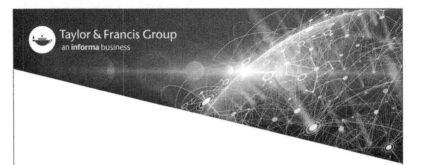

Made in the USA
Coppell, TX
23 May 2022

78074850R00109